Pinter

THE PLAYWRIGHT

THE LEARNING CENTRE
HAMMERSMITH AND WEST
LONDON COLLEGE
GLIDDON ROAD
LONDON W14 9BL

WITHDRAWN

D1514155

HAMMERSMITH WEST LONDON COLLEGE

338128

By the same author

THE THEATRE OF THE ABSURD
BRIEF CHRONICLES: ESSAYS ON MODERN THEATRE
MEDIATIONS: ESSAYS ON BRECHT, BECKETT AND THE MEDIA
AN ANATOMY OF DRAMA
ARTAUD
BRECHT: A CHOICE OF EVILS
THE FIELD OF DRAMA

Pinter

THE PLAYWRIGHT

Martin Esslin

Sixth edition

METHUEN DRAMA

Methuen Drama

Originally published in Great Britain in 1970
by Methuen & Co Ltd under the title
The People Wound: The Plays of Harold Pinter
Revised edition published in 1973 as
Pinter: A Study of his Plays by Eyre Methuen Ltd
Third, expanded edition published in 1977
Reprinted 1978
Fourth, expanded and revised edition published as a
Methuen Drama Paperback under the present title in 1982
by Methuen London Ltd
Corrected reprint 1984
Fifth, expanded and revised edition published by Methuen Drama in 1992
Sixth, expanded and revised edition published
in 2000 by Methuen Drama

Copyright © 1970, 1973, 1977, 1982, 1984, 1992 and 2000
by Martin Esslin

Martin Esslin has asserted his rights under the
Copyright, Designs and Patents Act, 1988, to be identified
as the author of this work

ISBN 0 413 66860 6 paperback

A CIP catalogue record for this book
is available from the British Library

This paperback edition is sold subject to the condition
that it shall not, by way of trade or otherwise, be lent,
resold, hired out, or otherwise circulated without the
publisher's prior consent in any form of binding or
cover other than that in which it is published and
without a similar condition including this condition
being imposed on the subsequent purchaser.

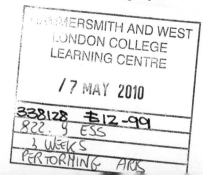
HAMMERSMITH AND WEST
LONDON COLLEGE
LEARNING CENTRE

17 MAY 2010

338128   £12-99
822. 9 ESS
3 WEEKS
PERFORMING ARTS

338128

Contents

Preface to the Sixth Edition

When the first edition of this book appeared in 1970 Harold Pinter had not yet reached the age of forty; he was still emerging from the collective label of 'angry young man' which had been fastened on the new wave of British playwrights of his generation by superficial journalistic opinion.

Now, at seventy, he has become an established public figure, deeply involved in the political debate of our time, and a writer who has become a 'contemporary classic'. His output of full-length plays has slowed down, yet within a series of shorter works an openly political strain has added a powerful new element to his *oeuvre*.

The present book, amended and revised over the years, has, it seems, continued to be of use to readers seeking information about Pinter's background and methods, and access to his still often enigmatic and intriguingly opaque plays. Hence perhaps the usefulness of a new edition that is fully up-to-date and deals with his latest work.

In embarking on this work, in the late nineteen sixties – and since –, I was fortunate to have been helped occasionally with my queries by Harold Pinter himself. He even allowed me to see some of his then as yet unpublished work, the early novel *The Dwarfs* and the play *The Hothouse*, which have since become freely accessible. But, as I pointed out, in the preface to the first edition of this book in 1970, while being deeply grateful to him for it, 'I must, however, emphasize that all the opinions about Pinter's work voiced in this book are entirely my own and expressed without fear or favour. Pinter very rightly refrains from commenting on the "meaning" of his work and I should not be surprised if he violently disagreed with some of the interpretations contained in this book.'

The literature about Pinter has grown to a veritable flood in recent years. The bibliography – selective as it must be – of this secondary literature has been brought up to date in this volume, as has the chronology of Pinter's career. And the plays he has produced since the last edition of this book appeared are treated in their time sequence, so that the section describing and analysing his output becomes a full account of his development as a playwright.

In the passages quoted from Pinter's plays three dots (. . .) signify a pause intended by the author, while four or more dots stand for words omitted in the quotation.

Winchelsea, East Sussex, July 2000   MARTIN ESSLIN

1

Chronology of a Career

1930   10th October: Harold Pinter born at Hackney, East London, the son of Hyman (Jack) Pinter, ladies' tailor, and his wife Frances (*née* Mann). Pinter believes that his father's family might have come to England from Hungary; the name Pinter does occur among Hungarian Jews, But there is also a family tradition that the name is of Spanish or Portuguese origin – Pinto, da Pinto or da Pinta – so that Pinters were originally Sephardic Jews. There is no reason why both these theories might not be correct, as Sephardic Jews frequently settled in East and Central Europe after the expulsions of the Jews from the Iberian peninsula. (Cf. Pete and Len talking about Mark's flat in *The Dwarfs*: 'LEN:. . . Everything in this house is Portuguese. PETE: Why's that? LEN: That's where he comes from. PETE: Does he? LEN: Or at least, his grandmother on his father's side. That's where the family comes from . . .')

1930–9   Pinter spends his childhood in the East End: 'I lived in a brick house on Thistlewaite Road, near Clapton Pond, which has a few ducks on it. It was a working-class area – some big, run-down Victorian houses, and a soap factory with a terrible smell, and a lot of railway yards. And shops. It had a lot of shops. But down the road a bit from the house there was a river, the Lea River, which is a tributary of the Thames, and if you go up the river two miles you find yourself in a marsh. And near a filthy canal as well. There is a terrible factory of some kind, with an enormous dirty chimney, that shoves things down to this canal. . . .My mother was a marvellous cook, as she still is. My father worked terribly hard. He worked a twelve-hour day, making

1

clothes in his shop, but eventually he lost the business and went to work for someone else. In the war he was an air-raid warden'.[1]

1939 At the outbreak of war, Pinter is evacuated to the country. 'I went to a castle in Cornwall – owned by a Mrs Williams – with twenty-four other boys. It had marvellous grounds. And it was on the sea. It looked out on the English Channel, and it had kitchen gardens. All that. But it wasn't quite so idyllic as it sounds, because I was quite a morose little boy. My parents came down occasionally from London. It was over four hundred miles there and back, and I don't know how they made it. It was terribly expensive, and they had no money. I came home after a year or so, and then I went away again – this time with my mother – to a place closer to London.'[2]

1944 Return to London. 'On the day I got back to London, in 1944, I saw the first flying bomb. I was in the street and I saw it come over. . . .There were times when I would open our back door and find our garden in flames. Our house never burned, but we had to evacuate several times. Every time we evacuated, I took my cricket bat with me.'[3]

1947 Pinter leaves Hackney Downs Grammar School. 'It was a ten-minute walk from my home. All boys – about six hundred of them. It was a good building. It was pretty awful, but it had great character, and some of the masters had, too. Especially my English master, Joseph Brearley. He's a very brilliant man. He's a great fellow. He's still there. He was obsessed with the theatre. I played Macbeth when I was sixteen, and he directed me, and then he directed me when

[1] Pinter, interview in *The New Yorker*, 25th February 1967. Harold Pinter now feels that he may well have overstressed the decay of the neighbourhood in which he grew up: 'There was indeed a soap factory . . . but it was actually two miles away at Bethnal Green. There were rundown Victorian houses but I did not live in one. The filthy canal was a mile away. I actually lived in a very pleasant environment and in a very comfortable terraced house. The house was immaculate. My father was forced to work very long hours, but through his industry and my mother's care we lived very well.'

[2] Pinter, *ibid*.

[3] Pinter, *ibid*.

I played Romeo. I went in for football and cricket at school and I was always chosen to run. My main ability was sprinting. I set a new school record – a hundred yards in ten point two but it's been broken since. The only universities I was thinking about were Oxford and Cambridge. But you had to know Latin, and I didn't know Latin. . . .'[4]

1948 Pinter applies for a grant to study acting at the Royal Academy of Dramatic Art. On the recommendation of R. D. Smith, the stage and radio producer, who is acting as assessor, he receives an LCC grant.

> He . . . found he hadn't the sophistication to cope with the other students. To escape he faked a nervous breakdown and, unknown to his parents, tramped the streets for months while continuing to draw a grant.[5]

'I went to RADA for about two terms, then I left of my own free will, I didn't care for it very much. I spent the next year roaming about a bit.'[6]

1948–9 On reaching the age of eighteen when he becomes liable for National Service, Pinter declares himself a conscientious objector. 'I was aware of the suffering and of the horror of war, and by no means was I going to subscribe to keeping it going. I said no'[7] He has to appear before two conscientious-objector tribunals. 'At my second tribunal, I took one of my close friends, Morris Wernick, to speak for me. The others took reverends. But I had no religious beliefs by then. There were a lot of colonels, with moustaches, at the tribunal. It was very, very stuffy. I took Wernick, and he made an immortal speech on my behalf. He said, "Now I *am* going into the army, so I am not a conscientious objector, but I can assure you, that you will never change *him*. It's a

---

    [4] Pinter, *ibid.*
    [5] Anon. 'Profile: Playwright on his own', *The Observer*, 15th September 1963.
    [6] Pinter, conversation with the author, 1967.
    [7] Pinter, interview in *The New Yorker*, 25th February 1967.

waste of time to try to persuade him to change his mind".[8]
Both tribunals refuse Pinter's application, he receives his
call-up papers, but persists in his determination not to go
into the army. Twice he has to appear before a magistrate.
'I expected to go to prison, but it was very simple. I was still
under twenty-one and it was a civil offence, and the magistrate fined me; then I went on another trial and the same
magistrate fined me again – ten pounds and then twenty
pounds. It need not have been like that at all, if I had had
another magistrate'.[9]

1950 *Poetry London*, No. 19, August 1950, publishes two
poems by Harold Pinter ('New Year in the Midlands' and
'Chandeliers and Shadows'). There is a bad printer's error
in this publication, with stanzas from the two poems having
been interchanged. So *Poetry London*, No. 20, November
1950, reprints 'New Year in the Midlands' together with two
new poems ('Rural Idyll' and 'European Revels'). But the
poet's name now appears as 'Harold Pinta'. This seems *not*
to have been a printer's error, as there is evidence that
Pinter signed some letters at that time with the 'Portuguese'
form of his name.

First efforts to obtain work as an actor. R. D. (Reggie)
Smith, who had got Pinter his RADA grant, gives him small
parts in radio features.

19th September: Pinter's first professional engagement as an
actor in a BBC Home Service broadcast *Focus on Football
Pools*.

31st October: *Focus on Libraries*.

1951 14th January: Pinter's first appearance in Shake-
speare. Recording of R. D. Smith's production of *Henry
VIII* for BBC Third Programme. Pinter plays the part of
Abergavenny. The production is first broadcast on 9th
February. Pinter resumes his training as an actor at the
Central School of Speech and Drama.

September: Starts his first engagement with Anew

---

[8] Pinter, *ibid*.
[9] Pinter, conversation with author, 1967.

McMaster's touring company in Ireland. 'He advertised in *The Stage* for actors for a Shakespearian tour . . . I sent him a photograph and went to see him in a flat near Willesden Junction . . . He offered me six pounds a week, said I could get digs for twenty-five shillings at the most, told me how cheap cigarettes were and that I could play Horatio, Bassanio and Cassio. It was my first job proper on the stage.'[10]

Poetry London, No 22, Summer 1951, publishes another poem ('One a Story, Two a Death') by 'Harold Pinta'.

Sept. 1951–Autumn 1952 Touring Ireland with Anew McMaster. The company includes a number of actors who later achieved prominence: Kenneth Haigh, Patrick Magee, Barry Foster. 'Mac travelled by car, and sometimes some of us did too. But other times we went on the lorry with the flats and props, and going into Brandon or Cloughjordan would find the town empty, asleep, men sitting upright in dark bars, cowpads, mud, smell of peat, wood, old clothes. We'd find digs; wash basin and jug, tea, black pudding, and off to the hall, set up a stage on trestle tables, a few rostrum [sic], a few drapes, costumes out of the hampers, set up shop and at night play, not always but mostly to a packed house (where had they come from?). . .'[11] 'Ireland wasn't golden always, but it was golden sometimes and in 1951 it was, all in all, a golden age for me and for others'.[12]

1953 Pinter appears in Donald Wolfit's classical season at the King's Theatre, Hammersmith; first meeting with the actress Vivien Merchant (Ada Thomson) with whom Pinter appears in small parts in *As You Like It*. Friendship with the actor – and, later, playwright – Alun Owen, another member of the company.

1954 Pinter decides to assume the stage name 'David Baron'.

1957–7 Acting in provincial repertory theatres: Colchester, Bournemouth, Torquay, Worthing, Richmond, etc.

[10] Pinter, *Mac*, London, Pendragon Press: 1968, pp. 7–8.
[11] p. 17, *ibid*.
[12] p. 16, *ibid*.

1956 While acting at Bournemouth Pinter meets Vivien Merchant again, they play leads opposite each other and get married.

1957 Pinter writes his first play *The Room*. At a party in London he had come across two men in a small room. One of them, a little man with bare feet, was 'carrying on a lively and rather literate conversation, and at the table next to him sat an enormous lorry driver. He had his cap on and never spoke a word. And all the while, as he talked, the little man was feeding the big man – cutting his bread, buttering it, and so on. Well, this image would never leave me,'[13] 'I told a friend, Henry Woolf, who was studying in the Drama Department of Bristol University, that I would write a play about them. I was working in a repertory company in Torquay, Devon, rehearsing one play in the morning and playing in another one at night. Woolf telephoned me and said he had to have the play, so I wrote it. It was *The Room*. It took me four days, working in the afternoons. Woolf directed it. On a Sunday night, when I wasn't acting, I went down to see the play. It seemed to go well. It excited me . . .'[14] *The Room*, in the production by the Drama Department of Bristol University, was so successful that Bristol's other drama school, attached to the Bristol Old Vic, also mounted a production, with which it participated in *The Sunday Times* student drama competition, held that year at Bristol. Harold Hobson, drama critic of *The Sunday Times* who acted as one of the judges of the competition, was so impressed by the play that he wrote about its performance (held on 20th December 1957); this drew the attention of a young impresario, Michael Codron, to Pinter. He asked for any other plays he might have written. Pinter submitted the two further plays he had written after *The Room*: *The Party* (later *The Birthday Party*) and *The Dumb Waiter*. Codron expressed interest in the former. The first performance of *The Room* also led to Pinter's acquisition of a first-rate,

---

[13] Pinter, quoted in *Time*, 10th November 1961.
[14] Pinter, interview in *The New Yorker*, 25th February 1967.

6

literary agent: 'After the first performance of *The Room* . . .
Jimmy Wax and I met accidentally in an attic in Bristol
(where I was on tour at the time). Susan Engel and myself
read *The Room* to him. He laughed a great deal and two
days later wrote to me suggesting he represent me. We have
been together ever since and have a very close relationship.
He has been a splendid agent.'

1958 29th January: Birth of Pinter's son, Daniel. 'Michael
Codron took an option on *The Birthday Party* and gave me
£50 just as Daniel was being born. The play was going to go
on, I think, in April. Vivien was in hospital, we actually had
nowhere to go when she came out. We had been offered a
double job at Birmingham, at the Alex (Alexander Theatre)
for the season, that would have meant £17 a week each,
which would have been an enormous salary for us. But I said
to Vivien: "I really think we should stay in London, because
I have the play coming on." But she could not take it as a
concrete thing, it was no more than a dream for her.
However, I insisted and we did stay in London . . . We
would in fact have done better to have gone to Birmingham,
but we didn't and my life just changed.'[15]

February: Pinter takes a flat in Chiswick, London.

28th April: First performance of *The Birthday Party* at the
Arts Theatre, Cambridge. (Meg: Beatrix Lehmann; Stanley:
Richard Pearson; Goldberg: John Slater. Directed by Peter
Wood).

19th May: First London performance of *The Birthday Party*
at the Lyric Theatre, Hammersmith. The reviewers of the
daily papers unanimously reject the play; Milton Shulman in
the *Evening Standard*, 20th May:

> *Sorry, Mr Pinter, you're just not funny enough.* Sitting through
> *The Birthday Party* at the Lyric, Hammersmith, is like trying to
> solve a crossword puzzle where every vertical clue is designed to
> put you off the horizontal. It will be best enjoyed by those who
> believe that obscurity is its own reward. Others may not feel up

[15] Pinter, conversation with the author, 1967.

to the mental effort needed to illuminate the coy corners of this opaque, sometimes macabre comedy. Not nearly as witty as Simpson's *The Resounding Tinkle* nor nearly as chilling as Ionesco's *The Lesson*, its appeal is based upon the same kind of irreverant verbal anarchy. But the fun to be derived out of the futility of language is fast becoming a cliché of its own. And Mr Pinter just isn't funny enough. . . .

The Times:

The first act sounds an offbeat note of madness; in the second the note has risen to a sort of delirium; and the third act studiously refrains from the slightest hint of what the other two may have been about.

The Manchester Guardian:

. . . What all this means, only Mr Pinter knows, for as his characters speak in non-sequiturs, half-gibberish and lunatic ravings, they are unable to explain their actions, thoughts, or feelings. If the author can forget Beckett, Ionesco and Simpson, he may do much better next time. . . .

21st May: Pinter in a letter to Donald McWhinnie, Assistant head of the BBC's radio drama department, who had shown interest in getting a radio play from him: '. . . .The Play has come a cropper, as you know. What else? The clouds. They are varied, very varied. And all sorts of birds. They come and perch on the window-sill, asking for food! It is touching. Thank you for your encouragement. . . .'
24th May: *The Birthday Party* is taken off after only a week's run. Total receipts for the week: £260 11s. 8d.
25th May: In *The Sunday Times* Harold Hobson comes to the defence of *The Birthday Party*:

One of the actors in Harold Pinter's *The Birthday Party* at the Lyric, Hammersmith, announces in the programme that he read History at Oxford and took his degree with Fourth Class Honours. Now I am well aware that Mr Pinter's play received extremely bad notices last Tuesday morning. At the moment I write these lines it is uncertain even whether the play will still be in the bill when they appear, though it is probable it will soon be seen elsewhere. Deliberately, I am willing to risk whatever reputation I have as a judge of plays by saying that *The Birthday Party* is not a Fourth, not even a Second, but a First, and that Mr Pinter, on the evidence of this work, possesses the most original, disturbing and arresting talent in theatrical London. I am anxious, for the simple reason that the discovery and encouragement of new dramatists of quality is the present most important task of the British theatre, to put this matter clearly and emphatically. The influence of unfavourable notices on the box office is enormous; but in lasting effect it is nothing. *Look Back in Anger* and the work of Beckett both received poor notices the morning after production. But that has not prevented those very different writers, Mr Beckett and Mr Osborne, from being regarded throughout the world as the most important dramatists who now use the English tongue. The early Shaw got bad notices; Ibsen got scandalous notices. Mr Pinter is not only in good company, he is in the very best company.

There is only one quality that is essential to a play. It is the quality that can be found both in *Hamlet* and in *Simple Spymen*. A play must entertain; it must hold the attention; it must give pleasure. Unless it does that it is useless for stage purposes. No amount of intellect, of high moral intent, or of beautiful writing is of the slightest avail if a play is not in itself theatrically interesting. Theatrically speaking *The Birthday Party* is absorbing. It is witty. Its characters . . . are fascinating. The plot, which consists, with all kinds of verbal arabesques and echoing explorations of memory and fancy, of the springing of a trap, is first rate. The whole play has the same atmosphere of delicious, impalpable and hair-raising terror which makes *The Turn of the Screw* one of the best stories in the world.

Mr Pinter has got hold of a primary fact of existence. We live on the verge of disaster. One sunny afternoon, whilst Peter May is making a century at Lords against Middlesex, and the shadows are creeping along the grass, and the old men are dozing in the Long Room, a hydrogen bomb may explode. That is one sort of threat. But Mr Pinter's is of a subtler sort. It breathes in the air. It cannot be seen, but it enters the room every time the door is opened. There is something in your past – it does not matter what – which will catch up with you. Though you go to the uttermost parts of the earth, and hide yourself in the most obscure lodgings in the least popular of towns, one day there is a possibility that two men will appear. They will be looking for you and you cannot get away. And someone will be looking for *them*, too. There is terror everywhere. Meanwhile it is best to make jokes (Mr Pinter's jokes are very good), and to play blind man's buff, and to bang on a toy drum, anything to forget the slow approach of doom. *The Birthday Party* is a Grand Guignol of the susceptibilities.

The fact that no one can say precisely what it is about, or give the address from which the intruding Goldberg and McCann come, or say precisely why it is that Stanley is so frightened by them is, of course, one of its greatest merits. It is exactly in this vagueness that its spine-chilling quality lies. If we knew what Miles had done, *The Turn of the Screw* would fade away. As it is Mr Pinter has learned the lesson of the Master. Henry James would recognize him as an equal. . . .Mr Pinter and *The Birthday Party*, despite their experience last week, will be heard of again. Make a note of their names.

18th July: After his first attempt to write a radio play *Something in Common* had – for reasons which are no longer ascertainable – failed to lead to a performance, the BBC commissions another sixty-minute radio play from Pinter.
27th October: The BBC acknowledges receipt of that script – *A Slight Ache*.
1959 28th February: World première of *The Dumb Waiter* – in German – at Frankfurt-am-Main.
11th May: *The Birthday Party* performed by the Tavistock Players at the Tower Theatre, Canonbury, Islington. The semi-amateur cast gives a first-rate performance, which rehabilitates the play in the eyes of some critics.
7th July: Pinter submits the synopsis of a new radio play, *A Night Out*, to the BBC
15th July: *One to Another*, a new Lyric Revue, opens at the Lyric, Hammersmith. It contains two sketches by Pinter, 'Trouble in the Works' and 'The Black and White'.
29th July: *A Slight Ache* broadcast in the BBC Third

Programme. (Edward: Maurice Denham; Flora: Vivien Merchant; Directed by Donald McWhinnie).

9th October: *A Night Out* completed.

10th December: *The Birthday Party* at the State Theatre, Braunschweig, Germany.

1960   21st January: *The Room* (Rose: Vivien Merchant; Mr Kidd: Henry Woolf, at whose instigation the play was written for Bristol; directed by Harold Pinter) and *The Dumb Waiter* (directed by James Roose-Evans) at the Hampstead Theatre Club. *The Times*:

> To find another artist with whom Mr Pinter may fruitfully be compared one must look farther afield than drama, or even literature, to Music – to Webern, in fact, with whose compositions Mr Pinter's plays have much in common. Like Webern he has a taste for short, compressed forms, as in his revue-sketches which are really complete plays five minutes long, and like Webern he inclines to etiolated pointilliste textures, forever trembling on the edge of silence, and to structures elusive, yet so precisely organized that they possess an inner tension nonetheless potent because its sources are not completely understood.

1st March: *A Night Out* broadcast in BBC Third Programme. (Albert Stokes: Barry Foster; The Girl: Vivien Merchant; Seeley: Harold Pinter; directed by Donald McWhinnie).

8th March: *The Room* and *The Dumb Waiter* transferred, with some cast changes, to the Royal Court Theatre. (*The Room* is now directed by Anthony Page).

22nd March: *The Birthday Party*, which has been accepted by Peter Willes, Head of Drama at Rediffusion-TV, after he had seen a revue sketch by Pinter, televised by ARD. (Meg: Margery Withers, who played the part in the Tavistock Players production; Stanley: Richard Pearson, who played it in the first stage presentation. Directed by Joan Kemp-Welch).

24th April: *A Night Out* televised by ABC-TV. (Albert Stokes: Tom Bell; The Girl: Vivien Merchant; Seeley: Harold Pinter; directed by Philip Saville).

11

27th April: *The Caretaker* opens at The Arts Theatre Club, London. (Mick: Alan Bates; Aston, Peter Woodthorpe; Davies: Donald Pleasence. Directed by Donald McWhinnie). *The Times*:

> *A Slight Play that Pleases and Dazes* . . . a slight, unrhetorical play with one set and only three characters . . . the pleasurable confusion in which Mr Pinter's writing leaves one. The surface of his works is simple and lucid – none of the individual things his characters say are very subtle or obscure. What is obscure however is the connection between any two things a character says (except on a stream-of-consciousness level) and even more the connection between what one character says and what another says afterwards. Even how the characters come to occupy the same room at the same time (together without togetherness) is as often as not kept from us. What part does the tramp-caretaker play in the lives of his ex-lunatic host and his brother? Why do they act as they do? How do they communicate, or do they communicate at all? We do not know, and strangely enough, while the play is on, it never occurs to us to worry about not knowing.

John Rosselli in *The Guardian*:

> . . . a fine play, consistently carried through apart from a few puzzling but not important details. . . . A particular virtue is that nowhere does Mr Pinter treat non-communication as an extraneous, rather banal 'point' to be made (compare Ionesco's *The Chairs*). It is knit with the people and the action. Yet one must still say that this plunging of audiences into the world of the shut-off mind is something that leads away from the main stream of art – whose main business, surely, is with the adult relationships we painfully try to keep and deepen. It is a fascinating byway and Mr Pinter's work literally fascinates; but one hopes he will move on.

Patrick Gibbs in the *Daily Telegraph*:

> . . . had *Waiting for Godot* never been written this piece would be judged to be masterly. As it is it appeared to be excessively derivative almost to the point of parody.

12

30th May: *The Caretaker* transfers to the West End, Duchess Theatre.

5th June: Kenneth Tynan in *The Observer*:

> With *The Caretaker*, which moved last week from the Arts to the Duchess, Harold Pinter has begun to fulfill the promise that I signally failed to see in *The Birthday Party* two years ago. The latter play was a clever fragment grown dropsical with symbolic content . . . the piece was full of those familiar overtones that seem to be inseparable from much of *avant-garde* drama. In *The Caretaker* symptoms of paranoia are still detectable . . . but their intensity is considerably abated; and the symbols have mostly retired to the background. What remains is a play about people.

21st July: *Night School*, a new television play by Pinter, broadcast by Associated Rediffusion-TV. (Walter: Milo O'Shea; Sally: Vivien Merchant; directed by Joan Kemp-Welch).

27th July: *The Birthday Party* opens at Actors' Workshop, San Francisco, directed by Glynne Wickham. (First professional performance of Pinter in USA)

29th October: *Der Hausmeister* (German version of *The Caretaker*) opens at the Düsseldorf Schauspielhaus.

2nd December: The radio play *The Dwarfs* broadcast by BBC Third Programme. (Len: Richard Pasco; Mark: Alec Scott; Pete: Jon Rollason; directed by Barbara Bray).

1961 15th January: Recognition from one of the strict upholders of tradition in the British theatre. Noël Coward writes in *The Sunday Times*:

> . . . at the moment . . . there is only one 'New Movement' straight play playing to good business in a London theatre – *The Caretaker* by Harold Pinter. This, to me, is in no way a strange phenomenon. Mr Pinter is neither pretentious, pseudo-intellectual nor self-consciously propagandist. True, the play has no apparent plot, much of it is repetitive and obscure, and it is certainly placed in the lowest possible social stratum; but it is written with an original and unmistakable sense of theatre and is impeccably acted and directed. Above all, its basic premise is

victory rather than defeat. I am surprised that the critics thought so well of it. Doubtless they were misled by the comfortingly familiary squalor of its locale and the fact that one of the principal characters is a tramp.

Noël Coward's admiration remained undiminished, and had indeed grown five years later:

> Pinter is a very curious, strange element. He uses language marvellously well. He is what I would call a genuine original. Some of his plays are a little obscure, a little difficult, but he's a superb craftsman, creating atmosphere with words that sometimes are violently unexpected.[16]

18th January: *A Slight Ache* staged as part of a triple bill, *Three* (together with one-act plays by John Mortimer and N. F. Simpson), at the Arts Theatre Club, London. (Edward: Emlyn Williams; Flora: Allison Leggatt; Matchseller: Richard Briers; directed by Donald McWhinnie).
27th January: *Le Gardien* (French version of *The Caretaker*) at the Théâtre de Lutèce in Paris, with Roger Blin as Davies, poorly received by the critics.
Le Figaro:

> (The Play) erects *misérabilisme* into a dogma, promotes starvation to the level of heroism, and glorifies the sordid and petty in boredom.

France-Soir:

> Either (the play) is an imposture, or the British have gone mad.

L'Humanité:

> . . . the rear-guard of the *avant-garde*.

[16] Interview in *The Sunday Telegraph*, 22nd May 1966.

21st February: In the London production of *The Caretaker* Pinter takes over the part of Mick from Alan Bates for four weeks.

11th May: *The Collection* broadcast by Associated Rediffusion. (Harry: Griffith Jones; James: Anthony Bate; Stella: Vivien Merchant; Bill: John Ronane; directed by Joan Kemp-Welch).

27th May: *The Caretaker* closes its run at the Duchess Theatre after 425 performances.

17th September: *A Night Out* staged by Leila Blake at the Gate Theatre, Dublin.

2nd October: *A Night Out* opens at the Comedy Theatre, London as part of a triple bill, *Counterpoint*, together with plays by David Campton and James Saunders.

4th October: *The Caretaker* opens at the Lyceum Theatre, New York. (With the London cast except that Robert Shaw had taken Peter Woodthorpe's place as Aston). Howard Taubman in the *New York Times*:

> Out of a scabrous derelict and two mentally unbalanced brothers Harold Pinter has woven a play of strangely compelling beauty and passion. *The Caretaker* which opened last night at the Lyceum, proclaims its young English author as one of the important playwrights of our day. . . . A work of rare originality, *The Caretaker* will tease and cling to the mind. No matter what happens in the months to come, it will lend lustre to this Broadway season.

1962 February: *The Caretaker* ends its New York run, having achieved much artistic but little commercial success. *The Collection* opens at the Aldwych Theatre, London, in a double bill with Strindberg's *Playing with Fire*. (Harry: Michael Hordern; James: Kenneth Haigh; Stella: Barbara Murray; Bill: John Ronane; directed by Peter Hall and Harold Pinter).

7th September: Pinter reads his story, *The Examination*, on BBC Third Programme.

November: Joseph Losey's film *The Servant*, after the novel by Robin Maugham, screenplay by Harold Pinter, opens in London.

12th December: Work starts on filmings *The Caretaker* in a derelict house (31, Downs Road, Hackney) not far from Pinter's childhood home. The production costs of about £30,000 have been raised by a group of showbusiness personalities, including Noël Coward, Richard Burton and Elizabeth Taylor, Peter Sellers, Peter Hall, Leslie Caron, etc. The film is directed by Clive Donner. The cast is the same as that of the New York run.

1963 28th March: *The Lover* broadcast by Associated Rediffusion. (Richard: Alan Badel; Sarah: Vivien Merchant; directed by Joan Kemp-Welch).

27th June: First screening of the film version of *The Caretaker* at the Berlin film festival.

1st July: The film version of *The Caretaker* wins one of the Silver Bears at the Berlin film festival.

18th September: *The Lover* and *The Dwarfs* open at the Arts Theatre Club, London. (*The Lover*, Richard: Scott Forbes; Sarah: Vivien Merchant; directed by Harold Pinter; *The Dwarfs*; Len: John Hurt; Pete: Michael Forrest; Mark: Philip Bond; directed by Harold Pinter and Guy Vaesen).

30th September: Joan Kemp-Welch's production of *The Lover* wins the Prix Italia for Television Drama at Naples.

23rd November: Harold Pinter, Alan Badel and Vivien Merchant receive Guild of British Television Producers and Directors awards for the script and leading performances in *The Lover*.

1964 January: The film version of *The Caretaker* starts its run in New York under the title *The Guest*.

February-March: The BBC Third Programme broadcasts nine short sketches by Pinter, some of which had already been staged in revue, while others had remained unperformed: *Last To Go; Applicant; Request Stop; That's Your Trouble; That's All; Interview; Trouble in the Works; The Black and White; Dialogue for Three*. (Director: Michael Bakewell).

2nd March: Pinter wins the British Screenwriters' Guild award for his screenplay of *The Servant*.

2nd June: Pinter reads his story *Tea Party* on the BBC Third Programme.

18th June: *The Birthday Party* revived at the Aldwych Theatre, London. (Meg: Doris Hare; Stanley: Bryan Pringle; Goldberg: Brewster Mason; McCann: Patrick Magee; directed by Harold Pinter).

1965 30th March: Pinter wins the British Film Academy Award for the best screenplay of 1964 for his adaptation of Penelope Mortimer's novel *The Pumpkin Eater* (directed by Jack Clayton, with Peter Finch and Anne Bancroft in the leading parts).

March: *The Homecoming* starts its pre-London tour.

25th March: The television play *Tea Party* broadcast by BBC1 in the series 'The Largest Theatre in the World' organized by the European Broadcasting Union, through which television organizations throughout Europe co-operate in joint commissions from leading authors. (Robert Disson: Leo McKern; Wendy: Vivien Merchant; Diana: Jennifer Wright; Willy: Charles Gray; directed by Charles Jarrott). Simultaneously, or in the following week, the play was also screened in France, Luxembourg, Belgium, Switzerland, Austria, Spain, Holland, Denmark, Sweden, Norway.

3rd June: *The Homecoming* opens at the Aldwych Theatre, London. (Max: Paul Rogers; Lenny; Ian Holm; Teddy: Michael Bryant; Ruth: Vivien Merchant; directed by Peter Hall).

Harold Hobson in *The Sunday Times*:

> . . . Harold Pinter's cleverest play. It is so clever, in fact so misleadingly clever, that at a superficial glance it seems to be not clever enough. This is an appearance only, but it is one for which Mr Pinter will suffer in the estimation of audiences, who will perceive an aesthetic defect that does not exist, in the place of a moral vacuum that does. . . . I am troubled by the complete absence from the play of any moral comment whatsoever. To

make such a comment does not necessitate an author's being conventional or religious; it does necessitate, however, his having made up his mind about life, his having come to some decision. . . .We have no idea what Mr Pinter thinks of Ruth or Teddy or what value their existence has. They have no relation to life outside themselves. They live; their universe lives: but not the universe.

October: Pinter achieves his first breakthrough in Paris with the production of *The Collection* and *The Lover* as a double bill, directed by Claude Régy and starring Delphine Seyrig.

15th November: Pinter appears in the part of Garcia in Sartre's *Huis Clos* on BBC Television, under the direction of Philip Saville.

1966 June: Pinter is awarded the CBE (Commander of the Order of the British Empire) in the Birthday Honours List.

11th October: *Le Retour (The Homecoming)* opens at the Théâtre de Paris. (Max: Pierre Brasseur; Lenny: Claude Rich; Ruth: Emmanuèle Riva; directed by Claude Régy).

November: World Première of the film *The Quiller Memorandum*, after the novel by Adam Hall, screenplay by Harold Pinter (with Alec Guinness; George Segal, Max von Sydow; directed by Michael Anderson).

20th December: *The Homecoming* opens at Boston.

1967 3rd January: *The Homecoming* opens at New York, at the Music Box. (The London production and cast, except that Michael Bryant's place in the part of Teddy was taken by Michael Craig). Walter Kerr in the *New York Times*, 6th January 1967:

. . . Mr Pinter is one of the most naturally gifted dramatists to have come out of England since the war. I think he is making the mistake, just now, of supposing that the elusive kernel of impulse that will do for a forty-minute play will serve just as handily, and just as suspensefully, for an all-day outing. *The Homecoming*, to put the matter as simply as possible, needs a second situation: We could easily take an additional act if the author would only scrap the interminable first. The tide must come in at least twice if we are to be fascinated so long by the shoreline.

28th February: *The Basement* is broadcast on BBC TV. (Stott: Harold Pinter; Jane: Kika Markham; Law: Derek Godfrey; directed by Charles Jarrot). This was originally written as a film script under the title *The Compartment* for a projected film – composed of three short subjects to be written by Beckett, Ionesco and Pinter and produced under the auspices of Grove Press, New York. Only one of these, Beckett's *Film* was completed.

February: First showing of the film *Accident* (from the novel by Nicholas Mosley, screenplay by Harold Pinter, directed by Joseph Losey; with Dirk Bogarde, Vivien Merchant, Stanley Baker, Delphine Seyrig).

28th March: *The Homecoming* wins the Tony award for the best play on Broadway.

May: *The Homecoming* is voted the best play on Broadway by the New York drama critics' circle and receives the Whitbread Anglo-American award for the best British play on Broadway.

27th July: Robert Shaw's play *The Man in the Glass Booth*, directed by Pinter, with Donald Pleasence in the lead, opens in London.

1968 21st January: The London press reports that Pinter refused to make the cuts demanded by the Lord Chamberlain in his new one-act play *Landscape*, which is to be staged by the Royal Shakespeare Company at the Aldwych Theatre. Eventually Pinter's insistence that the one or two offending four-letter words are essential leads to the abandonment of the plan to stage the play in the current season.

25th April: As radio is not subject to the Lord Chamberlain's censorship, *Landscape* receives its first, unaltered and uncut performance in the BBC's Third Programme. In the stereophonic production Peggy Ashcroft appears as Beth, Eric Porter as Duff, under Guy Vaesen's direction.

Autumn: Completion of the film version of *The Birthday Party* in London (Stanley: Robert Shaw; Meg: Dandy

19

Nichols; Goldberg: Sidney Tafler; McCann: Patrick Magee; directed by William Friedkin).

10th October: Stage versions of *Tea Party* and *The Basement* open at East Side Playhouse, New York.

9th December: The film of *The Birthday Party* opens in New York.

1969 January: *Silence* completed.

Screenplay of the adaptation of L. P. Hartley's novel *The Go-between* completed.

9th April: The sketch *Night* first performed as part of the evening of one-act plays about marriage by various authors, *Mixed Doubles*, at the Comedy Theatre, London. (Man: Nigel Stock; Woman: Vivien Merchant).

2nd July: *Landscape* and *Silence* open at the Aldwych Theatre, London. (In *Landscape*: Beth: Peggy Ashcroft; Duff: David Waller. In *Silence*: Ellen: Frances Cuka; Rumsay: Anthony Bate: Bates: Norman Rodway; both directed by Peter Hall).

17th September: *Le Gardien* (*The Caretaker*, newly adapted by Eric Kahane) opens at the Théâtre Moderne in Paris. B. Porot Delpech writes in *Le Monde*:

> The Théâtre Moderne is a thousand times justified in appealing against the bad reception accorded to *The Caretaker* by press and public in 1961 at the Théâtre de Lutèce. . . . In the meantime our sensibility has grown accustomed to the new Anglo-Saxon theatre. . . . A great play.

1970: Awarded the Shakespeare Prize of the Freiherr v. Stein Foundation, Hamburg.

1971 1st June: *Old Times* opens at the Aldwych Theatre, London. (Deeley: Colin Blakely; Kate: Dorothy Tutin; Anna: Vivien Merchant; directed by Peter Hall.)

October: *C'était hier* (*Old Times*) at the Théâtre Montparnasse, Paris.

November: *Old Times* at Billy Rose Theater, New York.

1972 29th April: *Alte Zeiten* (*Old Times*) at Thalia Theater, Hamburg.

1973 13th April: *Monologue* on BBC TV (The Man: Henry Woolf; directed by Christopher Morahan).

Autumn: Pinter appointed one of Peter Hall's Associate Directors at the National Theatre.

1975 23rd April: *No Man's Land* opens at the National Theatre at the Old Vic. (Hirst: Ralph Richardson; Spooner: John Gielgud; Foster: Michael Feast; Briggs: Terence Rigby; directed by Peter Hall).

15th July: *No Man's Land* transferred to the West End (Wyndham's Theatre).

30th September: *The Times* reports: 'Miss Vivien Merchant, aged 46, the actress, has cited Lady Antonia Fraser, aged 42, the author and wife of Mr Hugh Fraser, aged 57, Conservative MP for Stafford and Stone, and daughter of Lord Longford, in proceedings against her husband Mr Harold Pinter, aged 42, the playwright. A statement yesterday by a public relations firm acting for Mr and Mrs Pinter said the papers were filed on July 25.'

3rd December: *Monologue* broadcast on BBC Radio 3. (The Man: Harold Pinter; directed by Guy Vaesen).

1976 24th June: *Blithe Spirit*, directed by Pinter, opens in the National Theatre's Lyttelton auditorium.

17th November: The film version of Scott Fitzgerald's *The Last Tycoon* (Screenplay by Pinter) opens in New York.

1978 20th September: *Langrishe, Go Down* a screenplay based on the novel by Aidan Higgins that Pinter had adapted in 1970 but which was never filmed, broadcast by BBC TV, directed by David Jones with Jeremy Irons as Otto and Judi Dench as Imogen.

15th November: *Betrayal* opens at the National Theatre, Lyttleton auditorium. Directed by Peter Hall; with Michael Gambon (Jerry); Daniel Massey (Robert) and Penelope Wilton (Emma).

1980 24th April: *The Hothouse* (directed by Pinter) opens in London.

2nd August: *The Times* reports: 'Vivien Mercant, aged 51, the actress was granted a decree nisi in London yesterday against her husband, Harold Pinter, the playwright.'

27th November: Harold Pinter marries Lady Antonia Fraser.

1981   22nd January: *Family Voices* on BBC Radio 3.

13th February: *Family Voices* opens as a 'platform performance' at the National Theatre.

Summer: *The French Lieutenant's Woman* (screenplay by Harold Pinter, based on the novel by John Fowles) achieves a world wide success.

1982   27th March: *The Hothouse* (directed by Pinter) broadcast on BBC TV.

14th October: *Other Places*, a triple bill of short plays, *A Kind of Alaska, Victoria Station* and *Family Voices*, opens in the Cottesloe auditorium of the National Theatre.

1983 The film of *Betrayal* opens, directed by David Jones with Patricia Hodge, Jeremy Irons, Ben Kingsley.

Precisely (short sketch) published and performed.

1984 13th March: *One for the Road*, directed by Pinter with Alan Bates as Nicolas, opens at the Lyric Theatre Studio, Hammersmith London.

Other Places – with *One for the Road* substituted for *Family Voices* – directed by Pinter at the Manhattan Theatre Club, New York.

1985: Pinter and Arthur Miller visit Turkey as representatives of the PEN Club. Pinter is outraged by evidence of persecution and torture of political prisoners, especially writers. Expressing his disgust at US support of the Turkish regime at the US Ambassador's reception, he leaves.

Directs Tennessee Williams' *Sweet Bird of Youth* in London, with Lauren Bacall.

Screenplay: *Turtle Diary* (based on Russell Hoban's novel).

1986: The 'June 20th Society', a discussion group of liberal ideas, founded by Pinter and Lady Antonia.

1987: Screenplay: *The Handmaid's Tale* based on the novel by Margaret Atwood.

1988: 'Charter 88', a manifesto demanding a Bill of Rights and a written constitution for Britain, signed by Pinter and other leading left-wing intellectuals, including Salman Rushdie and John Mortimer.

20th October: *Mountain Language* (directed by Pinter) opens at the National Theatre.

Screenplay: *Reunion*, based on a novel by Fred Uhlman.

Screenplay: *The Comfort of Strangers*, based on the novel by Ian McEwan.

Screenplay: *The Heat of the Day*, based on a novel by Elizabeth Bowen.

1989: Screenplay: *Victory*, based on Joseph Conrad's novel.

1990: Screenplay: *The Trial*, based on Kafka's novel.

September: First publication of Pinter's early novel *The Dwarfs*. Revival of *The Homecoming*, directed by Peter Hall at the Comedy Theatre, London.

1991: Revival of *The Caretaker* with Donald Pleasence in his original part of Davies, at the Comedy Theatre, London.

April: Pinter symposium at Ohio State University, Columbus, attended by several hundred Pinter scholars. First public airing of the sketch *The New World Order* which Pinter has himself recorded, and first rehearsed reading of *Party Time*, of which Pinter has sent a copy.

26th October: *Old Times* in a television version adapted by Pinter screened by BBC 2.

31st October: *Party Time* opens at the Almeida Theatre, London, preceded by *Mountain Language*, both plays directed by Pinter.

1992 17th November: *Party Time* broadcast on Channel 4.

1993: Donates his manuscripts to the British Library.

7th September: *Moonlight* opens at Almeida Theatre, London. Directs *Oleanna* by David Mamet at the Royal Court Theatre.

1994: Works on screenplay of Nabokov's *Lolita (not used)*.

May: Pinter Festival, Gate Theatre, Dublin.

1995 15th March: Wins David Cohen British Literature Prize.

Chichester Festival: acts in *Hothouse*, directs *Taking Sides* by Ronald Harewood.

1996 12th September: *Ashes to Ashes* (directed by Pinter) opens at the Royal Court, Ambassadors Theatre.

1999 25th June: Violently attacks NATO bombing of Serbia in a speech to the Confederation of Psychologists in London.

2000 16th March: *Celebration* and *The Room* (directed by Pinter) open at the Almeida Theatre, London.

2

Background and Basic Premises

Since the nineteen-eighties Harold Pinter has become a leading, and passionate, campaigner on a variety of public issues: civil rights in Britain, American interventionism in Latin America, the plight of tortured writers in Turkey. And yet, when he first emerged as a playwright in the late nineteen-fifties and early sixties his work seemed to be at variance with the then prevailing strongly political trend in theatre exemplified by other young dramatists like Osborne, Wesker or Arden. His work gave the impression of being wholly unconcerned with political ideology or preoccupations. He himself, at the time, contributed to this impression. When, during the period of the Macmillan government's first negotiations about Britain's entry into the Common Market, *Encounter* asked a variety of public figures to give their views on the matter, Pinter's reply was the shortest of all: 'I have no interest in the matter and do not care what happens.'

Yet, while it is true that his plays at that period avoided openly political issues, in his attitude as a citizen and in his support for a variety of causes, Pinter has always been highly politically committed: 'I'm categorically anti the Americans in Vietnam. And I feel strongly in favour of Israel,' he said to an interviewer in April 1968.[1] And indeed, behind the highly private world of his plays, there also lurk what are,

[1] In search of Harold Pinter', by Kathleen Tynan in the *Evening Standard*, London, 26th April 1968.

after all, the basic political problems: the use and abuse of power, the fight for living-space, cruelty, terror. Only very superficial observers could overlook this social, this political side of the playwright.

Nor, if one looks at Harold Pinter's background, could these basic pre-occupations appear as anything but inevitable. The East End of London where Pinter grew up as a child of the nineteen-thirties was a political battlefield. A large Jewish population, mainly refugees from the great Russian pogroms of 1905, but swelled by newer arrivals after the First World War and, later, the victims of Hitler, was battling for a foothold and a livelihood among Cockneys, Chinese, Negroes and Irish. It was in the streets of the East End that Mosley's Fascists clashed with left-wing Jewish militants. And after the end of the Second World War these tensions did not die down.

'Everyone,' says Pinter, 'encounters violence in some way or other. I did encounter it in quite an extreme form after the war, in the East End, when the Fascists were coming back to life in England. I got into quite a few fights down there. If you looked remotely like a Jew you might be in trouble. Also, I went to a Jewish club, by an old railway arch, and there were quite a lot of people often waiting with broken milk bottles in a particular alley we used to walk through. There were one or two ways of getting out of it – one was a purely physical way, of course, but you couldn't do anything about the milk bottles – we didn't have any milk bottles. The best way was to talk to them you know, sort of "Are you all right?" "Yes, I'm all right." "Well, that's all right then, isn't it?" And all the time keep walking towards the lights of the main road. . . .We were often taken for Communists. If you went by, or happened to be passing a Fascist street meeting and looked in any way antagonistic – this was in Ridley Road market, near Dalston Junction – they'd interpret your very being, especially if you had books under your arms, as evidence of your being a Communist. There was a good deal of violence there, in those days.'[2]

[2] Lawrence M. Bensky, 'Harold Pinter' in *Writers at Work*. The *Paris Review* Interviews, Third Series, New York, Viking Press, 1967; London, Secker & Warburg, 1968, p. 363.

There can be little doubt that Pinter's radical pacifism, which led him, at the age of eighteen, to risk a prison sentence rather than do his national service, was a reaction to this experience of violence in the years of his boyhood and adolescence. To choose the path of the conscientious objector, however, *is* a deeply political act, but a political act of a peculiarly basic nature, involving, as it does, a refusal even to listen to the arguments for or against a particular war, a particular political situation. To a radical pacifist of this type all particular arguments pale into nothingness compared to the one essential fact that to be taking part in *any* war, in *any* fighting, must involve the taking of human life. A political decision at this deep, fundamental level can easily appear as a rejection of all politics on the more mundane level of daily debate. Pinter's attitude as a playwright is directly analogous to this paradox: determined to tackle his characters at the very root of their existence, he was led to a seeming neglect of the less essential aspects of their life and personality. When Kenneth Tynan pressed him on this point in a radio interview in 1960, asking him why his characters never seemed interested in sex (that was before *The Lover* and *The Homecoming*), politics or general ideas, Pinter replied that he was dealing with characters who stood at essential turning points in their lives: 'There is no reason to suppose that at one time or another they didn't listen to a political meeting, or they might even have voted . . . I'm dealing with these characters at the extreme edge of their living, where they are living pretty much alone, at their hearth, their home hearth . . . We all, I think . . . may have sexual relationships or go to political meetings or discuss ideas, but when we get back to our rooms and we are faced with a bed and we are either alone or with someone else, then . . . I don't think we go on long without ideas or political allegiances. . . . I mean, there comes a point surely, where this living in *the* world must be tied up with living in *your own* world, where you are – in your room. . . . Before you manage to adjust yourself to living alone in your room . . . you are not terribly fit and equipped to go out and fight the battles . . . which are fought mostly in abstractions in the outside world.'[3]

Existential adjustment, coming to terms with one's own being, precedes, and necessarily predetermines, one's attitude to society, politics and general ideas. Like Beckett and Kafka Pinter's attitude here is that of an existentalist: the mode of a man's *being* determines his *thinking*. Hence, to come to grips with the true sources of their attitudes, the playwright must catch his characters at the decisive points in their lives, when they are confronted with the crisis of adjustment to themselves, which precedes their going out into the world to confront society, its politics, its ideas and issues.

It is unlikely that Pinter could have been influenced, or even aware of, the philosophy of that originator of modern existentalism, Martin Heidegger, when he started to write his plays, or to formulate his ideas. All the more significant is it that Pinter, like Heidegger, takes as his starting point, in man's confrontation with himself and the nature of his own being, that fundamental anxiety which is nothing less than a living being's basic awareness of the threat of non-being, of annihilation. Pinter's people are in a room, and they are frightened, scared. What are they scared of? 'Obviously, they are scared of what is outside the room. Outside the room is a world bearing upon them, which is frightening . . . we are all in this, all in a room, and outside is a world . . . which is most inexplicable and frightening, curious and alarming'.[4]

Yet in Pinter's plays this existential fear is never just a philosophical abstraction. It is, ultimately, based on the experience of a Jewish boy in the East End of London, of a Jew in the Europe of Hitler. In talking about his first play, *The Room*, Pinter himself made this point very clearly: 'This old woman is living in a room which, she is convinced, is the

[3] Pinter, interviewed by Kenneth Tynan in the series *People Today*, BBC Home Service, 28th October 1960; pre-recorded 19th August 1960.
[4] Pinter, *ibid.*

best in the house, and she refused to know anything about the basement downstairs. She says it's damp and nasty, and the world outside is cold and icy, and that in her warm and comfortable room her security is complete. But, of course, it isn't; an intruder comes to upset the balance of everything, in other words points to the delusion on which she is basing her life. I think the same thing applies in *The Birthday Party*. Again this man is hidden away in a seaside boarding house . . . then two people arrive out of nowhere, and I don't consider this an unnatural happening. I don't think it is all that surrealistic and curious because surely *this thing, of people arriving at the door, has been happening in Europe in the last twenty years. Not only the last twenty years, the last two to three hundred.'*[5]*

Man's existential fear, not as an abstraction, not as a surreal phantasmagoria, but as something real, ordinary and acceptable as an everyday occurrence – here we have the core of Pinter's work as a dramatist. He acknowledged the influence of a number of writers: 'I read Hemingway, Dostoevski, Joyce, and Henry Miller at a very early age, and Kafka. I'd read Beckett's novels too, but I'd never heard of Ionesco until I'd written the first few plays'.[6] Of these he says Kafka and Beckett had made the greatest impression on him: 'when I read them it rang a bell, that's all, within me. I thought: something is going on here which is going on in me too'.[7] But whereas both Kafka and Beckett are moving in a surreal world of acknowledged phantasy and dream, Pinter, essentially, remains on the firm ground of everyday reality, even though in some of his earlier plays symbolic or even supernatural elements are later introduced into the action (the symbolic blind negro in *The Room*, the mysteriously operated food lift in *The Dumb Waiter*, the enigmatic matchseller in *A Slight Ache* who may well be merely the

[5] Pinter, interviewed by John Sherwood, BBC European Service, 3rd March 1960.
*My italics, M.E.
[6] Lawrence M. Bensky, *op cit*.
[7] Pinter, interviewed by John Sherwood, see above.

emanation of the two other characters' fears); but even in these plays the starting point is always a very real situation with the most closely observed real, even hyper-naturalistic dialogue, so that the phantasy element when it does make an appearance is clearly identifiable as the outward projection, the concretization, of these very real characters' dreams and anxieties. In the earliest of Pinter's plays, *The Room*, this attempt to introduce a symbol of death and alienation leads to a break in style and detracts from the play's effect. In the later instances these devices proved more effective; nevertheless Pinter gradually abandoned them and prefers now to remain within a firm framework of 'real' events.

And yet: Pinter is not a naturalistic dramatist. This is the paradox of his artistic personality. The dialogue and the characters are real, but the over-all effect is one of mystery, of uncertainty, of poetic ambiguity. An understanding of the cause of this strange paradox will go far towards helping us to find the key to Pinter's method and meaning, and the secret of his impact on the stage.

The first deviation from the usual realistically constructed play lies in the element of uncertainty about the motivation of the characters, their backgrounds, their very identity. Frequently this has led critics to accuse Pinter of deliberate mystification: is he withholding information from the audience merely to be able to tease them, like a crime writer who deliberately withholds or distorts the clues to the perpetrator of the crime in order to obtain cheap suspense.

Pinter's own reply to such accusations of bad faith is a categorical 'no'. When he received a letter which read: 'Dear Sir, I would be obliged if you would kindly explain to me the meaning of your play *The Birthday Party*. These are the points which I do not understand: 1. Who are the two men? 2. Where did Stanley come from? 3. Were they all supposed to be normal? You will appreciate that without the answers to my questions I cannot fully understand your play', Pinter is said to have replied as follows: 'Dear Madam, I would be obliged if you would kindly explain to me the meaning of your letter. These are the points which I do not understand:

1. Who are you? 2. Where do you come from? 3. Are you supposed to be normal? You will appreciate that without the answers to your questions I cannot fully understand your letter.'[8]

These, to Pinter, are genuine problems: the problems of identity, of motivation, of verification. They are also – so astonishingly is Pinter in tune with the thinking of our epoch – the basic problems of contemporary philosophy and literature.

'Sometimes,' Pinter confessed to an interviewer,[9] 'I don't know who I'm looking at in the mirror. There's no explanation for that face'. The question: 'Who am I?' is intimately linked with the question of motivation. Only if we know exactly *who* a character is, what his antecedents are, his tastes, his speed of reaction, his vocabulary, his personal values, can we predict with any accuracy how he will act in the future. '. . . the explicit form which is so often taken in twentieth century drama is . . . cheating. The playwright assumes that we have a great deal of information about all his characters, who explain themselves to the audience. In fact, what they are doing most of the time is conforming to the author's own ideology. They don't create themselves as they go along, they are being fixed on the stage for one purpose, to speak for the author who has a point of view to put over. When the curtain goes up on one of my plays, you are faced with a situation, a particular situation, two people sitting in a room, which hasn't happened before, and is just happening at this moment, and we know no more about them than I know about you, sitting at this table. The world is full of surprises. A door can open at any moment and someone will come in. We'd love to know who it is, we'd love to know exactly what he has on his mind and why he comes in, but how often do we know what someone has on his mind or who this somebody is, and what goes to make him and make him what he is, and what his relationship is to

[8] *Daily Mail*, London, 28th November 1967.
[9] Marshall Pugh, in the *Daily Mail*, London, 7th March 1964.

others?"[10] Indeed, in the novel, the omniscient narrator, the author who knew every motivation of his characters and freely told his readers about it, went out with Henry James. In drama, where the apparent absence of a narrator, the apparent objectivity of the action presented on the stage, has masked the problem, the omniscient author remained the rule even during the period of naturalism, when the theory underlying the practice of playwrights actually called for total objectivity. Even Ibsen and Gerhart Hauptmann felt compelled to motivate their characters totally and to disclose their motivation to the audience.

It is this cocksureness of the playwrights (their claim to be in a position to know all about their characters and what makes them tick) which Pinter, with his radical and uncompromising attitude of total sincerity, not only rejects but regards as a form of intolerable arrogance on the part of the writers concerned. How, in the present state of our knowledge of psychology and the complexity and hidden layers of the human mind, can anyone claim to know what motivates himself, let alone another human being?

We do not know, with any semblance of certainty, what motivates our own wives, parents, our own children – why then should we be furnished with a complete dossier about the motivations of any character we casually encounter on the stage? Hence Pinter's rejection of the conventional exposition in drama, which, in a few bold and clever strokes, purports to introduce the principal characters to us with a handy do-it-yourself kit to decipher their origin, background and motivations – all in the first ten to fifteen minutes of the action.

In the programme brochure of the performance of Pinter's *The Room* and *The Dumb Waiter* at the Royal Court Theatre on 8th March 1960 – Pinter's second professional appearance as a dramatist on the London stage – there lay a single, unsigned, printed sheet of paper, clearly Pinter's own attempt to forewarn the audience:

[10] Pinter, interviewed by John Sherwood, see above.

Given a man in a room and he will sooner or later receive a visitor. A visitor entering the room will enter with intent. If two people inhabit the room the visitor will not be the same man for both. A man in a room who receives a visit is likely to be illuminated or horrified by it. The visitor himself might as easily be horrified or illuminated. The man may leave with the visitor or he may leave alone. The visitor may leave alone or stay in the room alone when the man is gone. Or they may both stay together in the room. Whatever the outcome in terms of movement the original condition, in which a man sat alone in a room, will have been subjected to alterations. A man in a room and no one entering lives in expectation of a visit. He will be illuminated or horrified by the absence of a visitor. But however much it is expected, the entrance, when it comes, is unexpected and almost always unwelcome. (He himself, of course, might go out of the door, knock and come in and be his own visitor. It has happened before.)

We all have our function. The visitor will have his. There is no guarantee, however, that he will possess a visiting card with detailed information as to his last place of residence, last job, next job, number of dependents, etc. Nor, for the comfort of all, an identity card, nor a label on his chest. The desire for verification is understandable but cannot always be satisfied. There are no hard distinctions between what is real and what is unreal, nor between what is true and what is false. The thing is not necessarily either true or false; it can be both true and false. The assumption that to verify what has happened and what is happening presents few problems I take to be inaccurate. A character on the stage who can present no convincing argument or information as to his past experience, his present behaviour or his aspirations, nor give a comprehensive analysis of his motives is as legitimate and as worthy of attention as one who, alarmingly, can do all these things. The more acute the experience the less articulate its expression.

This statement, here reproduced in full, contains the germ of quite a number of Pinter's plays beyond the two which it introduced: certainly *The Birthday Party*, *The Caretaker*, *The Homecoming* are already present in embryo in the permutations of possibilities arising from someone waiting in a room, who may or may not receive a visitor, may or may not stay with him, may or may not leave. One of the earliest texts by Pinter to have been published, 'Kullus', a prose poem in dialogue form dated 1949 (when Pinter was barely more than eighteen years old), already contains this very situation:

I let him in by the back door.
There was a brisk moon.
   – Come in.
He stepped inside, slapping his hands, into the room.
   – Go on, Kullus. Go to the fire.
He stooped to the grate and stretched his fingers.
   – You do not welcome warmth,
said Kullus.
   – I?
   – There is no meeting. There is separation. . . .

A girl is introduced into the room. Eventually she asks:

   – which is your room?
she said.
   – I am no longer in my room. . . .[11]

It is the very same situation which, much later, Pinter developed at length in his television play *The Basement*, but which is present in so many of his other plays.

There is thus a remarkable consistency and continuity in Pinter's basic philosophy. The progammatic statement, here quoted at length, shows the close affinity between Pinter's ideas and those held by the school of the *nouveau roman* in France. Like these writers Pinter rejects the author's right to creep inside his characters and to pretend to know what makes them act, even how they feel. All he can do is to render a meticulously accurate account of the movement which takes place, to give a description of the situation at the beginning, before the intrusion, and to note the changes that have taken place at the end. But – if the playwright

---

[11] 'Kullus' in Pinter, *Poems*, London: Enitharmon Press, 1968, pp. 22–4.

cannot claim to know what his characters feel, what makes them act as they do, what then can he communicate to an audience? He can convey his impression of the structure, the pattern of a situation, the movement of its change as it unfolds, again in a pattern, like the movement of a dance; and, on observing this, the author can also communicate his own sense of mystery, of wonder at this strange world of patterns and structures, of beings that move by mysterious and unpredictable impulses, like fish in a huge aquarium. Is that *enough* for an author, a playwright to communicate to an audience which has been used to be offered, in the theatre, complete accounts, with built-in motivation and full explanation of the actions of well-defined characters?

After all, Pinter might argue, we hardly get more than that in real life. We see two people arguing, perhaps starting to fight, in the street. A crowd gathers around them and watches in fascination. It is most unlikely that this crowd could ever get a clear idea about the issues involved in the quarrel, let alone the antecedents and personalities of the two men themselves. And then, after a police car has arrived and taken the two contenders to the police station, the crowd disperses and may never know what the fight was about. And yet that fight had meaning: it communicated something about the stresses, the violence, the heartbreak of life in a big city; and it had something of a poetical validity – as an expression of the mood, the atmosphere of the time, as a metaphor even for all the unhappiness, the tragedy of the human condition. The bystander whose eyes were open, who was sensitive enough to react to the emotional climate of that street incident, could gain an insight, quite a deep insight, into life, a greater awareness, perhaps, of its true nature than if all the facts, all the motivations could have been offered him on a plate (which in reality they hardly ever could), for after all, the opaqueness, the impenetrability of other people's lives, their feelings, their true motivations, is, precisely, an essential feature of the true quality of the world and of our own experience of it.

There is nothing very unusual in these considerations if we

apply them, not to drama, but to a kindred form of literature – poetry. What else is a poem but a pattern, a structure of images, loosely connected, of glimpses of nature, movements, gestures, flashes of insight, snatches of conversation, juxtaposed not to furnish an argument or an explanation, or even a description of the world, but as metaphors for a mood, an intuition of another human being's inner world.

Pinter's first ambition was to write poetry; basically he has remained a lyric poet whose plays are structures of images of the world, very clear and precise and accurate images, which however, and that is the point, never aspire to be arguments, explanations or even coherent stories, aiming to satisfy the audience's craving for vicarious experience through involvement in a nicely rounded incident; instead, Pinter's plays present us with a situation, or a pattern of interlocking situations, designed to coalesce into a lyrical structure of moods and emotional insights.

This, however, does not mean that there is not a great deal of dramatic incident, suspense, witty characterization or pointed dialogue in Pinter's plays. While the overall effect is lyrical, the detail is intensely dramatic. Indeed, the indeterminacy of the characters, the ambiguity of events, heightens the dramatic tension: is the old man in *The Caretaker* really called Davies, or is he called Jenkins? Why is Stanley in *The Birthday Party* being pursued by two sinister figures? Has Stella in *The Collection* been unfaithful to her husband? Why does Ruth in *The Homecoming* accept the offer to become a prostitute so calmly? These questions are not raised by Pinter to be answered; nor are they, as his critics sometimes suggest, raised gratuitously merely to create spurious curiosity and suspense. They are raised as metaphors of the fact that life itself consists of a succession of such questions which cannot, or will not be capable of an answer.

'My characters', Pinter has said, 'tell me so much and no more, with reference to their experience, their aspirations, their motives, their history. Between my lack of biographical data about them and the ambiguity of what they say there

35

lies a territory which is not only worthy of exploration but which it is compulsory to explore. You and I, the characters which grow on a page, most of the time we're inexpressive, giving little away, unreliable, elusive, evasive, obstructive, unwilling. But it's out of these attributes that a language arises. A language . . . where, under what is said, another thing is being said.'[12]

Basically a lyric poet, Pinter is deeply concerned with words, their sound, their rhythm, their meaning. 'I have mixed feelings about words . . . Moving among them, sorting them out, watching them appear on the page, from this I derive a considerable pleasure. But at the same time I have another strong feeling about words which amounts to nothing less than nausea. Such a weight of words confronts us, day in day out, words spoken . . . words written by me and others, the bulk of it a stale, dead terminology, ideas endlessly repeated and permutated, become platitudinous, trite, meaningless. Given this nausea, it's very easy to be overcome by it and step back into paralysis. I imagine most writers know something of this kind of paralysis. But if it is possible to confront this nausea, to follow it to its hilt and move through it, then it is possible to say that something has occurred, that something has even been achieved.'[13]

The tension in Pinter between the delight in words, the love of vivid, vital language on the one hand, and the nausea caused by the contemplation of the vast mass of dead, atrophied language which daily confronts us, is matched by the tension between his characters' inarticulateness, the spontaneity with which they themselves utter their speech, and his own craftsmanship, his determination to *shape* what he writes.

'Given characters', he says, 'who possess a momentum of their own, my job is not to impose on them, not to subject them to a false articulation, by which I mean forcing a

[12] Pinter, speech to the Seventh National Student Drama Festival in Bristol, *Sunday Times*, London, 4th March 1962.

[13] Pinter, *ibid*.

character to speak where he could not speak, making him speak in a way he could not speak, making him speak of what he could never speak. The relationship between author and characters should be a highly respectful one, both ways. And if it's possible to talk of gaining a kind of freedom from writing, it doesn't come by leading one's characters into fixed and calculated postures, but by allowing them to carry their own can, by giving them a legitimate elbow room. This can be extremely painful. It's much easier, much less pain, not to let them live.

'I'd like to make it quite clear at the same time that I don't regard my own characters as uncontrolled, or anarchic. They're not. The function of selection and arrangement is mine. I do all the donkey work, in fact, and I think I can say that I pay a meticulous attention to the shape of things, from the shape of a sentence to the overall structure of the play. This shaping, to put it mildly, is of the first importance. I'm not in favour of diarrhoea on the stage. But I think a double thing happens. You arrange *and* you listen, following the clues you leave for yourself, through the characters. And sometimes a balance is found, where image can freely engender image and where at the same time you are able to keep your sights on the place where the characters are silent and in hiding. It is in the silence that they are most evident to me.'[14]

Silence thus is, for Pinter, an essential, an integral part, and often the climax of his use of language. He has been reproached with a mannerism of silence, an excessive use of long pauses. These strictures are true, but again they seem to me to err in so far as they attribute mercenary motives to what is, to this particular playwright, simply part of his creed as a poet and craftsman, a highly personal way of experiencing, and reacting to, the world around him. And indeed: if we try to listen, with an ear unburdened by an age-old tradition of stage dialogue, to the real speech of real people, we shall find that there are more silences, longer pauses than those allowed tby stage convention. And also that a great deal of

[14] Pinter, *ibid*.

what *is* spoken, in effect, qualifies as little more than silence: 'There are two silences. One when no word is spoken. The other when perhaps a torrent of language is employed. This speech is speaking of a language locked beneath it. That is its continual reference. The speech we hear is an indication of that we don't hear. It is a necessary avoidance, a violent, sly, anguished or mocking smokescreen which keeps the other in its place. When true silence falls we are still left with echo but are nearer nakedness. One way of looking at speech is to say it is a constant strategem to cover nakedness'.[15]

The discovery that stage dialogue is a strategem to cover nakedness, that therefore what is said is merely a chain of rocks and small islands supported by a vast mountain range beneath the sea's surface, this discovery is not Pinter's but was first made by Chekhov. In the fourth act of *The Cherry Orchard* Varya and Lopakhin actually talk about some article of clothing Varya is looking for, but beneath that trivial exchange there runs Lopakhin's ability to summon up the courage to propose to her, and *her* inability to give the conversation a turn that might force him into it. Lopakhin asks her 'What are you looking for?' Varya replies, 'I packed the things myself, yet I can't remember. . . .(*A pause*)'. And in that pause, that hesitation on both sides to speak the first word, to end the silence, lies the turning point of the destiny of these characters. This example – and one could find dozens of others in Chekhov – shows the relation between this kind of 'oblique' dialogue and the pause. It is the pause which shows to the audience that the real preoccupation of the characters, the unspoken subtext, is going on beneath the surface, but that it is unable to come into the open. Pinter has developed this Chekhovian technique much further than his master; in Chekhov's plays there is still a very great deal which is explicit in the traditional convention of stage dialogue; Pinter is able to put far more into the form of 'oblique' dialogue, to let far more of the real emotional tension of a situation shine through the interstices of monosyllabic utterance.

[15] Pinter, *ibid*.

38

One of the labels by which criticism of Pinter has been bedevilled is that of a theatre of non-communication. Lopakhin's failure to declare himself, Varya's inability to make him speak, would clearly also come into this category, so that even if the label fitted, the thing itself could by no means be regarded as a novelty, an invention of the mid-fifties of this century. But, of course, what is involved is not a failure, let alone an impossibility of communication, merely a *difficulty* of explicit communication. 'I think', Pinter said, 'that we communicate only too well, in our silence, in what is unsaid, and that what takes place is continual evasion, desperate rearguard attempts to keep ourselves to ourselves. Communication is too alarming. To enter into someone else's life is too frightening. To disclose to others the poverty within us is too fearsome a possibility. I'm not suggesting that no character in a play can ever say what he in fact means. Not at all. I have found that there invaribaly does come a moment when this happens, where he says something, perhaps, which he has never said before. And where this happens, what he says is irrevocable, and can never be taken back'.[16]

A playwright so fascinated by the difficulty, the terror, the pitfalls of communication will inevitably be fascinated by words and their multifarious uses to disclose and to disguise meaning. Pinter's theatre is a theatre of language; it is from the words and their rhythm that the suspense, dramatic tension, laughter and tragedy spring. Words, in Pinter's plays, become weapons of domination and subservience, silences explode, nuances of vocabulary strip human beings to the skin. Not even his severest critics have ever cast doubt on Pinter's virtuosity in the use of language. His 'tape-recorder' ear has often been praised. And rightly: few English playwrights before him have displayed so acute an observation of the mannerisms, repetitions and nonsensicalities of the vernacular as it is actually spoken. But there is more to Pinter's use of language than merely accurate observation. In

[16] Pinter, *ibid.*

fact, what sounds like tape-recorded speech is highly stylized, even artificial. It is his ability to combine the appearance of total reality with complete control of rhythm and nuance of meaning which is the measure of Pinter's stature as a poet. Pinter's dialogue is as tightly – perhaps *more* tightly – controlled than verse. Every syllable, every inflection, the succession of long and short sounds, words and sentences are calculated to a nicety. And it is precisely the repetitiousness, the discontinuity, the circularity of ordinary vernacular speech which are here used as formal elements with which the ingredients from which he takes the recurring patterns and artfully broken rhythms *are* fragments of a brilliantly observed, and often hitherto overlooked, *reality*, he succeeds in creating the illusion of complete naturalness, of naturalism.

An introductory chapter is not the place for a detailed study of Pinter's linguistic techniques. We shall return to the subject after an analysis of Pinter's work, play by play. What must be stressed at this point is the essentially *dramatic* nature of his use of language. Brecht demanded that the language of drama should be *gestural*, i.e. that the syntax and rhythm of each sentence alone should force the actor into making the appropriate gesture and movement. Pinter's use of language eminently fulfils Brecht's requirement. The speech rhythms of the tramp Davies in *The Caretaker* positively cry out for the impotent stabbing movement of his gesture, Aston's casual style of speech in the same play totally implies and dictates the slowness of his movements, his stillness while endlessly trying to fix an electric plug.

Equally dramatic is the way in which Pinter uses language as a vehicle and instrument of dramatic *action*. Words become weapons in the mouths of Pinter's characters. The one who gets hold of the more elaborate or more accurate expression establishes dominance over his partner; the victim of aggression can be swamped by language which comes too thick and fast, or is too nonsensical to be comprehended: this happens, above all, to Stanley in *The Birthday Party*, who is subjected to a process of brainwashing through a torrent of incomprehensible questions and assertions fired at him by the two terrorists.

The precision, economy and control which Pinter exercises over the language of his dialogue firmly links him to the tradition of contemporary English high-comedy. No wonder that Noël Coward, the leading representative of that tradition, has saluted Pinter as one among the 'new wave' of British dramatists whose craftsmanship in the use of language he respects and admires. The fact that he can quite legitimately be related to Kafka and Beckett on the one hand, and to Oscar Wilde and Noël Coward on the other, is highly characteristic of Pinter's originality, his ability to work on a multiplicity of different levels. Insofar as his plays are firmly rooted in real speech and real situations he appears naturalistic – and was, in fact, originally lumped together with the social realist 'kitchen sink' school; insofar as he eschews motivation and questions the very nature of reality his plays can be seen as structures of lyrical images of an unverified, unverifiable and therefore dreamlike world between fantasy and nightmare; insofar as his observation of linguisitic quirks is uncannily sharp, his dialogue must be considered as one of the most realistic representations of the genuine vernacular of the mid-twentieth century; but, because the real speech of real people is to a large extent composed to solecism and tautology, it can also be likened to nonsense-poetry and the literature of the absurd. From one angle of vision this world of inhibited, half-conscious, inarticulate people surrounding themselves with irrational anxieties is grotesque and comic, from another point of view it will appear pitiable and tragic.

This kind of ambivalence, indeed of multivalence, Pinter might argue, is in itself a realistic trait; for reality itself is equally multivalent. When Leonard Russell, during the run of *The Caretaker* in London, addressed an open letter to Pinter, deploring the gales of laughter about the unhappy plight of the old tramp in the play, Pinter replied: 'An element of the absurd is, I think, one of the features of the play, but at the same time I did not intend it to be merely a laughable farce. If there hadn't been other issues at stake the play would not have been written. Audience reaction can't be regulated, and no one would want it to be; nor is it easy to analyse. But where the comic and the tragic (for want of a better word) are closely interwoven, certain members of the audience will always give emphasis to the comic as opposed to the other, for by so doing they rationalize the other out of existence. On most evenings at the Duchess there is a sensible balance of laughter and silence. Where, though, this indiscriminate mirth is found, I feel it represents a cheerful patronage of the characters on the part of the merrymakers, and thus participation is avoided. This laughter is in fact a mode of precaution, a smoke-screen, a refusal to accept what is happening as recognizable (which I think it is) and instead to view the actors (*a*) as actors always and not as characters and (*b*) as chimpanzees. From this kind of uneasy jollification I must, of course, dissociate myself. . . . As far as I'm concerned, *The Caretaker* is funny, up to a point. Beyond that point it ceases to be funny, and it was because of that point that I wrote it.'[17]

This statement is the definition of Pinter's own, personal brand of tragi-comedy: plays which can be very funny up to the point when the absurdity of the characters' predicament becomes frightening, horrifying, pathetic, tragic. 'Comedies of menace' they have been called (in a term first used in 1957 by David Campton in the subtitle of his play *The Lunatic View*, and first applied to Pinter by Irving Wardle in an article which appeared in *Encore* in September, 1958). The term, which echoes the sobriquet 'comedy of manners', has its justificiation. For, as Pinter pointed out in his letter to Leonard Russell, much of the laughter that accompanies his plays up to that point where they cease to be funny, is already the laughter of precaution against panic, the whistling in the dark of people who are trying to protect themselves against the menace, the horror, which lies at the, core of the action they are witnessing. Even when that

[17] Pinter, *The Sunday Times*, London, 14th August 1960.

laughter tends to be patronizing, when it displays the audience's delight in their superiority over characters who are struggling to express even the simple things in intelligible language, even there it is mingled with the uneasy realization that, basically, even the more articulate among us have the same difficulties with vocabulary, syntax and the logical arrangement of our thought. But this is only one, and the least frightening aspect, of Pinter's tragi-comic vision of the world. The real menace which lies behind the struggles for expression and communication, behind the closed doors which might swing open to reveal a frightening intruder, behind the sinister gunmen and terrorists, behind the violence, the menace behind all these menacing images is the opaqueness, the uncertainty and precariousness of the human condition itself. How can we know who we are, how can we verify what is real and what is fantasy, how can we know what we are saying, what is being said to us? 'I'm speaking', Pinter once said as he began to make a speech, 'knowing that there are at least twenty-four possible aspects of any single statement, depending on where you're standing at the time or on what the weather is like.'[18] This is a jocular expression of a state of affairs, but it cannot hide the fact that the state of affairs – which is a true one – is disconcerting and a potential source of terror.

A writer who – naively – believes that reality is simple, clearly defined and can be tackled with confidence from a firm viewpoint, can plan and calculate his work with far greater confidence and foresight than a poet of Pinter's cast of mind, who sees the world as mysterious, multi-faceted and unfathomable. Such a poet can merely follow the outlines of his vision; his working method will have to be highly intuitive; 'All I know', Pinter has said, 'is that blank sheet of paper in front of me, and then, when it's filled, I can't believe it. I don't throw away many sheets of paper that are filled. I do, of course, go over the sheets of paper

[18] Pinter, speech to students at Bristol, *The Sunday Times*, 4th March 1962.

many times. I regard myself as an old-fashioned writer. I like to create character and follow a situation to its end. I write visually – I can say that. I watch the invisible faces quite closely. The characters take on a physical shape. I watch the faces as closely as I can. And the bodies. I can't see a consistency in my work. I have no idea whether the plays have a consistency or have not. Each play is quite a different world. The problem is to create a unique world in each case with a totally different set of characters. With a totally different environment. It's a great joy to do that.'[19]

The starting point is sometimes no more than a situation. Two people in a room. A few words. At the time when he had just begun work on what later became the play *Landscape* Pinter is quoted as having said: 'I've started a couple of pages of something quite different. A new form and I'm diving. It's simply, as it stands, about a woman around fifty. That's all I bloody well know. I don't know where she is . . .'[20] So intuitive a writer could not possibly have an axe to grind, a philosophy to propagate. 'I only formulate conclusions after I've written the plays. I've no idea what I'm obsessed with – just so pleased to see the words on paper. . . .'[21]

It is from the conjunction of this type of obsessive vision and an accomplished craftsman's sense of form and style that this kind of work must spring. The method of work illumines the seeming contradiction also between the meticulous outward reality of the characters and their speech, and the dreamlike, nightmarish quality of the plays as a whole. Intuitions of the obsessive intensity which Pinter describes when he talks about his method of work *are* daydreams, almost hallucinations. Their very realism is part of their menace: it is the clarity of outline of the most frightening of nightmares. The dreamer of such dreams may not be aware of their inner consistency; yet, on closer analysis, they will be bound to reveal to a dispassionate observer such a

[19] Pinter, in *The New Yorker, loc. cit.*
[20] Kathleen Tynan, 'In Search of Harold Pinter', Part Two, *Evening Standard*, London, 26th April 1968.
[21] *Ibid.*

consistency, which is no more and no less than the structure of the dreamer's personality itself. That is why the work of artists of Pinter's stature can also, though not solely, or even mainly, be open to a psychoanalytical approach. Not to yield any revelations about the author's personality and problems, but to explain the impact of work on audiences. It is not the private, personal element in such works of art which exercises that appeal, but precisely the element which the author *shares* with the rest of mankind. That is the secret of the impact of Oedipus or Hamlet. That Pinter's work is open to analysis of this kind, precisely because it has a similar impact, is the contention of this study.

In a very early manuscript which must date back to Pinter's late teens or early twenties, he clearly, brilliantly, in some ways prophetically, describes just this quality of a major dramatist. The text is fairly cryptically entitled 'A Note on Shakespeare'. It starts:

The mistake they make, most of them, is to attempt to determine and calculate, with the finest instruments, the source of the wound. They seek out the gaps between the apparent and the void that hinges upon it, with all due tautness. They turn to the wound with deference, a lance, and a needle and thread.

At the entrance of the lance, the gap widens. At the use of needle and thread, the wound coagulates and atrophies in their hand.

Shakespeare writes of the open wound, and through him, we know it open and know it closed. We tell when it ceases to beat, and tell it at its highest peak of fever.

In attempting to approach Shakespeare's work in its entirety, you are called upon to grapple with a perspective in which the horizon alternately collapses and reforms behind you; in which the mind's participation is subject to an intense diversity of atmospheric.

Once the dedication has begun however, there is no other way but to him.

One discovers a long corridor of postures; fluid and hardened at the quick; gross and godlike; putrescent and copulative; raddled; attentive; crippled and gargantuan; crumbling with the dropsy; heavy with elephantiasis; broody with government;

severe; fanatical; paralytic; voluptuous; impassive; muscle-bound; lissome, virginal; unwashed; bewildered; humpbacked; icy and statuesque. All are contained in the wound which Shakespeare does not attempt to sew up or re-shape, whose pain he does not attempt to eradicate. He amputates, deadens, aggravates at will, within the limits of a particular piece, but he will not pronounce judgement or cure. Such comment as there is, is so variously split up between characters, and so contradictory in itself, that no central point of opinion or inclining can be determined.

'He himself is trapped in his own particular order, and is unable to go out at a distance to regulate and forestall abortion or lapses in vraisemblance. He can only rely on a "few well chosen words" to bring him through any doubtful patch.

He belongs of course, ultimately, to a secret society, a conspiracy, of which there is only one member; himself. . . .'

There follows, in this remarkable description of a great playwright's existential situation, a long catalogue of the self-contradictory elements, the multitude of bizarre personalities which that playwright, whom the young author chooses to call Shakespeare, carries within himself. The text ends with this summing up: 'The fabric breaks. The wound is open. The wound is contained. The wound is peopled.'

'A Note on Shakespeare' dates back to the time of Pinter's earliest efforts as a writer. All the more remarkable is its insight into the creative process of the kind of dramatist into which he himself was later destined to develop. For out of the wound of existential anguish springs the playwright's effort to come to terms with the world and its mystery, its suffering, its bewildering multiplicity. The wound, the playwright's eye, his perception of the world, is open: that is why all the world enters into it. The wound is the world. And the world is the wound. And – because the world's suffering and anguish is the anguish and the suffering of other people as well as of the mind behind the open eye, the open wound – the wound *is* peopled.

3

Analysis

Early Poetry

When he emerged as a dramatist in 1957 Pinter was twenty-seven years old. But he had published poems since before he was twenty. Two poems, 'New Year in the Midlands' and 'Chandeliers and Shadows', appeared in the August 1950 number of *Poetry London*. Unfortunately the ends of the two poems got confused in the printing. *Poetry London* tried to make amends by publishing 'New Year in the Midlands' again in the following number (November 1950), while 'Chandeliers and Shadows' had to wait till 1968 to appear in its correct form in the slim volume of *Poems* published by the Enitharmon Press.

'New Year in the Midlands', although couched in a Dylan-Thomas-like idiom of concentrated exuberance, already contains Pinter's sharp eye for the dreamlike quality of the world in all its sordid reality:

> . . . and here am I,
> Straddled, exile always in one Whitbread Ale town,
> Or such.
> Where we went to the yellow pub, cramped in an alley bin,
> A shoot from the market,
> And found the thin Luke of a queer, whose pale
> Deliberate eyes, raincoat, Victorian,
> Sap the answer in the palm. . . .

The thin, pale queer in the raincoat is already a Pinter character in embryo. 'Chandeliers and Shadows' on the other hand, with its motto from *The Duchess of Malfi* ('I'le goe hunt the badger by owle-light: 'tis a deed of darknesse') – omitted in the 1968 reprint – contains its intimation of the baroque, fantastic Pinter of plays to come:

> . . . Yet I, lunatic from lunatic spheres,
> Shall run crazy with lepers,
> And bring God down the chimney,
> A tardy locust,
> To plunder and verminate man's pastures, entirely.

('You verminate the sheet of your birth' is one of Goldberg's accusations against Stanley in *The Birthday Party*). There is much adolescent love of unusual and archaic words in this and others of Pinter's early poems ('floodlit emperies', 'Palsied stomacher', a 'necromantic cauldron of crosses' in this one poem alone), but the imagery is strong and haunting; it betrays the author's grasp of the poetic quality of the *situations* his imagination thrusts upon him. For these poems are clearly written in a state of obsession with words, under the spell of an irresistible impulse. Hence some of them are so private in their surrealist automatic writing that they scarcely yield a meaning to the outsider. 'One a Story, Two a Death', for example, a longish narrative poem which appeared in the Summer 1951 issue of *Poetry London* and was not reprinted in the collected volume of 1968, starts with the cryptic stanzas:

> Brought in a bowl of flaming crocuses
> In an ebon mirrorless age,
> Let fall to her face
> Till her cheeks lit in tongues.
>
> Who would laugh and call Zello,
> See how scorched is the boy,
> Who would laugh at the arrow
> I should plunge in her eye . . .

There is a dead girl in the poem who is visited by the poet; but little more can be discerned in the darkness of its whirling images. Yet here too some of the images of the plays already appear –

The giant Negro tones in ether his flute –

foreshadowing the symbolic death figure of the Negro in *The Room*.

'Where in his cape walks the Negro,
Growing flowers on his groin.'

In another poem from *Poetry London*, not reprinted in the collected edition, 'European Revels', we meet one of the destructive females of the later Pinter as well as violent men, reminiscent of the killers in *The Dumb Waiter*, the terrorists in *The Birthday Party* –

Her men lovers plasterlads, who
Felled rich women in the moon's Zodiac.

There is in these poems, as indeed in the early and long unpublished novel *The Dwarfs* (which will be discussed in connection with the play of the same title), the recurring character of a young man, who, like Len in *The Dwarfs*, like Aston in *The Caretaker*, has a tendency to talk too much and too intensely and fears the moment when society, the outside world, or his growing up, will put a stop to this stream of exuberant, mad talking:

Only the deaf can hear and the blind understand
The miles I gabble.
Through these my dances of dunce and devil,
It's only the dumb can speak through the rubble.
Time shall drop his spit in my cup,
With this vicious cut he shall close my trap
And gob me up in a drunkard's lap.
All spirits shall haunt me and all devils drink me;

O despite their dark drugs and the digs that they rib me,
I'll tear off my terrible cap.[1]

(Note the use of assonant rhymes, alternating between a and u sounds: gabble/rubble; cup/trap.) The parallels, particularly to Aston's situation, seem difficult to overlook. The same is surely true of the short poem 'The Anaesthetist's Pin' (1952) which introduces that instrument linked to 'the amputator's saw' and ends:

> At that incision sound
> The lout is at the throat
> And the dislocated word
> Becomes articulate.

Which seems to indicate that the operation is – as in the case of Aston in *The Caretaker* – concerned with curing an excess of speech ('the dislocated word'), hence the 'amputation' and the 'anaesthetist's pin' may well stand for a lobotomy or electric shock treatment.

The earliest text in the volume of *Poems* is dated 1949 and had remained unpublished until that volume appeared almost twenty years later. This is the dialogue prose poem 'Kullus' which has already been discussed in the previous chapter and contains the motif of the room and the intruder which pervades Pinter's work from *The Room* to *The Basement*. Kullus, a character who clearly played a considerable part in the young writer's imagination also makes an appearance in the poem 'The Task' (1954). And again he is linked to the image of the room:

> The last time Kullus, seen,
> Within a distant call,
> Arrived at the house of bells,
> The leaf obeyed the bud,
> I closed the open night
> And tailormade the room.

[1] I shall tear off my terrible cap, 1951.

does not know anyone who might want to talk to her. But when Mr Kidd hints that the stranger might come into the room when Bert is present, she relents. Let him be asked to come quickly. Mr Kidd leaves. Again Rose is left by herself. And now again the door has become the focal point of suspense and tense expectation. When it opens, what will it disclose?

At last the door does open; there enters a blind Negro; Riley he calls himself. Rose reacts to him with all the symptoms of disgust, fear, even race hatred.

But Riley has a message for Rose. From whom? From her father.

Your father wants you to come home.

And Riley calls Rose by a different name:

Come home, Sal.

And, indeed, it seems that Riley is not only a messenger from Rose's – Sal's – father, but that he *is* her father.

RILEY: I want you to come home.
ROSE: No.
RILEY: With me.
ROSE: I can't.
RILEY: I waited to see you.
ROSE: Yes.
RILEY: Sal.

Now Rose acquiesces in being called Sal, although only a few moments earlier she had angrily asked not to be called by that name. And she even, in what is clearly a moment of truth, confesses that her life is almost intolerable:

The day is a hump. I never go out.

It is a moment of great lyrical intensity, for the phrase is simple, but memorable.

At this moment Bert comes back. He has returned from his trip into the night. And – again a shock effect achieved by the simplest of means, for the first time in the play – he speaks. He speaks about having come back safely, although 'they got it dark out', although 'they got it very icy out'. Then, in a speech of some length, he describes how hard he drove his van: 'I caned her along. She was good'. The erotic overtones of this impassioned outburst about the van, always referred to in the feminine gender, are unmistakable.

> . . . I use my hand. Like that. I get hold of her. I go where I go. She took me there. She brought me back.

It is only now that Bert becomes aware of the intruder. With a single exclamation: 'Lice!' he attacks the Negro, throws him out of his armchair and kicks his head against the gas stove, until he lies motionless on the floor. Rose clutches her eyes. She has gone blind.

The Room is a remarkable first play: the dialogue is already masterly; each character has his own style of speech and the wittily observed vernacular with its rambling syntax and tautologies is brilliantly modulated into the intensity of the poetic climax between Rose and Riley. The suddenness of the brutal ending, which comes as a complete surprise, also has a tremendous impact.

It is only the use of the perhaps too overtly symbolical and poetic figure of the blind Negro which might be felt as a break in style: for whereas in the rest of the play the dream-like and poetic quality arises directly from the realistic detail, here we are confronted almost with a cliché metaphor, an allegorical figure from a different – a neo-romantic, or pre-Raphaelite *genre*.

The room, the relationship between the brutal husband and his sentimental wife, who is tormented by dark forebodings and existential fears, is seen in entirely realistic and psychologically accurate terms; indeed, the older couple –

Bert/Rose – is subtly contrasted with the young couple, Mr and Mrs Sands, who are looking for a room; their relationship also shows the signs of tension between a more intelligent woman and a lazy and dull man who dominates her by sheer brutality. (Mrs Sands says she saw a star outside; Mr Sands has not seen it; he simply decrees that she did not see a star.) So the young couple could be Rose and Bert at an earlier stage. The mystery and dreamlike anxiety that pervades the first half of the play, in fact, emerges from the contrast between the clarity and realism of these well observed features and the layers of darkness which envelop this pool of light: the night outside, the basement, the large, unexplored house with its uncertain number of floors; this is a Rembrandtesque technique of chiaroscuro, and most effective in creating an atmosphere of foreboding and uncertainty. The blind Negro, on the other hand, who has been lying in the basement for days and who appears to bring Rose a message from her past, is all too manifestly a symbol, an allegory. He has been lying down below and had foreknowledge of the future – that room number seven would soon be vacant – he must therefore be a being from beyond the confines of this world: a dead man or a messenger of death, perhaps Rose's own dead father. His blackness and his blindness reinforce these allegorical implications. The blindness which strikes Rose at the end belongs to the same category of symbolism – it must mean the end of her relationship with Bert, but probably more than that: her own death.

The character of the old caretaker – or landlord? – Mr Kidd, combines the realistic and the symbolical elements in a far more successful manner. His inability to recall the number of floors in the house, for example, certainly reinforces the eery, dreamlike atmosphere, yet it also can be quite realistically explained as the result of his senility or hardness of hearing. Yet it cannot just be a physical disability, or even mental deterioration, which would wholly explain Mr Kidd's uncertainty about his own background (about which he has not even been asked). '*I think my mum was a Jewess. Yes, I wouldn't be surprised to learn that she was a Jewess.*' Not even a high degree of feeblemindedness would explain this degree of uncertainty, particularly as Mr Kidd displays no symptoms of mental incapacity in bringing Rose the message from her visitor, or in persisting in trying to get it to her. The inference is that Mr Kidd may simply be an inveterate liar or mystifier. After all, when he has been talking a good deal about his sister, and has left the room, Rose's reaction is: 'I don't believe he had a sister, ever.' Here Pinter's use of uncertainty about what his characters say and mean, can thus still be seen as somewhat mechanical and arbitrary. He hardly ever makes this kind of mistake in his later work.

It is very characteristic of Pinter that the element of race hatred (which, as we know, must have overshadowed his childhood in the East End of London) pervades the play without ever being directly pushed into the foreground. Mr Kidd's strange vagueness about his own origins introduces the subject, which breaks to the surface with brutal clarity when Bert assaults the blind Negro with the exclamation 'Lice!'; here Bert's motivation must be one of racial hatred; after all, he has not even taken the trouble to find out why the Negro is in his room; thus, he must be attacking him merely as an object of instant racial revulsion. That Rose's father is sending a Negro to her with his message, or that Rose's father himself might be that Negro, must surely also be a fact of considerable significance. The name by which her father, or his messenger, addresses Rose is Sal – Sarah? – which might indicate that the woman who now calls herself Rose – an *English* Rose? – not only lives with Bert under a false name, but perhaps may also be concealing her true origin and identity; this would give Mr Kidd's musings about *his* possible Jewish origin a painful irony in Rose's eyes. And the knowledge that she is living in Bert's room, in his household, under false pretences, as an outsider concealing her hated foreign origin, would also explain Rose's eagerness to please, her fear of the surrounding world, her terror of discovery and expulsion, the strain under which she is living which makes each day a hump to be climbed. Consciously – or subconsciously – as far as the author is concerned, this might be the source of the existential anxiety that pervades this play and so much of Pinter's other work. Again and again Rose congratulates herself on living in a warm room rather than downstairs in the dark and damp basement – in the underworld of the dead, from which her dead father is calling for her. As a Jew in the world of Auschwitz she would indeed be a fugitive from death. Is this the reason why, when she finally shows her true feelings to the blind Negro, she says, several times: *I have been here*, as though she wanted to say, here, among strangers, in an alien land? The blindness and blackness of the messenger are, in themselves, symbols of death. That he is called Riley might be an additional pointer to his representing Rose's origins among a despised, underprivileged group.

Such speculations should not be taken as more than hints of possible lines of interpretation of just one of the many strands that make up this short, but characteristically richly textured play. The poetic quality of such work springs, precisely, from the multiplicity of possible approaches, the ambivalence and ambiguity of the images of which it is composed. It must also be stressed that, of course, the audience is neither meant nor required to become consciously aware of all the possible significances of the symbols and images; what comes across to them is a total impression: the author's anxiety which he communicates through this texture of images. Another strand, which, however, doubles and reinforces the same existential emotion, could be isolated from the images of Rose's fear that she might lose her man's love, her fear of being abandoned, her feeling of inadequacy. In the final minutes of the play these two strands coalesce: for shortly before Bert brutally assaults the racial outcast – and indirectly Rose as a member of his group, whatever it might be – he also unmistakably reveals that she has failed to hold his affection; Bert's account of his trip in his van clearly shows that his sexual energy is no longer focused on Rose; the van, which Bert treats as a 'she', has

59

ousted her from his affections. The journey into the winter night becomes an act of intercourse with its own triumphant orgasm. No wonder Rose is totally annihilated as the play ends.

The Dumb Waiter

The Dumb Waiter, also in one act, uses the same basic situation as *The Room*. Again we are in a room enclosed by a dark, mysterious world outside. Again the people in the room are watching, in dreadful suspense, a door which is certain to open. Moreover, in this case we are, from quite an early point in the play, made aware of the fact that whoever it will be who enters by the door will have to die. For the two people in the room are professional assassins, Ben and Gus by name, working-class Cockneys. They are working for a mysterious organization which sends them, from time to time, across country on missions of this kind; at first they are told no more than the bare name of the town to which they have to go and the address at which they will have to call; then they just have to stay there and await further instructions. When these arrive they must liquidate their victim; then they have to get back as quickly as they can; they don't even know who it is that disposes of the bodies: who cleans up the room where the execution has taken place. As soon as they are back at base, they have to stay at home waiting for the next phone call with the next address for the next execution.

This basic situation in *The Dumb Waiter* is a highly contrived one; it is as though it had been worked out *in order* to provide a new and ingenious variation on the room-door-suspense syndrome. On the other hand, the hired killers are, after all, a well-worn and familiar device of the gangster film and the stage thriller; Pinter as a seasoned rep actor must have regarded it as pretty commonplace and easily acceptable as a starting point. In any case: the variation on the opening situation of *The Room* is brilliantly ingenious and intelligent.

Rose, in *her* room, looking at *her* door, was clearly a victim-to-be. Ben and Gus are looking at the door waiting for the victim to walk into the trap. This provides a very different element of suspense and a very different focus for the spectator's fears and hopes. Moreover, with the born dramatist's instinct, Pinter has a spectacular surprise up his sleeve. The audience is watching the door, the *only* way into the room. But there *is* another opening, out into the dark, menacing, outside world. Neither the people in the room nor the audience have noticed that, between the two beds on which the men are lolling, there is a panelled opening. Suddenly that panelling is pulled up and reveals that the basement room in which we are, must, originally, have been the kitchen of a café or restaurant: for behind it there is a 'dumb waiter'. We know that the two men are waiting for their victim in a totally uninhabited, derelict house. Who then is working the dumb waiter? Moreover in the tray that comes down the two killers find chits of paper with orders; at first these are for very ordinary English fare: Soup of the day. Liver and onions. Jam tart. But gradually the orders become more and more outlandish: Macaroni Pastitsio. Ormitha Macarounada. Bamboo Shoots. Water Chestnuts and Chicken. Char Siu and Beansprouts. The two killers, who, after all are just loyal employees trying to serve their masters, and eager to obey orders, make desperate attempts to fulfil these orders as well as they can. Gus, the more intelligent of the two – and therefore also more tormented by doubt and guilt feelings – ransacks his luggage to find old biscuits, a packet of crisps, a small bottle of milk, a packet of tea. These efforts reveal to Ben, who clearly is the senior partner, that Gus has been less than candid with him, having concealed the fact that he did possess a packet of potato crips so as not to have to offer him a few. . . .

Gus repeatedly asks how it can happen that demands for food should come into the kitchen of a derelict building. Again and again the two men try to convince the supernatural power bombarding them with impossible demands that, they have nothing to send. Finally they discover that, as is usual in restaurant kitchens, there is a speaking tube next to the dumb waiter; it even has the whistle through which one can announce one's desire to communicate with the other end upstairs. Ben tries to do so and hears a voice complaining that the Eccles cake was stale, the chocolate was melted. On top of all that, the mysterious voice is asking for tea. Now Ben and Gus have been trying to make themselves some tea ever since they arrived; they had discovered that the gas in the flat was working off a meter, and they did not have a shilling to put in between them. Gus is indignant about the impertinence of an unseen presence which is asking him to make tea although it already knows that he has no shilling. Angrily he leaves to drink at least a glass of water in the kitchen. When he is gone, the speaking tube begins to whistle. Ben is getting his instructions from above. The victim, it seems, has arrived. And now the door opens – a man is pushed in. It is Gus, without his jacket, his holster, his revolver. So it is Gus who is the victim! The two partners face each other, staring at each other, as the curtain falls. Will Ben kill his mate? The question remains unanswered.

The symbolism, the intervention of supernatural powers, is thus even more obvious in *The Dumb Waiter* than it is in *The Room*. Nevertheless the play marks a considerable step forward in the development of Pinter's personal style. It is, for instance, far more clear here that the supernatural forces which come into play are expressions of the subconscious motivations of characters which, in themselves, are drawn with extreme realism. Ben and Gus, the Cockney killers, are sharply observed and most accurately characterized by their use of language.

From the first it is clear that there is a dangerous degree of tension between these two. They don't trust each other. Gus is in the process of developing guilt feelings; his discipline is getting slack. The last victim was a girl and so the job was an unusually messy one:

What a mess. Honest, I can't remember a mess like that one. They don't seem to hold together like men, women. A looser texture, like. Didn't she spread, eh? She didn't half spread. Kaw!

Thus the dissolution of the partnership is clearly foreshadowed – just as the precariousness of the relationship between Bert and Rose which finally erupts into symbolic violence in *The Room* – and the violent end becomes the concretization of this hostility. We are, consequently, in an area of dream imagery. Because the two men are operating in a world the workings of which they do not understand (an organization which functions entirely above their heads), because they carry out instructions which seem without meaning to them, they have become specially irritable; each of them unloads his own insecurity, his guilt-feelings, and the boredom which comes from doing incomprehensible things, upon the other.

If we disregard the bizarre detail of the initial assumption behind the occupation Gus and Ben pursue, we can see without any great difficulty what it is that the supernatural trappings of the play describe: no more and no less than the process of alienation to which men are subjected in a highly organized industrial society, which denies to the individual, particularly the individual of low intelligence and insight in the lower ranks, any real understanding of its working; and the frustration this engenders, the violence into which this frustration is bound to erupt. After all: is an army so different from the organization which employs Gus and Ben? In an army too men are sent to destinations where they have to await further orders as to when they are to start to shoot. Nor does the machinery by which orders pass in an army differ so very much from the manner in which Gus and Ben receive theirs. (Remember: Pinter was a conscientious objector and is a determined opponent of any organization which requires its members to use violence).

These reflections may point towards an interpretation of *The Dumb Waiter*. But they should not be taken too far or too literally. It is the essence of dream imagery of this kind that the concretized metaphors which it puts upon the stage are, by their very nature, ambiguous, ambivalent, and significant on a multiplicity of different levels. Ultimately what is being conveyed is a complex existential situation – through its emotional tone: and in this case it is the emotional situation of simple people in a social context which is beyond their powers of comprehension.

The failure – on the part of Gus and Ben – to understand the workings of their organization, their frustration and irritation finds its expression in the dialogue, which bristles with their difficulties of communication. Again and again they become entangled in linguistic knots which they are unable to unravel: the famous exchange about whether one says 'I'll light the kettle' or 'I'll light the gas' is just one among many similarly funny and revealing passages. The battle of wills, the battle between two different outlooks on life, different temperaments, is translated into a battle between different views of language.

> BEN: If I say go and light the kettle I mean go and light the kettle.
> GUS: How can you light a kettle?
> BEN: It's a figure of speech! Light the kettle. It's a figure of speech!
> GUS: I've never heard it.
> BEN: Light the kettle! It's common usage!
> GUS: I think you've got it wrong.
> BEN (*menacing*): What do you mean?
> GUS: They say put on the kettle.
> BEN (*taut*): Who says?
> *They stare at each other, breathing hard.*
> (*Deliberately.*) I've never in all my life heard anyone say put on the kettle.
> GUS: I bet my mother used to say it.
> BEN: Your mother? When did you last see your mother?
> GUS: I don't know, about –
> BEN: Well, what are you talking about your mother for?
> *They stare.*
> Gus, I'm not trying to be unreasonable. I'm just trying to point something out to you.
> GUS: Yes, but –
> BEN: Who's the senior partner here, me or you?

GUS: You.

BEN: I'm only looking after your interests, Gus. You've got to learn, mate.

GUS: Yes, but I've never heard –

BEN (*vehemently*): Nobody says light the gas! What does the gas light?

GUS: What does the gas – ?

BEN (*grabbing him with two hands by the throat, at arms' length*): THE KETTLE, YOU FOOL!

The dispute about language is here quite manifestly a dispute about authority, a fight for dominance. Yet in the very next exchange, Ben is again threatened. Gus has consented to go and make the tea. But he hesitates. He wants to try out the matches (which, mysteriously, have been pushed in under the door, when they complained about not having any left – a first intimation that there are mysterious powers about).

GUS: I want to see if they light.

BEN: What?

GUS: The matches.

Ben's 'What?' is full of the fear that Gus might be persisting in his error, that he might reply: 'if they light *the gas*.' He is relieved at Gus's reply. At first the matches don't light. When they finally are seen to be working, Ben says, 'wearily':

Put on the bloody kettle for Christ's sake.

Unconsciously he has surrendered, by using Gus's phrase rather than his own. The stage direction is quite explicit here:

BEN *goes to his bed, but realizing what he has said, stops and half turns. They look at each other.*

This hostile look foreshadows the final confrontation of executioner and victim. *The Dumb Waiter* may thus, ultimately, be about the relationship between a pair of human beings, on the pattern of Beckett's *Nec tecum, nec sine te* in *Waiting For Godot*. There is always a death-wish at the bottom of these insoluble tensions. The supernatural forces driving us to murder our fellow human being are our subconscious desires and fantasies of aggression.

The Birthday Party

Pinter's first full-length play combines elements from the two one-acters which he wrote in the same period of his life: the room, the safe haven, menaced by an intrusion from the cold outside world, is here a seedy boarding house in a seaside resort, where Stanley Webber, a not so very young man in his late thirties, has found refuge from the troubles of life. His landlady, Meg, a simple, elderly woman, who looks after him with exaggerated solicitude and who obviously regards him as a son – but also as a kind of lover – recalls the character of Rose in *The Room*. And the two emissaries of a mysterious and brutal organization who arrive to fetch Stanley away from Meg – a Jew, Goldberg, and an Irishman, McCann – have a good deal in common, both in their function and in their manner of operation, with the two hired killers in *The Dumb Waiter*. But these characters have become far more complex in the three-act play. The situation which forms the starting point for the action is also far more realistically treated, at least in its tangible, external detail, and thus acquires considerably greater power as a poetic metaphor.

Meg's husband, Petey, who is almost as silent as Rose's man Bert in *The Room* but in a kindly, benevolent way, and Lulu, the buxom girl from next door, complete the sextet of characters; they too are treated with complete realism. The only area of darkness that remains concerns the reason *why* Stanley is hiding from the world, why Goldberg and McCann have come to spy him out.

Stanley, we learn, had come to the seaside resort in question as the pianist of a concert party who appeared at the pier. He even tells the story of an occasion when, so he claims, he gave a concert on his own in London; in Lower Edmonton to be exact, which, after all, is anything but a major centre of artistic activity. But now he has been idle for months, hardly goes out of the house (perhaps because he is too lazy to shave and dress, but perhaps because he is afraid of being recognized?), pours contempt upon his landlady, who stifles him with her motherliness, yet seems totally dependent on her – an adult who has regressed to the status of a babe in arms. That Stanley is disappointed in the world which has rejected him becomes clear from his account of a second concert he was supposed to give:

> They carved me up. Carved me up. It was all arranged, it was all worked out. My next concert. Somewhere else it was. In winter. I went down there to play. Then, when I got there, the hall was closed, the place was shuttered up, not even a caretaker. They'd locked it up. . . . A fast one. They pulled a fast one. I'd like to know who was responsible for that. . . . All right, Jack, I can take a tip. They want me to crawl down on my bended knees. Well I can take a tip . . . any day of the week.

We learn this *before* the arrival of the two terrorists; clearly, Stanley *has* offended some powerful force. But who are *they* who want him to crawl down on his bended knees? And *what* could he, a harmless pianist, have done to *them*?

On the day on which the action of the play starts – Pinter preserves the unities of time and place and compresses the action into a time-span of about twenty-four hours – Meg, who is always spoiling Stan with her oversolicitous infatuation, wants to surprise him with a gift. To motivate the present, she maintains it is his birthday, although it is almost certainly nothing of the sort, and, indeed, Meg probably does not even know the actual date of his birthday. In the course of the opening scenes of the play Lulu, the girl from next door, arrives with a big parcel, containing Stanley's present. She is a girl of vulgar vitality and tries to arouse Stanley's interest, to get him to go out with her. But Stanley will not allow himself to be seduced.

When Goldberg and McCann arrive – they have obviously been looking for Stanley all over the town – Meg blurts out the fact that it is Stanley's birthday. And Goldberg, who likes playing the part of a highly sociable fellow, suggests they should give him a party, to which Lulu is also to be invited. Stanley, who has beaten a hasty retreat when the two intruders appeared on the scene, returns after they have gone upstairs; and Meg unveils her present: he is after all, a musician and as he has no piano in the house, she is giving him another musical instrument. A drum. A boy's drum. At first Stanley is stupefied. But, then, he puts the drum round his neck and begins to beat it, in a normal rhythm at first, but then more and more wildly and uncontrolled. It is clear: Meg has succeeded in making him regress to the status of a little boy, a child. Thus the savagery of his reaction seems to signify the depth of his despair; for Stanley seems to understand the meaning of his acceptance of the little boy's drum only too well. His 'savage and possessed' drumming concludes the first act.

The second act is devoted to the 'birthday party' itself, the ritual of Stanley's destruction by his two pursuers. At first, before the party has started, Stanley still tries to escape. But McCann, the brutal Irish terrorist, blocks his efforts to get out with increasingly open threats of violence. Petey, Meg's quiet husband, a deckchair attendant on the promenade, will not be present at the party. He has to go to his chess club. But Lulu comes and immediately succumbs to Goldberg's routine seducer's tricks. Stanley, who has been subjected to a weird surrealist cross-examination by his tormentors before the party got under way, follows the proceedings from a corner of the room, where he sits silent and apathetic, while the alcohol begins to flow and Goldberg indulges in sentimental recollections of his past family life. (The episodes he recounts are, however, strangely contradictory; even Goldberg's own first name varies between Nat and Simey). A game of blind man's buff forms the climax of the party. Stanley has his eyes bandaged; and McCann breaks Stanley's glasses in the process. Blinded, Stanley steps into his newly acquired drum (thus destroying the last vestige of his status as an artist? or putting an end to his being Meg's little boy?). Then, at last he catches Meg:

> *His hands move towards her and they reach her throat.*
> *He begins to strangle her.*

At this point the lights go out. Lulu is heard screaming. When at last McCann finds a torch, we see Lulu lying spread-eagled on the table and Stanley bending over her. As Goldberg and McCann move towards him, menacingly, he begins to giggle.

> *The torch draws closer. His giggle rises and grows as he flattens himself against the wall. Their* [i.e. Goldberg's and McCann's] *figures converge upon him. Curtain.*

Thus Stanley, having tried to strangle Meg and to rape Lulu, seems to have gone out of his mind as the avenging representatives of the organization finally lay hands on him.

Act three: The next morning. Meg who remained unaware throughout 'the party' of what was going on is asking Petey whether Stanley is feeling better. Petey, who witnessed something of the tortures to which Stanley was being subjected upstairs in his room during the night, tries to keep her in the dark about the true state of her beloved lodger. Outside the door there stands a large black car, which, as we later learn, belongs to Goldberg. The two intruders appear and from their conversation we gather that the things that were done to Stanley in the night were pretty horrible and disgusting, Even McCann refuses to go upstairs and to enter Stanley's room. And Goldberg, who seemed most vigorous the night before, now looks aged, deprived of his vitality. He is on the point of collapse, and McCann has to blow into his mouth to revive him with a kind of 'kiss of life'. Lulu comes and accuses Goldberg of having seduced and exploited her. Petey feebly tries to protect Stanley from being taken away by his tormentors. Without any success.

69

Goldberg says he knows a doctor who can look after Stanley. They will take him there. And so Stanley is brought downstairs. He is in a state of catatonic trance, unable to speak, without any human reaction; but dressed most respectably in 'a dark, well-cut suit'. He carries a bowler hat in one hand and his broken glasses in the other. 'He is clean-shaven.' Goldberg and McCann subject him to another flood of verbiage, reminiscent of the previous brainwashing scene, but this time composed of clichés about recovery, treatment, recuperation and success in the conventional world:

GOLDBERG: We'll make a man of you.
MCCANN: And a woman.
GOLDBERG: You'll be re-orientated.
MCCANN: You'll be rich.
GOLDBERG: You'll be adjusted.
MCCANN: You'll be our pride and joy.
GOLDBERG: You'll be a mensch.
MCCANN: You'll be a success.
GOLDBERG: You'll be integrated.
MCCANN: You'll give orders.
GOLDBERG: You'll make decisions.
MCCANN: You'll be a magnate.
GOLDBERG: A statesman.
MCCANN: You'll own yachts.
GOLDBERG: Animals.

But Stanley can only reply with inarticulate gurgles. Then they take him away – to Monty, where he'll get 'treatment'.

Meg, still unaware of what has happened, returns from her shopping. She asks whether Stanley has come down yet. Petey hasn't the heart to tell her the truth. And Meg muses over the wonderful party they have had:

I was the belle of the ball. . . .Oh yes. They all said I was. Oh, it's true. I was. . . . I know I was.

A play like *The Birthday Party* can only be understood as a complex poetic image. Such an image exists, simultaneously, on a multitude of levels. A complex pattern of association and allusion is assembled to express a complex emotional state; what the poet tries to communicate by such an image is, ultimately, the totality of his own existential anxiety.

It is clear that the chief agent of this anxiety is Goldberg, the dominant partner in the team of terrorists. In his poem 'A View of the Party' (dated 1958, the year of the first performance of the play), Pinter himself puts Goldberg into the centre:

The thought that Goldberg was
A man she might have known
Never crossed Meg's words
That morning in the room.

The thought that Goldberg was
A man another knew
Never crossed her eyes
When, glad, she welcomed him.

The thought that Goldberg was
A man to dread and know
Jarred Stanley in the blood
When, still, he heard his name.

Goldberg thus might be more than merely the *agent* of the evil power pursuing Stanley; he might be that power itself. At the same time, in the second part of the poem it is suggested that Goldberg and McCann might, essentially, be forces in the mind – *thoughts*:

The thought that Goldberg was
Sat in the centre of the room,
A man of weight and time,
To supervise the game.

The thought that was McCann
Walked in upon this feast,
A man of skin and bone,
With a green stain on his chest.

So Goldberg and McCann are concrete men of weight and time, skin and bone, and yet they are also essentially thoughts. This ambivalence between the concrete reality of his characters and their simultaneous force as dream images, symbols, thoughts, is of the essence of Pinter's poetic personality; and it is here stated as clearly as he could ever be expected to define it.

Another point made very clear in this remarkable poem, 'A View of the Party', is the theme of the room, the home from which Stanley is expelled. Pinter describes the party itself; and then continues:

> And Stanley sat – alone,
> A man he might have known,
> Triumphant on his hearth,
> Which never was his own.
>
> For Stanley had no home.
> Only where Goldberg was,
> and his bloodhound McCann,
> Did Stanley remember his name.

Finally: the image of blindness falling, which we already know from *The Room* and which recurs in a number of Pinter's other plays, is clearly present in *The Birthday Party*. For the poem closes with the lines:

> A man they never knew
> In the centre of the room,
> And Stanley's final eyes
> Broken by McCann.

The breaking of the glasses by McCann thus corresponds to the blinding of Rose in *The Room*.

Pinter's poem is entitled 'A View of the Party'. Just *a* view, one among many possible ones.

What, then, could Goldberg and his organization represent?

On one level it is fairly clear – particularly from the final image of Stanley in the uniform of respectable, bourgeois gentility – that Stanley is the *artist* whom society claims back from a comfortable, bohemian, 'opt-out' existence. This, it seems, is possible because he is an artist who has doubts about his creative ability; he has not worked for a long time; he has come down, from a piano to a little boy's drum; and even that he breaks in his clumsiness in the game of blind man's buff.

On another level *The Birthday Party* might be seen as an image of man's fear of being driven out from his warm place of refuge on earth. The play would then, like Beckett's *Endgame*, emerge as a morality about the process of death itself, a kind of modern *Everyman*. In the first act Stanley teases Meg with a threat which seems to be a long-standing one between them:

STANLEY (*advancing*): They are coming today.
MEG: Who?
STANLEY: They are coming in a van.
MEG: Who?
STANLEY: And do you know what they've got in that van?
MEG: What?
STANLEY: They've got a wheelbarrow in that van.
MEG (*breathlessly*): They haven't.
STANLEY: Oh yes, they have.
MEG: You're a liar.
STANLEY (*advancing upon her*): A big wheelbarrow. And when the van stops they wheel it out, and they wheel it up the garden path, and then they knock at the front door.
MEG: They don't.
STANLEY: They're looking for someone.
MEG: They're not.
STANLEY: They're looking for someone. A certain person.
MEG (*hoarsely*): No, they're not!
STANLEY: Shall I tell you who they're looking for?
MEG: No!
STANLEY: You don't want me to tell you?
MEG: You're a liar!

At this moment there *is* a knock at the front door. Meg goes out and one hears a voice saying: 'Hullo Mrs Boles. It's come.' (A very typically Pinteresque shock-effect, after the long build up about the van and the wheelbarrow!) It turns out that the visitor is Lulu and what has come is the parcel with Stanley's present. Yet there can be little doubt that the van with the wheelbarrow in it, with which Stanley frightens Meg, is a hearse with a coffin. Stanley does not specify *who* it is that will be taken away in the wheelbarrow. It might be Meg, and Meg's reaction might therefore be her fear of her own death; but Stanley might also be frightening her with the prospect of *his* disappearance. In the light of the later events in the play it becomes clear that, above all, Stanley's game to frighten Meg is merely a projection of his fear that someone will come to take *him* away. Goldberg's black car at the end would then also represent a hearse, while Stanley's correct dress, his speechlessness, and his blindness would be an image of him laid out, and lying in state, as a corpse. In *The Room* Rose's fear of losing her home is clearly the fear of death; the coming of the Negro who calls at her home is, therefore, in my view, a signal of her impending death. Goldberg and McCann *could* also be seen as messengers, sent out to transport a human being into the nether world: Goldberg, with his pronounced Jewish family feeling and his sentimentality, could then be seen as a grotesque caricature of Jehovah, the Lord over life and death, while the brutal torturer McCann could represent a projection of Stanley's fears of the physical suffering in the hour of extinction.

On another plane again, that of psychological archetypes, *The Birthday Party* might also be seen as an image, a metaphor for the process of growing up, of expulsion from the warm, cosy world of childhood. That Meg, with her crushing combination of motherliness and senile eroticism, is a mother-image seen from the viewpoint of an Oedipus complex, needs no particular stress. Stanley is reluctant to leave the warm, though seedy, nest which Meg has built for him. He is afraid, not only of the outside world, but also of sexuality outside the cosy mother-son relationship. That is why he refuses to 'go out' with Lulu (in both senses of the phrase: having a girl friend and going out into the world). And that is why, at the climax of his mental crisis, his 'birthday party', he first attacks Meg, the mother-figure, perhaps for not *resisting* the destruction of their relationship, not being aware of the meaning of the presence of Goldberg and McCann; why we, then, find him trying to rape Lulu. He *has* been driven away from infantile sexuality, and is being pushed into the adult relationship (hence also Goldberg's provocative love play with Lulu in Stanley's presence). It is because the individual's feelings in this crisis are ambivalent that Stanley's actions are ambivalent and charged with aggression both against the mother-figure (whom he despises for the very dependence in which he lives and yet cannot reject because he is too lazy, too weak to brave the world on his own) and the girl whose attraction frightens him and therefore evokes feelings of hatred and aggression. Moreover: if Meg is a mother-figure with overtones of subconscious incestuous yearnings, then Goldberg, with his exaggerated Jewish family feelings, is a father-figure *par excellence*. In that case Stanley's fear of the avenging angels sent by 'the organization' would be an expression of his guilt feelings for his incestuous impulses, his dread of punishment by the father-figure. It is noteworthy that Petey in many ways resembles Bert in *The Room*: he also hardly talks, lets himself be pampered by his wife, and goes out of the house for long periods; but while Bert is savage and brutal, Petey is mild. Bert's brutality reappears in that of Goldberg and McCann. In other words: one figure has been split into three components.

Seen from this angle, Stanley's removal in the garb of the respectable hardworking suburban breadwinner would be an image of the adult's nostalgic leavetaking from the cosy, comfortable, warm, cared-for world of his childhood, his view of the adult world as one of Adam driven out from Paradise to earn his daily bread by the sweat of his brow.

These are just three possible levels of interpretation of a play like *The Birthday Party*. There may be many others.

What must be stressed, however, is that there is *no contradiction* between these different aspects. As in all poetic imagery there is a deep and organic connection between the multiple planes on which the layers of ambiguity of the imagery operate. For example: the process of growing up is in itself an image, and a metaphor of dying: one incarnation of the self dies, to make room for another which is being born to take its place. Rites of initiation are also very often closely related to funeral rites. Equally: society driving an artist towards respectable work closely corresponds to the transition from childhood to the workaday world of the adult. All children can be seen as living for play and self-expression. In that sense all children are artists, and the process of growing up is one of losing the emotional range, the irresponsibility and freedom of the artist.

Thus, on closer examination the different levels of approach will be seen merely as different aspects of the same, immensely complex, immensely relevant, and immensely *true* poetic metaphor for a basic human situation, an existential archetype embodied in a play like *The Birthday Party*. And it is precisely the realism, the reality of the concrete situation portrayed, which gives the poetic image its solidity and power. Each of the characters is endowed with his own linguistic personality: the slowness and softness of Meg, Goldberg's mental agility, McCann's brutality, they are all firmly delineated by the way they speak. But, here again, the language also provides a poetic texture of images which parallel and reinforce the metaphorical aspect of the action. The seemingly nonsensical brain-washing sessions in which Stanley is drowned in a welter of quick-fire questions and statements by the two terrorists contain innumerable references to the main metaphors of the play. ('What would your old mum say, Webber?' 'Why did you kill your wife?' 'Why did you never get married?' 'You contaminate womankind.' 'You verminate the sheet of your birth' – just to pick out a few from a long list of projections of Stanley's guilt feelings, culminating in: 'What makes you think you exist? You're dead. You're dead. You can't live, you can't think, you can't love. You're dead. You're a plague gone bad. There's no juice in you. You're nothing but an odour?' These are the *thoughts*, Stanley's thoughts, externalized by the characters of Goldberg and McCann!)

Both in treatment and subject matter *The Birthday Party* shows affinities with another masterpiece which is also a metaphor of an existential crisis of a similar nature: Kafka's *The Trial*, where, after all, the hero also suffers from unaccountable guilt feelings and is also, at the end, taken away to his execution by two angels of death in the guise of respectable-looking gentlemen. But Pinter's play, his first mature contribution to dramatic literature, is a wholly individual, wholly original creation.

A Slight Ache

Originally conceived as a radio play, *A Slight Ache* has also been performed on the stage. But in its radio form the play is bound to be more effective, because then it can remain open whether the central character, the matchseller, who never speaks, actually exists or is no more than a projection of the two other characters' fears.

A Slight Ache is the first of Pinter's plays which is based on a middle-class idiom: Edward and Flora are an affluent middle-class couple, who live in a large country house surrounded by gardens. Edward used to be in business, now he regards himself as something of an intellectual; he mentions that he is engaged on writing a book on Space and Time; on another occasion he refers to his plans for a work on the Belgian Congo.

The play starts with Edward and Flora at breakfast; their dialogue about trival matters shows – as does the dialogue between Ben and Gus at the opening of *The Dumb Waiter* – that there is considerable tension between them. Do wasps 'bite' or 'sting'? The question leads to a bitter altercation. And the wasp which has strayed on to the breakfast table is trapped in a marmalade jar by Edward and, after prolonged torture, killed by having boiling tea water poured over it. Edward, who has complained about a slight ache in his eyes, rejoices in the thought that the hot water will *blind* the wasp:

> . . . Tilt the pot. Tilt. Aah . . . down here . . . right down . . . blinding him . . . that's . . . it.

Again we thus find the image of blindness – as in *The Room* and *The Birthday Party* – which seems to be equated with sexual inadequacy and death. Also the episode around the wasp shows the depth of bitterness, hatred and cruelty which lurks behind the polite voices and formal manners in this marriage. Edward and Flora are worried: For some time, about two months, an old man with a tray has been standing at the back entrance to their garden, trying to sell matches to passers-by. But hardly anybody ever passes there. So what is that old man trying to do? Edward seems to be afraid of the old man; to find out what he is after he proposes to invite him in and to put some questions to him. He asks Flora to go and get him. As he does not speak throughout the play, this old matchseller is, in the radio version, no more than silence, nothingness. It is one of the great advantages of radio that it is, among all the performing arts, the only one able to put the absolute void on to the stage of the audience's imagination. (Ingmar Bergman's famous film *The Seventh Seal* started as a radio play: there too the figure of Death appeared as pure silence; far more effectively than in the film, where he had to be turned into a lay figure clad in a black cloak.) In the stage version and on television the matchseller's menace is considerably reduced when he can be seen as a very ordinary old man; and his silence, which is terrifying in the radio version, becomes a somewhat embarrassing sign of idiocy.

Edward's attempts to draw the matchseller into conversation turn, confronted with the visitor's speechlessness, into a nervous monologue which, getting increasingly hysterical, exposes the snobbery, intellectual pretences, and selfishness of the speaker. Edward can no longer stand it, and asks Flora to lead him out into the garden (he seems weakened; the slight ache from which he suffered initially has grown into a general loss of vitality, the start of the descent into the decay of old age).

Now it is Flora's turn to try and get the old man to speak. He reminds her of a poacher she once met in her youth:

> I had an encounter with a poacher once. It was a ghastly rape, the brute. High up on a hillside cattle track. Early spring. I was out riding on my pony. . . . Of course, life was perilous in those days. It was my first canter unchaperoned. . . . Years later, when I was Justice of the Peace for the county, I had him in front of the bench. He was there for poaching. That's how I know he was a poacher.

In other words: the encounter with the old matchseller provokes Flora into the sexual fantasies of her youth about possible first, unchaperoned 'canters' and being set upon by wild men. And in spite of the old man's 'vile smell' she gradually works herself up into sexual excitement about him:

> Hmmnn, you're a solid old boy, I must say. Not at all like a jelly. All you need is a bath. . . . I'm going to keep you. I'm going to keep you, you dreadful chap, and call you Barnabas.

But when Edward returns Flora tries to keep him out of the room by pretending that the old man is dying. Edward retorts with a furious verbal attack on his wife: 'You lying slut. Get back to your trough!' Flora goes out, Edward is again left alone with the matchseller. Now he talks about his youth, his athletic prowess, cricket; his surveying the sea from a hill through a telescope, following the path of three-masted schooners. Is the old man laughing about him? Or is he crying in grief for Edward's plight? A fever has Edward in its grip. He falls on the floor complaining about the germ he caught in his eyes. Has he gone blind? It seems so: for now he believes the matchseller looks 'extraordinarily youthful'. He asks the matchseller to lead him out into the garden: 'Take my hand.'

Flora has come in. The matchseller goes over to her. She hands Edward the matchseller's tray, and leaves the room with the old man.

Who or what is the matchseller? That he is not meant as a realistic character is clear enough. Hence his awkward effect in stage performance. One senses the incompatibility of his concreteness with his symbolic quality.

For Edward the matchseller is the focal point of his anxiety; he may indeed be that which starts as a slight ache and ends with Edward's loss of his personality – perhaps even his sight – and his expulsion from Flora's bed. The matchseller had to stand outside the garden gate. Now it is Edward who is handed his tray, presumably to stand outside. In other words: Edward's fate is closely analogous to Rose's in *The Room*. She too is visited by a symbolic figure who had been waiting for her outside. She too is stricken with blindness and presumably loses her warm home to be expelled into the cold of the ·basement: death, Edward's expulsion – as Stanley's in *The Birthday Party* – could therefore also be a metaphor for his dying. Hence the matchseller, whom Flora experiences as the return of sexual desire, a liberation from a hated, impotent husband (the matchseller to her appears 'not at all like a jelly'), is simply Edward's death. Hence the mysterious figure, whom Edward fears, represents to Flora a return to sex and to life.

In *A Slight Ache* Pinter very convincingly demonstrated that his mastery of dialogue transcended the limits of the low life vernacular; his ear for the absurdity of the clichés of middle-class speech proved to be as mercilessly accurate as his ability to expose the idiocy of proletarian solecisms. But essentially the imagery remains the same: the intruder waiting outside whose coming ends in the expulsion and destruction of one of the main characters, and who may be an angel of death; the tension between two closely related but antagonistic partners, which expresses itself in disputes about the finer points of language; the motherly but sexually active and aroused woman, the man, who is incapable of love; the coexistence of extreme realism and the symbolism of the dream.

A Night Out

A Night Out was also, originally, written as a radio play, but soon after its first transmission it was also performed, with great success, on television, and has also since then occasionally been staged. It is the first of Pinter's plays which remains on an entirely realistic level throughout, and eschews all supernatural or openly symbolist effects, as well as the elements of enigma and mystery which pervade plays like *The Birthday Party* and *A Slight Ache*.

Albert Stokes is a young man of about twenty-eight who lives with his mother and is entirely dependent on her – a relationship in some ways resembling that of Stanley and Meg in *The Birthday Party*. Albert's mother is so possessive that for her his announcement that he has to go out for the evening, to an office party, constitutes almost an act of desertion and rebellion.

But this time Albert is determined to have his way. He must attend the party which his boss is giving for an aged colleague about to retire. At a coffee stall by a railway arch Seeley and Kedge, two of Albert's office friends, are already waiting for him. When Albert, having defied his mother, arrives, he is still uncertain whether he should, in fact, go through with it and go to the party. His friends tease him as a mother's boy.

At the party spirits are high. Gidney, the firm's accountant, who has a grudge against Albert, persuades two of the secretaries to embarrass Albert by playing on his shyness in the presence of girls. While the boss makes a speech celebrating the long service of the guest of honour, one of the girls cries out that someone 'touched' her. It was, in fact, Mr Ryan, the aged guest of honour: this, at least in the television version, is made clear by the way he looks innocently up to the ceiling with a knowing smile on his lips. But suspicion fastens on Albert, the situation becomes distinctly uncomfortable, and he flees. When he gets back home his mother receives him with a flood of reproach and abuse. Albert loses his temper, grabs an alarm clock and begins to hit his mother with it. He hears her scream and rushes out into the street, convinced that he has gravely hurt, perhaps even killed her.

Back at the coffee stall, he is accosted by a prostitute; he follows her home, as he is clearly afraid to go back to his own house.

The tart, who behaves in a most genteel, ladylike manner and talks of her little girl, whose photograph adorns the mantelpiece, tries to find out more about Albert. He does not say much, but hints that he works in films. An alarm clock in the prostitute's room recalls the incident with his mother to him. When the girl nags him about having dropped some cigarette ash onto her carpet, he becomes violent; she too has now recalled the image of the dominant female in his life; he rebels, and throws his burning cigarette down, on purpose. When the tart protests, he grabs her alarm clock and threatens to kill her. The girl is terrified; he tears the little daughter's photograph from the frame and exposes her lies: the photograph is more than twenty years old and has obviously nothing to do with the tart. Albert throws her half a crown and leaves.

He is back home. His mother, surprisingly, is alive and well. She tells him that she forgives him:

> You're good, you're not bad, you're a good boy . . . I know you are . . . you are, aren't you?

But there is no reaction from Albert. As the play ends, we are left in the dark as to whether the power situation in the household has changed or not. Has Albert's show of domination over the prostitute given him the confidence to dominate his mother too? His silence could imply that. But, equally, it might mean that he has surrendered and resigned himself to a life of dependence.

The great success of *A Night Out*, particularly when it was shown on television, was based largely on the brilliantly realistic dialogue: the conversation about football at the coffee stall, the party chat, and the acutely observed tone of genteel refinement of the prostitute's speech.

The parallels with *The Birthday Party* are fairly clear: not only the analogy betwen Albert's dependence on his mother and Stanley's on Meg, but also the resulting fear of sex with other women. Albert too is being tormented by men who do know how one gets on with girls and who tease him about his innocence and bashfulness. Albert's aggression against first his mother and then the tart, exactly corresponds to Stanley's attacks on Meg and Lulu during *his* party. There is a difference, however: Stanley attacks Lulu as the embodiment of the sexuality he fears, while Albert raises his hand against the tart because she turns out to be exactly as nagging as his mother. But, on the other hand, it is equally clear that the attack on the prostitute also arises from Albert's feelings of inferiority, his rage about his inability to approach the prostitute as a sexual object. Albert hates both aspects of the feminine principle: the sexual demand of the prostitute, i.e. woman as a challenge to his sexual potency; and the mother's claim to dominance over him as head of her family, as a person entitled to his respect, gratitude and servitude. The girls who tease him during the party can thus be seen as further embodiments of the first challenge, painful reminders of Albert's sexual inadequacy.

A Night Out can therefore be regarded as an elegant and subtle set of variations on the theme of man's confrontation with aspect of the feminine principle: Albert flees from the mother who enslaves him; at the party he meets the sexual provocation of the girls from the typing pool, which reminds him of his fear of that other aspect of woman; and finally, in the prostitute, where, being a paying customer, he *could* assert his sexuality without fear of rejection, he discovers that here too he cannot escape the other side of the feminine principle: the nagging gentility of the mother's figure. And when he returns home from his wild night out, the mother is still there; not even the extreme act of violence to which he resorted has been able to free him. Or has it?

That is the question with which we are left.

The Hothouse

The Hothouse remained unpublished and unperformed for more than twenty years. When Harold Pinter lent me a copy of the play as I was writing the first edition of this book, the title page bore the inscription: 'Final Draft. Discarded play'. When the play was finally published in 1980 it carried an author's note:

> I wrote *The Hothouse* in the winter of 1958. I put it aside for further deliberation and made no attempt to have it produced at the time. I then went on to write *The Caretaker*. In 1979 I reread *The Hothouse* and decided it was worth presenting on the stage. I made a few changes during rehearsal, mainly cuts.

The Hothouse is clearly related to the synopsis of a radio play that Pinter submitted to the BBC on 12th November 1958, and in a further extended form on 23rd December of the same year. The first idea for this play, which was to show doctors in a psychological research station wrapped up in their own personal affairs and intrigues while the patients suffered in soundproof cells, clearly came between the completion of *A Slight Ache* and the emergence of Pinter's first truly realistic play *A Night Out*. *The Hothouse* also takes place in a kind of psychological research station or mental home in the country (officially referred to by the staff as a 'rest home') and is written in an idiom of grotesque farce which points in the direction of Ionesco. Yet there are a number of very significant parallels with *The Caretaker*.

The 'rest home' in *The Hothouse* is a government establishment. The inmates bear numbers instead of names, while the staff, led by an ex-army officer called Roote, are grotesquely and monosyllabically named Lush, Hogg, Beck, Budd, Tuck, Dodds, Tate, Peck, Gibbs, Lamb, Cutts, Tibb and Lobb. Miss Cutts, the only woman in the cast, has an affair with the superintendent as well as with his aide, Gibbs. Gibbs and Cutts use the newest member of the staff, Lamb, as the guinea pig for experiments, in the course of which he is connected to electrodes and wildly tormented, while his torturers flirt and laugh. This can be seen as a grotesquely farcical variant on Aston's experience in the mental hospital in *The Caretaker*. Moreover, one of the inmates of the 'rest home' has died; when his mother comes to inquire after him, she is fobbed off with a 'cock and bull' story about his having been transferred to another home. Even the name Jenkins – Davies's alias – appears briefly in the original script of *The Hothouse*, when the superintendent discusses the possibility of giving the inmates their names back:

> One of the purposes of this establishment is to instil that confidence in each and every one of them, that confidence which will one day enable them to say 'I am . . . Jenkins', for example. Not easy, not easy, agreed, but it makes it doubly difficult if they're constantly referred to as 5244, doesn't it? We lose sight of their names and they lose sight of their names.

(For publication and performance, Pinter changed Jenkins to Gubbins.)

Lamb, the victim in *The Hothouse*, is subjected by Miss Cutts to a cross-examination which contains elements of Stanley's brainwashing in *The Birthday Party*, but also relates to Aston's fear of women; in the first act of *The Caretaker* Aston tells Davies of an incident in a café when a woman suddenly touched his hand and asked him: '. . . how would you like me to have a look at your body?' Aston's reaction is:

> . . . To come out with it just like that, in the middle of this conversation. Struck me as a bit odd.

In *The Hothouse* Miss Cutts is equally embarrassing, but in a grotesquely heightened vein:

CUTTS: Are you virgo intacta?
LAMB: What?
CUTTS: Are you virgo intacta?
LAMB: Oh, I say, that's rather embarrassing. I mean in front of a lady –
CUTTS: Are you virgo intacta?
LAMB: Yes, I am, actually. I'll make no secret of it.
CUTTS: Have you always been virgo intacta?
LAMB: Oh, yes, always. Always.
CUTTS: From the word go?
LAMB: Go? Oh, yes. From the word go.

(Pinter used this particular episode in one of his revue sketches, *Applicant*.)

Strange things go on in *The Hothouse*. Not only has one patient died, but another, a woman, has given birth to an illegitimate baby. In the end Gibbs reports to a bureaucrat in Whitehall that the entire staff have been killed – by the inmates? or, indeed, by Gibbs himself? – in an orgy of bloodshed. The play ends with the poor forgotten victim, Lamb, in the sound-proof room, still 'sitting in the chair, earphones and electrodes attached, quite still'. In the post-production edition of the play (1982) this became: 'He sits still, staring, as in a catatonic trance'.

It is as though Aston's experience in the hospital had been wildly heightened and exaggerated to form the subject matter of an entire play.

The grotesque figures in *The Hothouse* are caricatures, gargoyles rather than human beings, while in *The Caretaker* some of the same subject matter has been expressed through fully rounded – although still mysterious and unmotivated – *characters*. Lamb's experience in *The Hothouse* is in the form of the wild nightmare of a patient in a mental hospital, Aston's tale in *The Caretaker* is the same experience recollected in sober tranquillity. The numbered patients in *The*

Hothouse have, in *The Caretaker*, been transmuted into Davies's – or Jenkins's? – anxiety about his insurance card – which after all also bears a number, but in sober reality – and *his* uncertainty about his real name and identity. The grotesque caricature of the revue sketch dialogue about Lamb's virginity from the word go has, in *The Caretaker*, become the very real awe and fear in which Aston, mentally and perhaps physically maimed by his treatment, stands of women who put embarrassing propositions to him.

In the light of Pinter's subsequent development in *The Caretaker* it appears that *The Hothouse* marks the point at which Pinter decided that his future lay in the area of realism – images of the real world which are raised to the level of becoming metaphors for the human condition by the mere mysteriousness already inherent in reality itself (and the great difficulty we all have in drawing a dividing line between what is real, what is imagined and what is a dream, a day-dream or a fantasy) rather than using the method of direct distortion of reality into grotesque fantasy images.

The fact that, more than two decades after he wrote it, Pinter did decide to release the play and to direct it himself shows that by that time he had won sufficient detachment from the situation when he had to make the choice in which direction he should go on developing. In 1979 he could look at that early play as simply another one among the examples of his earliest style which, by then, had become a well-established, if now surpassed, phase of his history as a playwright.

The Caretaker

With *The Caretaker* Pinter finally achieved his breakthrough in the theatre. Donald McWhinnie, the radio producer who had helped Pinter over his difficult period after the failure of *The Birthday Party* two years earlier, directed the play at the Arts Theatre Club; and Donald Pleasence, one of the finest character actors on the English stage, played the part of the tramp Davies.

The Caretaker is a three-act, three-character play. Mick and Aston are brothers, the younger in his late twenties, the older – Aston – in his early thirties. Mick we gather (but one can never be quite sure about the truth of what is said about a character in a Pinter play) is a successful businessman of sorts; he owns a small van and seems to be dabbling in buying and selling properties. For his elder brother, Aston, he has bought an old, derelict house in a western suburb of London. Only one room in this house is habitable. Aston has, rather vaguely, been given the task of converting the whole house. In the meantime the one habitable room is cluttered up with old furniture and other junk which Aston has acquired; and even this room has a leaking ceiling; a bucket hangs from the roof to catch the water which drips through.

Aston is a slow, awkward man who incessantly fiddles with screwdrivers and handsaws, but he is good-natured and ready to help his fellow human beings. The play opens, after a brief, tantalizing and mysterious silent inspection of the room by Mick, with Aston bringing in an old tramp whom he has saved from being beaten up in a brawl in a café. The tramp, Davies, informs him that he had been working as a cleaner in that café and that he had refused to remove a bucket of rubbish:

> It's not my job to take out the bucket! They got a boy there for taking out the bucket. I wasn't engaged to take out buckets.

It was out of this incident that the fight developed. Davies, it seems, not only insists on doing only jobs appropriate to his station in life, but is also filled with race hatred:

> All them Greeks had it, Poles, Greeks, Blacks, the lot of them, all them aliens had it [i.e. a place to sit down in a work break]. And they had me working there . . . they had me working . . .

All them Blacks had it, Blacks, Greeks, Poles, the lot of them, that's what, doing me out of a seat, treating me like dirt.

So the old tramp emerges in the first minutes of the play as an epitome of some of the worst traits of the British workman: prone to get involved in quarrels about who should do what job, xenophobic, lazy and ill-tempered. Moreover he is bitter, weak and constantly deceiving others as well as himself. He tells Aston that he is not really called Davies, for example. His name is Jenkins. At least he has got an insurance card under the name of Jenkins. Yet, when further questioned, he reverts to Davies. Davies is his real name:

Mac Davies. That was before I changed my name.

To get his papers in order, Davies, or Jenkins, has to get to Sidcup, but to get there he would need good shoes; and good shoes are hard to come by.

Aston is sorry for the old man, and invites him to stay with him in his room for a few days until he gets fixed up. He will even try to find some decent shoes for him. He gets a second bed ready. Davies can hardly believe his luck.

The next morning Aston mildly complains that Davies has been talking in his sleep. He hotly denies it and attributes it to 'them Blacks. . . . Next door'. Aston wants to go out. Davies is astonished to find that, nevertheless, he will be allowed to remain alone, he can hardly understand that he is trusted not to steal some of the many pieces of junk piled high in the room. He is even given the second key by Aston. But he is frightened by the electric fire, and the old gas stove, which is not even connected to the mains. When he is left alone in the room, Pinter has again succeeded in establishing, out of Davies's lack of self-confidence and his nervousness about the menace of these objects, an atmosphere of threat, mystery and horror. At this moment, Mick, the younger brother, slides into the room and eventually frightens Davies out of his wits by suddenly seizing him from behind and treating him as though he *was* a burglar.

Act Two takes up the action immediately at the point where it left off – in a typically Pinteresque *coup de théâtre* shock effect – with Mick's brutal intrusion into Davies's solitude. Mick cross-examines Davies, rapidly alternating between brutality and a politeness which might be cruelly ironic or, indeed, even genuine. He seizes Davies's trousers and has become very threatening again, when Aston returns, and Mick's attitude immediately changes to one of matter-of-fact inquiry about the house, with Davies's presence seemingly forgotten. It is Aston who draws Davies back into the conversation, by telling him that he has got his bag from the café where he had left it the night before. There follows another bout of teasing by Mick, who grabs the bag repeatedly so that it rapidly passes from one of the characters to the next in a seemingly endless round. Then, as mysteriously as he has come, Mick goes again; Davies asks:

DAVIES: Who was that feller?
ASTON: He's my brother.
DAVIES: Is he? He's a bit of a joker, en'he?

With almost motherly solicitude Aston gives Davies a number of things he has bought for him. Even the bag, it turns out, is not really Davies's; somebody else had taken it at the café. So Aston has bought another bag for him at some second-hand stall, together with a bundle of clothes.

It is clear that Aston is happy to have someone to look after. He goes so far as to offer the homeless tramp a permanent home:

ASTON: You could be . . . caretaker here, if you liked.
DAVIES: What?
ASTON: You could . . . look after the place, if you liked . . . you know, the stairs and the landing, the front steps, keep an eye on it. Polish the bells.

Davies can hardly believe his good fortune, but at the same time his sour, querulous nature asserts itself and his acceptance is vague, half-hearted; what would happen if the people who are 'after him' came to the door and rang the bell and he, as caretaker, had to go and open?

The same evening: Davies returns to the room, having gone out; he tries to switch on the light, it does not work. A sudden loud and eerie noise puts him into a state of extreme panic. Mick, who is using a vacuum cleaner, had plugged it into the lamp socket, hence the darkness and the sudden noise. When the light is on again, Davies is discovered trying to defend himself by holding a knife in his hand, ready to strike any attacker. But Mick, the suave, quick-witted brother, has become polite and considerate to Davies, complains about his brother's laziness, and – to Davies's amazement – also offers him the position of caretaker. Only, he wants references. Davies, at first uncertain as to which of the two brothers is the owner of the house, promises that he will be able to bring these as soon as he can get down to Sidcup. Recognizing the obvious superiority of the younger brother, Davies now regards him as the one he has to play up to and, weak as he is, he is not able to resist the temptation to speak ill of his benefactor, Aston.

The next morning: now there is a growing tension between Aston and Davies. Davies can't sleep by an open window and complains about the rain coming in. Aston must have fresh air to sleep. But then, obviously from a deep longing to be friends and to communicate, Aston begins to tell Davies the story of his life. There was a time when he was as nimble and as communicative as his brother. Indeed, he 'talked too much'. And he had hallucinations. He was taken to a mental hospital. A doctor informed him that he ought to have treatment, something would have to be done to his brain. But Aston refused:

Well, I wasn't a fool. I knew I was a minor. I knew he couldn't do anything to me without getting permission. I knew he had to get permission from my mother. So I wrote to her and told her

91

what they were trying to do. But she signed their form, you see, giving them permission.

He tried to escape; in vain. He was subjected to electric shock treatment. That is why he has become slow, unable to work, except on his own, pottering about the house which he is supposed to redecorate. As Aston finishes his long speech, the curtain falls on Act Two.

This moment of Aston's self-revelation seals Davies's fate. Weak and beset by terrible feelings of inferiority, he simply cannot resist the temptation to take advantage of Aston's confession; confronted with a man who has been to a mental hospital, who admits his inadequacy, Davies is unable to react with sympathy, with gratitude for the maimed man's kindness, his offer of friendship. He must enjoy the thrill of treating his benefactor with the superiority of the sane over the lunatic. Transferred to the lower levels of contemporary society, this is the *hybris* of Greek tragedy which becomes the cause of Davies's downfall.

As Act Three opens – two weeks later – it still seems as though Mick might really have meant his offer to Davies, that he should become his caretaker in the house, and take over the supervision of the redecorations. In a passage of ecstatic description he outlines his dream of seeing the derelict house as a luxurious penthouse: the language of furniture advertisements and glossy weeklies is here transformed into a kind of visionary poetry. Davies is in a state of euphoria and sees himself as Mick's friend; he complains about Aston and asks Mick to speak to him and to tell him that from now on he, Davies, will be in command. But Mick, who clearly has merely been tempting the old man to show his true nature, departs with a mere 'Yes . . . maybe I will.'

Aston returns. He has at last got hold of a pair of shoes for Davies. But Davies finds fault with them. He clearly no longer wants to walk to Sidcup.

In the night when Aston again complains about Davies's talking in his sleep and making noises, Davies reacts with the anger and contempt of the dominant partner, and even resorts to pulling out his knife. When Aston suggests that the time may have come when Davies should try to find somewhere else to live, he retaliates by announcing that he has been put in charge, and that it might be Aston who would have to go. Aston merely puts Davies's things in his bag and hands it to him. Davies goes, but he is sure that he will be back.

The same evening: Davies has returned, in Aston's absence, and is denouncing Aston to Mick. Mick appears to be listening sympathetically, but when Davies goes so far as to suggest Aston should 'go back where he come from', i.e. the mental hospital, Mick's attitude changes abruptly to one of savage irony. He treats Davies as an impostor who had pretended to know about interior decoration:

> Ever since you come into this house there has been nothing but trouble. Honest. I can take nothing you say at face value. Every word you speak is open to any number of different interpretations. Most of what you say is lies. You're violent, you're erratic, you're just completely unpredictable. You're nothing else but a wild animal, when you come down to it. You're a barbarian. And to put the old tin lid on it, you stink from arse-hole to breakfast time.

In his anger Mick picks up and smashes the figure of the Buddha which is one of Aston's favourite pieces in the room. Davies is speechless. Aston returns. The two brothers look at each other. 'Both are smiling, faintly'. Mick begins to speak but is unable to form a coherent sentence, probably because he cannot bring himself to confess to having smashed the Buddha, and leaves the room. Aston sees the broken pieces, then goes to his bed and begins to work on his electric plug.

Davies makes a feeble attempt to regain his favour, by withdrawing any harsh words he may have said. But Aston is adamant. The play closes with Davies desperately pleading for the room, the home he has now lost, while Aston stands silently by the window with his back turned to him. Davies's words stick in his throat. He stands silently by the door as the curtain falls. We know that he will have to go, that he has lost his last chance in life.

The final scene, with one of the characters about to leave, certain to leave, yet not seen to be leaving is strongly reminiscent of the concluding image in Beckett's *Endgame*. There Clov's leaving would mean the end of the room's owner, here it is the one who is driven away whose life is thereby forfeited. There are echoes here, too, even of *Waiting for Godot*: the tramp, the two complementary brothers, the shoes that will not fit; in Beckett's play the two main characters are waiting for salvation to come, in Pinter's one of the characters is within sight of salvation and is then driven out of paradise by his own original sin. Yet *The Caretaker* is, at least on the surface, far more naturalistic. Originally Pinter was thinking of a violent end – perhaps the killing of the old man by the two brothers. But he realized in time that this was quite unnecessary; that Davies's expulsion from paradise would be far more tragic, precisely through Aston's apathy.

The Caretaker marks the decisive consolidation of Pinter's abandonment of obvious symbolism, supernatural devices and even the chiaroscuro effects of the mysterious killers in *The Birthday Party*: the renunciation of the violent end was a further step in this direction.

In *The Room*, in *The Birthday Party* and in *A Slight Ache* the main character was living in an undefinable dread of an outside intruder who might expel him from his home. In *The Caretaker* the situation is reversed: here a homeless wanderer is fighting to gain a foothold in a home. And this time his loss of his home is not merely the outcome of the workings of mysterious fate; it is the direct consequence of his own shortcomings, his original sin: his inability to resist the easy satisfaction of glorying in his superiority over the ex-inmate of an asylum, his overconfidence in playing one brother off against the other. It is Mick who plays the role of the snake in this re-enactment of Adam's expulsion from paradise: by apparently accepting Davies's inane boasts, his complaints about Aston, he has deliberately provoked him into revealing the worst side of his nature. Had Davies been able to show true kindness, genuine sympathy towards Aston after he had been made aware of his past history, he could have established a genuine relationship with him, could have benefited from the offer of friendship implied in that generous gesture of confidence. But poor Davies, whose own inferiority finds an outlet in his hatred of Negroes, Indians and Greeks, simply is not capable of even realizing the meaning of such a gesture. This makes Davies a highly significant and symptomatic character in an age in which an inability by large numbers of human beings to transcend such primitive emotions of racial hatred (which is merely the reverse side of their own deep feelings of inadequacy, their lack of insight and empathy into the plight of other human beings) has become one of the most dangerous threats to peace. Here again we can see that Pinter's apparent lack of political commitment by no means prevents him from dealing with the basic problems of our time.

The character of Aston throws an interesting light on that of Stanley in *The Birthday Party*. If Lamb's plight at the hands of Miss Cutts and Gibbs in *The Hothouse* exaggerates Stanley's experience into an even wilder sphere of sadistic torture phantasies, Aston's story reduces it into the terms of sober, clinical realism. Aston tried to escape from the shock treatment; had he succeeded he might well have hidden, like Stanley, in some seaside boarding house, he might well, like Stanley, have feared the men who would be looking for him to take him back. The reason why Aston was taken to hospital was that he talked too much and too volubly, to the point of having hallucinations; in other words, he was living a life of heightened sensibility and imagination; he was, in some senses, an artistic personality who had to be forcibly reduced to sober respectability.

This, again in a somewhat less extravagant vein, is closely analogous to Stanley's situation, his attempts at becoming a concert artist. Moreover: in *The Birthday Party* Meg – the mother figure – is unable to see what the sinister men who want to brainwash Stanley are after. In *The Caretaker* the mother, from whom Aston expected sympathy and protection, signs the document giving the doctors permission to subject her son to electric shock treatment. Like Aston, Stanley is firghtened of women. Aston was outraged by the woman who propositioned him in a café; Stanley refuses Lulu's suggestion that he should 'take her out'.

The third character in *The Caretaker*, Mick, is the play's most original creation; he has much in common with Len, the equally sleek pimp of *The Homecoming*; in some of his habits of speech, his tendency to indulge in long and circumstantial stories which he obviously invents on the spur of the moment as he tells them, he resembles Goldberg in *The Birthday Party*; he seems, in the end, to be taking his brother's part in dealing with Davies; hence, at least from Aston's point of view, he is not, as Goldberg is from Stanley's, a hostile character. Yet we can never be sure of his motives, or indeed, what part he played at the time of Aston's rape at the hand of the psychiatrists. The way in which the characters of the two brothers complement each other also suggests, however, that ultimately Mick and Aston – like Didi and Gogo in *Waiting for Godot* – could be seen as different sides of the same personality. Mick could then stand for the worldly, Aston for the deeper emotional aspects of the same man. Or in terms of their creator – after all every character an author brings to life can be regarded as an emanation of one aspect of *his* personality – Mick might stand for the actor, Aston for the poet.

The solid reality of the circumstances and characters in *The Caretaker*, and the fact that this reality has all the indeterminacy, open-endedness and mystery of real life, becomes the basis for its effectiveness on a higher plane – the plane of the poetic image, the metaphor for a greater and more general truth, the powerful, universal archetype. This, ultimately, is due to the extreme clarity and truth with which the play represents the real world (which includes the extreme lucidity of the description of its very opaqueness and mystery!); the spectator's sense of reality gets sharpened to the point when he suddenly perceives ordinary and everyday events which he had not heretofore noticed with such intensity of insight that they transcend themselves and become symbolic of a whole category of experience. It is the experience of the Buddha's encounters with the sick man, the old man and the corpse; or of Newton's observation of the apple falling from the tree; here, as in the experience of a spectator confronted with a slice of real life which he is made to see in blinding clarity, the real old man, the real, ordinary apple, became archetypes of cosmic significance and illumined areas of knowledge and experience that had up to that moment remained dark and void of significance.

That sick man, that old man, that corpse who changed the Buddha's life, were at that moment in history as ordinary and everyday as millions like them; by being perceived in that particular way by that particular great personality they became universal symbols, the centre of a great myth of human existence: archetypes of the human condition.

I do not want to strain the analogy too far, nor to suggest that the characters in the play we are discussing can aspire to the lofty universality of one of the great myths of mankind; I merely want to show how the realistic representation of the particular *can* transcend itself – through the poetic truth and power of the manner of the representation – and assume the significance of the symbol, the mythical, the archetypal. The individual and particular – observed with the perception and represented with the creative power of a real poet – can thus become the metaphor of its own deeper, general, all-embracing significance.

Considerations like these are, I believe, fundamental to an understanding of a play like *The Caretaker* and indeed most of Pinter's work. Mick and Aston on the one hand, Davies on the other, are meticulously observed individuals; but they are also archetypes. Archetypes, for example, of the conflict between two young men and an old one, of the battle between the sons and the father. The idea may, at first sight, seem far fetched. But there is an unmistakable indication in the text that it nevertheless has some validity.

When Mick first meets Davies his reaction is:

You remind me of my uncle's brother. . . . To be honest, I've never made out how he came to be my uncle's brother. I've often thought that maybe it was the other way round. I mean that my uncle was his brother and he was my uncle. But I never called him uncle. As a matter of fact I called him Sid. My mother called him Sid too. It was a funny business. Your spitting image he was . . .

Who is one's uncle's brother? Another uncle – or one's father. As Mick's mother never called Sid his uncle, it follows that the man, of whom Davies reminds Mick, was Mick's father.

If Davies is a father-figure, his rejection and expulsion at the end of the play would explain the power and poignancy of the play's final image – an old man realizing that he has to go, a young man impassively accepting this fact, unwilling and unable to do anything about it. And this is the way in which Davies reaps the reward of his unthinking assumption of superiority towards Aston: there is surely here an element of the tragic guilt of all parents.in their children's eyes: that they persist far too long in maintaining the stance of superiority over them which was appropriate when they were helpless infants but becomes intolerable to them when they reach adolescence and maturity. In bringing Davies home, Aston expressed a yearning for a human relationship with a father-figure; he has tried his best: it did not, it could not work. Mick's attitude was hostile and cynical from the outset: yet his seeming acceptance of Davies, his flattery and false politeness, also embody something of the sons' tactics towards the generation of the fathers: flattery and subservience in the sure foreknowledge that the days of their power and superiority are numbered.

The image of the sons chasing the father out of the house might also – on a different level again – be seen as a projection forward of the sons' *wish* to express their aggressiveness against the father-figure. Aston's account of his experience at the hands of the doctors, his helplessness when brutally manhandled and manipulated as a passive object, contains a good deal of the child's feeling of helplessness towards the parents who decide his destiny; the doctors tormenting Aston thus become another aspect of the father-figure. And it is surely significant that Aston, who appealed to his mother for help, was let down by her. As a wish-fulfilment image Davies would be a weakened and degraded version of the father, someone who has all the presumption and arrogance of the real father but is so weak and contempt-ible in other ways that the son's aggression can find a free and full outlet against him.

The Caretaker is a play without a woman: but the repressed hate/love for the mother pervades the struggle of the sons with the father-figure, just as in *A Night Out* the shadow of Albert's late father falls powerfully across his love-hate relationship with his mother. The doctors in the mental hospital where Aston was treated castrated him – to punish him for his Oedipal desires – with the consent and connivance of his mother. By taking an attitude of superior-ity, treating him as a mental defective, as those doctors did, Davies assumes the same role. And this is what makes the two brothers finally unite against the old man.

These suggestions are not brought forward as dogmatic statements of the 'true meaning' or hidden content of the play, but merely as indications as to the possible sources of its power, its richness as a poetic metaphor of man's predic-ament. Such an indication of a possible direction in which its hidden layers of meaning might be explored does not exclude a multitude of other approaches: Aston's attempts at making his room habitable have been seen as an image of man's struggle for order in a chaotic world; it has been said that Pinter is preoccupied with the age-old human instinct to fight for territory and that therefore his preoccupation with rooms and homes to be defended or to be conquered reflects man's deep instinctual nature. There is an element of truth in all these interpretations, provided we keep in mind that they are all *equally* relevant and that they are not intentional on the part of the author. The starting point is *not* the possible interpretation: but the concrete image – two young men, an old one, a room. The more concretely, individually and realistically this situation is enacted and thereby explored in depth, the greater its complexity and richness of human associations will become, the wider the general implications which radiate outward from this central image like waves spreading from a stone thrown into a pond.

The Caretaker is the first of Pinter's plays to have achieved this complete synthesis between utter realism in the external action and the poetical metaphor, the dream image of eternal archetypes on the deeper – or higher – levels of impact. Much of the play's initial success was undoubtedly due to the wit and accuracy of the dialogue and the number of laughs to which it gave rise. Davies is a brilliantly comic creation and audiences tend to laugh about his weakness and his own unawareness of these weaknesses. But at the same time Davies is also a figure of menace, the intruder who might well – if Mick is not shamming – succeed in driving Aston from his room and depriving him of his place in the world. It is Mick's mystery and indeterminacy which is thus the pivot of the action. The economy and elegance with which this trio of inter-related characters is handled is truly remarkable. And, in contrast to some of Pinter's earlier plays, there is nothing arbitrary or forced about either the plot or the characters. Even the episode when Mick breaks the Buddha at the climax of his diatribe against Davies, which has been criticized for importing an element of spurious symbolism, is, in my opinion, quite devoid of any such aspect. Aston collects bric-à-brac of all sorts, the Buddha was one of the things he picked up as possible ornaments for the house; his bringing Davies home was another example of the same naïve tendency to pick things up and bring them home. Thus Mick's destruction of the Buddha at the moment when he has decided to get rid of Davies *is* a symbolic action, but one which is completely motivated by the real situation in which he finds himself at that moment. He vents his rage against Davies on an object which reminds him of his brother's failing that led to the appearance of Davies in the house.

The episode with the statue of the Buddha is thus a good

example of the way in which Pinter has, in *The Caretaker*, fused the real and the symbolic: the presence of the Buddha in the room is a symbol, but also the direct realistic consequence of Aston's habit of picking up useless things ('Picked it up in a . . . in a shop. Looked quite nice to me. Don't know why . . . Yes, I was pleased when I got hold of this one. It's very well made') and its destruction by Mick has the same double character and function. In other words: what we do in life concretizes itself in the objects with which we surround ourselves and these become symbolical of our character. Because Aston tends to pick up useless things without much thought, he also picks up Davies. And because Mick has no use for things which merely clutter up the place and have no function, he destroys the Buddha and brings about the expulsion of Davies.

The solidity and organic motivation of this particular symbolic element in *The Caretaker* shows what a long way Pinter had travelled since his use of the over-obvious and arbitrary symbol of the blind Negro in *The Room*, the mysterious orders for food in *The Dumb Waiter* or even the speechless matchseller in *A Slight Ache*.

The same is true of Pinter's use of silence: Rose talks to Bert in the opening scene of *The Room* without getting an answer or a reaction. This is theatrically effective, but fairly arbitrary; we never get an explanation for Bert's silence. The same is true of the matchseller in *A Slight Ache*. He simply does not speak. In the radio version it becomes wholly arbitrary. In the final scene of *The Caretaker* we again have a character who speaks and another who does not respond: Aston who 'remains still, his back to (Davies), at the window'. But this time we know why Aston does not answer:

Listen . . . if I . . . got down . . . if I was to . . . get my papers . . . would you . . . would you let . . . would you . . . if I got down . . . and got my . . . (*Long silence*).

The long silence which closes *The Caretaker*, and which is both wholly real and, at the same time, a powerful poetic

101

metaphor, is anything but arbitrary. The whole course of the play has organically, logically and inevitably led up to it.

With *The Caretaker* Pinter had acquired mastery of one of the strongest instruments in his armoury as craftsman, and the one which probably is most characteristic of his artistic personality – the use of silence.

Night School

Night School was written for television and broadcast, by no means unsuccessfully, by Associated Rediffusion TV in July 1960; yet Pinter felt dissatisfied with the play, did not include it in any of the volumes of his collected plays and refused to sanction further performances; he once said that he repudiated the play because it struck him as too obviously and mechanically 'Pinteresque', as though it were a copy of a play by Pinter rather than a genuine work. But in the summer of 1966 he returned to it and rewrote it for radio in a version which he regards with far greater sympathy and which appeared in the sixth volume of his plays, published in 1967.

And indeed, the theme of *Night School* is a very typically Pinteresque one; again it is a matter of a room and a struggle for its possession. Walter, a small-time crook, who tries to make a living by forging Post Office savings books, has just been released from prison and is being welcomed home by his two old aunts, Annie and Milly (who mother him in the same over-sweetly sentimental manner with which Meg looked after Stanley in *The Birthday Party*). Walter is looking forward to getting back to his old room in the aunt's house; but they inform him that in his absence they have been compelled to let the room. Walter is shattered and indignant. The aunts are full of praise for the lodger who now shares their house: Sally Gibbs, a schoolteacher, is pretty, intelligent, tidy and so keen on her further education that she attends night school three times a week to learn languages.

Walter is determined to win back his room and above all his bed. But when he meets Sally he also is impressed by her; perhaps he might get back into his own room and bed by becoming Sally's lover?

Determined to impress the girl by suggesting that he is, in fact, a far more romantic type of criminal that he really is, a fierce and successful gunman, he asks her permission to look for something – a gun? – in his (now her) room by himself. In rummaging around in the cupboard Walter finds a photograph which shows Sally with some gentlemen in a dress and situation which suggests that she is in fact working as a dance hostess in a night club. He pockets the photograph. When Sally is asked if she had ever been a dancer she hotly denies that she ever goes out to dance.

Walter is determined to find out the truth about Sally and so he turns for help to an acquaintance who, he knows, is familiar with the world of night clubs: Solto, a man of Levantine origin (he speaks of his youth in Athens, but it seems more likely that he is in fact a Cypriot), is the owner of the house which Walter's aunts inhabit and is from time to time invited to tea there. Walter, who also wants to borrow money from Solto to get started in some more legitimate business but is fobbed off by him, asks him to try and find the identity of the girl in the photograph (without revealing that she in in fact the lodger in the house). Solto, who is struck by the girl's looks, promises to do his best.

One evening Walter succeeds in getting himself invited to Sally's room for drinks. While the two aunts take turns in listening to the conversation through the keyhole, he tries to impress Sally by wild stories about his life as a gunman and convict. When Sally seems ripe for an erotic approach after having consumed a lot of drink, Walter takes the initiative. He begins to assert his authority by ordering Sally about:

Cross your legs. (*Pause.*) Uncross them. (*Pause.*) Stand up. (*Pause.*) Turn round. (*Pause.*) Stop. (*Pause.*) Sit down. (*Pause.*) Cross your legs. (*Pause.*) Uncross your legs. (*Silence.*)

103

The printed version is the radio version; so it remains uncertain whether Sally actually does the actions she is ordered to perform. Even in the television version the matter might have remained uncertain by showing Walter in close-up and leaving Sally's actions to the imagination of the audience. What is even more uncertain is whether Walter's exercise of his authority is the prelude to love making or merely the expression of his impotent infantile sadism. On the analogy of the scene between Albert and the prostitute in *A Night Out*, which bears considerable resemblance to it, I should be inclined towards the latter hypothesis. Yet the decision is left with each member of the audience.

The scene shifts to a night club where Solto has in fact identified the girl in the photograph, Sally. He asks for the manager of the place, an old pal, to introduce him to her. As he likes her very much he makes up to her and invites her to spend the weekend with him in his bungalow by the sea; quite casually he reveals that someone called Walter, an aquaintance of his and a small-time crook, had asked him to try and find her. Sally is deeply upset that Walter will now learn that she is working as a night club hostess (whether she is in fact a school teacher in the daytime as well and is merely trying to supplement her earnings by nightwork, or whether she is a full-time entertainer, is left open).

The same night Solto comes to see Walter and informs him that he has been quite unable to locate the girl in the photograph. In fact he doubts whether such a girl ever existed.

And the next morning Sally has gone. She evidently could not face Walter again, knowing that he knows her night-time occupation. So Walter has his room back; but he has also lost what might have been the only chance in his life to find a human being who could have become a real partner for him.

Night School thus combines the theme of the struggle for a room with the equally typical Pinteresque theme of the net of lies by which people mutually obscure their real selves from each other and impede genuine contact. Walter has told Sally that he is a romantic gunman. Solto has revealed to her that this was a lie. Sally has told Walter that she is a schoolteacher who goes to night school. The photograph has revealed to him that this was a lie. Neither of them can face the other in the knowledge that they know the truth. Had they had the courage to be frank about themselves, they might have found each other: after all, they are ideally suited to each other: a small-time crook who wants to go straight would be just the right partner for a girl who wants to get out of being a near-prostitute. In fact their real identities match each other far better than their fantasy personalities of the big gangster and the demure little schoolmarm.

The two tragi-comic protagonists are set against three brilliantly drawn grotesques: the two aunts who eavesdrop on the young people's confrontation but are too senile and too deaf to understand what is going on (very much like Meg in *The Birthday Party*) and who spin voluptuous fantasies around food; and Solto, who also lives in his own world of fantasy: grandiose tales of his exploits in Australia and the world of opulence with which he tries to seduce Sally to spend the weekend with him.

Night School may be minor Pinter, yet it is a highly polished example of his technique and contains some of his funniest dialogue; it is also very characteristic of some of his main preoccupations. The character of Sally, who oscillates between schoolteacher and whore, foreshadows the double nature of Sarah in *The Lover* and, above all, Ruth in *The Homecoming* who also fuse the respectable woman and the prostitute. Solto is a direct continuation of the Goldberg character in *The Birthday Party* and the two aunts are expansions of the simple-minded motherliness of Rose in *the Room* and Meg in *The Birthday Party*. Walter, the small-time crook, is clearly related to the two gunmen in *The Dumb Waiter* but also contains elements of Albert Stokes, the impotent clerk of *A Night Out*. The plot with its tissue of deceptions foreshadows the much more mature treatment of the same theme in *The Collection*.

The Dwarfs

Written as a radio play and later transferred to the stage, *The Dwarfs* is one of Pinter's less successful works. Nevertheless it is of considerable importance for an understanding of the sources of its author's basic preoccupations. For this short play is based on, and is a distillation from, Pinter's earliest major effort as a writer, the novel *The Dwarfs* on which he worked from ca. 1950 to 1956 and which thus antedates his playwriting. For more than thirty years Pinter withheld the novel from publication. He eventually published it in 1990, preceded by a note which said: 'I wrote *The Dwarfs* in the early fifties, before I began writing plays. I didn't offer it for publication at the time. In 1960 I extracted some elements from the book and wrote a short play under the same title. . . . In 1989 I read the book for the first time in many years and decided it would benefit from further work. This work consisted mainly of cuts. I cut five chapters which seemed to me redundant and reorganised or condensed a number of other passages. Despite this reshaping the text is fundamentally that written over the period 1952–1956.' The novel derives directly from the milieu of his boyhood and adolescence in the east of London. The play therefore represents one of the earliest strata of Pinter's development and can allow us to gain an insight into the motivations of his writing, particularly if we compare it with the novel.

The play, *The Dwarfs*, consists of a sequence of dialogues and monologues involving three characters, young men in their late twenties, Len, Pete and Mark, who have been close friends from boyhood when the play starts and have drifted apart when it ends. Only once, in the course of the play, are all three characters together; mostly we witness encounters and conversations between two at a time who then often discuss the third. Only one of the three, Len, appears alone in a series of monologues; Len is the one who is obsessed with the 'dwarfs' of the title: he imagines these tiny, dirty creatures rummaging in his yard, offering him scraps of food; from these hallucinations it is quite clear that Len, like Aston in *The Caretaker*, is undergoing a crisis, a mental breakdown. He has been leading an irregular and eccentric life for some time and when the play opens he is working as a porter on nightshift at Euston station (in the radio version: in a later stage version it is Paddington):

> The trains come in, I give a bloke half a dollar, he does my job, I curl up in the corner and read the timetables.

Mark, who, like Pinter, is of Portuguese origin ('Or at least, his grandmother on his father's side. That's where the family comes from') is well off and frequently absent from his house to which his two friends have access. In the original radio version his occupation was obscure: in the novel and in the later (1956) stage adaptation we learn that in fact, like Pinter when he wrote the novel, he is an actor who occasionally goes to take up engagements outside London.

There is little action in the play, but a great deal of discussion and meditation; Len falls ill and gets better; he tells Mark that Pete thinks he is a fool and thereby destroys Mark's friendship for Pete. The play ends with Len's sense of loss after emerging from his mental illness: the dwarfs have left. He is alone in a prosaic, antiseptic, ordered world and regrets the glorious warmth of chaos. (Cf. Brecht's treatment of a very similar theme in *The Jungle of the Cities* which ends with the line: 'The chaos is used up. It was the best time.') In Len's words:

> . . . they say nothing. Either they've gone dumb or I've gone deaf. Or they've gone deaf and I've gone dumb. . . . They've cut me off without a penny. . . . It's unsupportable. I'm left in the lurch. Not even a stale frankfurter, a slice of bacon rind, a leaf of cabbage, not even a mouldy piece of salami, like they used to sling me in the days when we told old tales by suntime . . .
>
> And this change. All about me change. The yard as I know it is littered with scraps of cat's meat, pig bollocks, tin cans, bird brains, spare parts of all the little animals, a squelching, squealing carpet, all the dwarfs' leavings spittled in the muck, worms

stuck in the poisoned shit heaps, the alleys a whirlpool of piss, slime, blood and fruit juice.

Now all is bare. All is clean. All is scrubbed. There is a lawn. There is a shrub. There is a flower.

It is the desolation of the young man emerging from the wild whirlpool of steaming adolescence into the bare, ordered world of respectability.

The subject matter of *The Dwarfs* therefore is, essentially, the identity crisis which marks the transition from adolescence to maturity. While the play eliminates much of the concrete detail of this experience and reduces it to its essential, major issues, the novel is far more specific: here the bond that holds the three young men together is clearly described as that of the close community of adolescents, the tribal unit of a gang of young men:

> In fact [Pete is reported as saying in the novel] he was not sure whether they might not be said to constitute a church of a kind. They were hardly one in dogma or direction, but there was common ground and there was a framework. At their best they formed a unit, and a unit which, in his terms, was entitled to be called a church; an alliance of the three of them for the common good, and a faith in that alliance.

In the play the relationship between the three friends from which the action starts is never so explicitly spelled out and the audience's relative ignorance about the nature of their ties seems to me to be one of the weaknesses of the play. Here Len occupies the centre of attention to a much greater extent and so his problem is far more in focus. And Len's problem is clearly also that of an identity crisis:

> For me, you see, I don't grow old. I change. I don't die. I change again. I am not happy. I change. Nor unhappy. But when a big storm takes place I do not change. I become someone else, which means I change out of all recognition, I am transformed from the world in which I suffer the changes I suffer, I retreat utterly from the standpoint where I am subject to change, then

with my iron mask on I wait for the storm to pass. But at the same time it is, I admit, impossible in these moments to sit quite still without wanting to go back. It's also impossible not to feel the itch to go forward. I must learn restraint.

Later in the play, in a conversation with Mark, Len broaches the central problem of human identity:

The point is, who are you? Not why or how, not even what. I can see what, perhaps, clearly enough. But who are you? . . . What you are, or appear to be to me, or appear to be to you, changes so quickly, so horrifyingly, I certainly can't keep up with it and I'm damn sure you can't either. But who you are I can't even begin to recognize, and sometimes I recognize it so wholly, so forcibly, I can't look, and how can I be certain of what I see? You have no number. Where am I to look, where am I to look, what is there to locate, so as to have some surety, to have some rest from this whole bloody racket? You are the sum of so many reflections. How many reflections? Whose reflections? Is that what you consist of? What scum does the tide leave? What happens to the scum? When does it happen? I've seen what happens. But I can't speak when I see it. I can only point a finger. I can't even do that. The scum is broken and sucked back. I don't see where it goes, I don't see when, what do I see, what have I seen? What have I seen, the scum or the essence?

Here – and this I consider a key to a great deal of Pinter's work – the uncertainty about the speaker's own identity merges into his uncertainty about the identity of others and into the general problem of *verification*: in a system of shifting reflections of further reflections where there can be no certainty whether what we see is the scum or the essence, how can any firm basis be found from which to survey the world? This, we can now understand in the light of our recognition of the problem, is also the hidden mainspring of the quest for a firm point in the world which is concretized in the image of the room which Pinter's characters so often try to defend against the assaults of the outside world or try to conquer for themselves. Len's first monologue makes this clear. This room which is, or ought to be, the fixed centre point of his universe is beginning to shift and that is the onset of his mental crisis:

> This is my room. This is a room. There is wallpaper, on the walls. There are six walls. Eight walls. An octagon. This room is an octagon. . . . This is a journey and an ambush. This is the centre of the cold, a halt to the journey and no ambush. This is the deep grass I keep to. This is the thicket in the centre of the night and the morning. There is my hundred-watt bulb like a dagger. It is neither night nor morning. . . . Here is my arrangement and my kingdom. . . .

But when the stability is disturbed:

> The rooms we live in . . . open and shut. . . . Can't you see? They change shape at their own will. I wouldn't grumble if only they would keep to some consistency. But they don't. . . . I am all for the natural behaviour of rooms, doors, staircases, the lot. But I can't rely on them.

Pete also has his nightmares: he tells Len of a dream in which he saw himself in a tube station with a girl. There was some sort of panic and suddenly the faces of all the people in that crowd were peeling off.

> When I looked at the girl I saw that her face was coming off in slabs too, like plaster. Black scabs and stains. The skin was dropping off like lumps of cat's meat. . . . Then I thought, Christ, what's my face like? Is that why she's staring? Is that rotting too?

In this scene clearly the familiar post-war nightmare of atomic bomb attack has also merged into the questioning of one's own identity. In comparison with Len, who holds the centre in the play with his long monologues (which also devote considerable attention to the personalities of his two friends), Pete and Mark are fairly shadowy figures; they are seen from Len's point of view.

In the novel this is not so. A comparison between the novel and the play illumines a good deal of Pinter's method as a dramatist. For in the novel all the gaps which give the play its intriguing and elliptic construction are filled in. Above all we are quite clearly in the East End London of Pinter's boyhood and adolescence: Hackney and Bethnal Green, the buses one takes to get to the West End both in the daytime and at night, the river Lea and the marshes, even the evil-smelling soap factory which Pinter mentions in his own recollections of his childhood, they are all there, meticulously detailed and concrete. The three young men themselves are far more concrete. We learn, for example, that two of them are Jewish – Len Weinstein and Mark Gilbert – while one of them, Pete Cox, is non-Jewish. We learn that Len is mad about higher mathematics and Bach and that he avidly reads the Bible, that Pete works as an accountant in a city firm but is also a skilled tailor who makes clothes for his friends. There can be little doubt that there is a wealth of first-hand observation of the real places and people of Pinter's early years in the novel, that it, in fact, represents a veritable storehouse of the raw material from which much of Pinter's later work is drawn. If, for example, Len was a real character whom Pinter knew as well as Pete and Mark know him in the novel (and there can be little doubt about that) we are clearly in the presence of the prototype of Aston or Stanley, while the sleek and elegant Mark bears some of the features of Mick in *The Caretaker* or Lenny in *The Homecoming*. (On page eight of the manuscript of the novel we even find the phrase: 'it was a good homecoming'.)

Moreover Pete and Mark are also manifestly the proto-types of the two men fighting for a girl in *The Basement* or jealously confronting each other in *The Collection*. For in the novel there is a fourth major character who has been omitted in the play of *The Dwarfs*, a girl, Virginia, who is a schoolteacher, like Sally in *Night School*, and turns into a frequenter of Soho night clubs as she does. While it is from Len in the play that Mark learns that Pete thinks him a fool,

111

in the novel he hears it from Virginia, while making love to her after she has deserted Pete, her boyfriend of long standing. Virginia must be the prototype of numerous later split female characters in Pinter's plays who vacillate between respectability and whoredom: the genteel prostitute in *A Night Out*, the wife/whore in *The Lover*, the faithless wife who may not have been faithless at all in *The Collection* and, above all, Ruth in *The Homecoming*.

In the novel Virginia is rejected by Pete because she presumes to talk about Shakespeare when he maintains that she knows nothing about the subject. They are briefly reconciled, but eventually she cannot take Pete's domineering attitude, deserts him for an American to whom she has been introduced by a girl friend of hers who has become a call-girl in Soho and presumably also takes up that trade, at least part time. It is only after she has thus changed her character and turned into a 'whore' that she briefly becomes Mark's mistress. The end of the friendship between Pete and Mark comes when Mark, to revenge himself for Pete's alleged intellectual contempt for him, tells him that he slept with Virginia the previous night.

The world of the four young people in the novel of *The Dwarfs* is an intensely emotional one, full of passionate intellectual discussions, midnight visits to each others' houses, an extrovert life more reminiscent of the continent of Europe than of other parts of England. But, then, the East End, and particularly the Jewish East End, of London must have been more like nineteenth-century Russia, Hungary, Austria or France than the conventional pattern of English life. What is astonishing in the novel is the brilliance of the numerous dialogues which not only foreshadows Pinter's later mastery of stage dialogue but also illustrates the high level of his awareness of language, his intensive preoccupation with the nuances of spoken English, which also, to some extent, may be the outcome of his milieu: a young man, aware of alien origins and backgrounds, determined to master his environment and its language. There is a scene in the novel, when Pete Cox is shown in his office in the City encountering an old school mate who also works there and who is being interviewed by a senior partner in the firm, where Pinter clearly indicates how alien and indeed ridiculously stiff the conventional middle-class world outside the East End appeared to him at that time.

The novel of *The Dwarfs* is a very original and astonishingly finished book – and by no means imitative, although there are passages which are unmistakably influenced by Joycean internal monologue. These are above all Pete's thought sequences, while Len's monologues are already very much in Pinter's own idiom. It shows his fine ear and good judgement that in the play Len's monologues have been preserved almost intact, while Pete's have been largely omitted.

The transition from the novel to the play also reveals Pinter's recognition that in the more objective genre of drama much that can be shown and discussed in a novel must go; and that, indeed, the economy and reticence of drama suited his own artistic personality far better than the more explicit narrative form. In discussing the poetry of certain writers Len, in the novel, makes a point of immense relevance to Pinter's approach:

> Do you know what these people do? Len said. They climb from word to word, like stepping stones.
> He walked about the room, demonstrating.
> – Like stepping stones. But tell me this. What do they do when they come to a line with no words in it at all? Can you answer that? What do they do when they come to a line with no words in it at all? Can you tell me that?

To write those lines of poetry that have no words at all in them, Pinter had to turn to drama. Those lines with no words at all in them are the pauses which climax the dialogue. The poetry of the stage is indeed the only poetry that can produce great lines with no words in them at all.

Why did Pinter omit Virginia in the play of *The Dwarfs*? My guess is that he wanted to avoid the conventional subject matter of the erotic triangle; that also, perhaps, he might, at that early stage in his career as a dramatist, not have felt able to deal with so complex a female character; but, above all, that he felt that the girl as a mere catalyst of the break-up of the friendship, the alliance, the church, of the three friends, was little more than a chance motivation rather than a truly organic one; that that friendship was bound to disintegrate in any case, so that the actual reason for its disintegration was inessential and would have distracted the audience's attention from the inevitable features of the process. Such considerations certainly have a great deal of force. The question here, however, is whether, having retained so much of the framework of the novel, Pinter actually succeeded in creating a dramatic structure which could stand in its own right and fully convey what he intended, without obscurity, without setting before the spectators – or the radio audience – a riddle which they were unable, because ill equipped, to solve.

The play of *The Dwarfs* may be a partial failure. It nevertheless contains some of Pinter's most interesting, significant and beautiful writing.

The Collection

Having acquired a reputation for his handling of low vernacular English with a series of plays which, with the solitary exception of *A Slight Ache*, involved working-class or lower middle-class people, Pinter moved into the West End of London and into a more elegant and sophisticated milieu with *The Collection*. The four characters in this play – originally written for television but since frequently performed on the stage – all come from the world of the rag trade. Harry Kane is a successful middle-aged man in the wholesale clothing business who lives in what is clearly a homosexual ménage, with a young designer, Bill Lloyd, whom he has discovered. The peace of their household is disturbed by the intrusion of James Horne, who runs a boutique with his wife Stella; James has been told by Stella that she had been unfaithful to him with Bill – during a visit to Leeds, where the season's collections were being shown. According to Stella's story Bill, who was staying at the same hotel, had followed her to her room and, taking advantage of her loneliness, more or less raped her.

Is Stella's story true? Can it be true? And can anyone not directly involved ever know, ever verify, whether it is true or not? The basic situation is reminiscent of Pirandello's *Cosi è (se vi pare)* – *Right You Are (If You Think You Are)* – where two, and eventually three, incompatible stories confront each other without hope of verification. The difference is that in Pirandello's play either one, two or all three of the characters involved may be mad and therefore unable to realize the true situation. In *The Collection* it is not a matter of madness but of subtle conscious or subconscious motivations. At first sight Bill, who has been shown as a member of a homosexual ménage, seems most unlikely to have committed so brazen a heterosexual act of aggression. And, indeed, when confronted with James, he denies the whole story. After a bout of rough treatment by the wronged husband however, he tells him another version of the incident:

> The truth . . . is that it never happened. . . . All that happened was . . . you were right, actually, about going up in the lift . . . we . . . got out of the lift, and then suddenly she was in my arms. Really wasn't my fault, nothing was further from my mind, biggest surprise of my life, must have found me terribly attractive quite suddenly, I don't know . . . but I . . . I didn't refuse. Anyway, we just kissed a bit, only a few minutes, by the lift, no one about, and that was that – she went to her room. The rest of it just didn't happen. I mean, I wouldn't do that sort of thing. I mean that sort of thing . . . it's just meaningless.

And yet, immediately afterwards, when James tries to substantiate his story by bringing in the further detail that while he, James, phoned Stella, Bill was sitting on her bed, Bill corrects him:

Not sitting. Lying.

So is he teasing James? And by outdoing James's more lurid details, throwing doubts on his own earlier, partial, admissions?

Harry, Bill's middle-aged flat-mate, who clearly has extremely possessive feelings about the young man, has become suspicious by the mysterious telephone calls and traces of secret visitors in his flat. James, the wronged husband, on the other hand, is becoming fascinated with Bill: he tells Stella that he wants to go and see him again; that he had dinner with him the previous evening (which we, the audience know is not true, or at least not entirely: this gives us a means of gauging the readiness of the characters involved to make up stories by enlarging and elaborating minor details). He begins to praise Bill:

> . . . I've come across a man I can respect. It isn't often that you can do that, that that happens, and really I suppose I've got you to thank. . . . Thanks.

While this may well be the irony of the injured party and a way to rub salt into the wife's wounds, there is also an element of genuine feeling behind it:

> I mean, you couldn't say he wasn't a man of taste. He's brimming over with it. Well, I suppose he must have struck you the same way. No, really, I think I should thank you, rather than anything else. After two years of marriage it looks as though, by accident, you've opened up a whole new world for me.

While James goes back to visit Bill once again, Harry comes to see Stella. When confronted with James's persecution of Bill, Stella denies the whole story:

> I mean, Mr Lloyd was in Leeds, but I hardly saw him, even though we were staying at the same hotel. I never met him or spoke to him . . . and then my husband suddenly accused me of . . . it's really been very distressing.

In the meantime James and Bill are engaged in a highly ambivalent confrontation which oscillates between extreme friendliness and sudden outbursts of hatred; it culminates in a sort of duel with knives. When Bill tries to catch a knife thrown against his face by James, he cuts his hand. At this moment Harry, who has been watching them from the background, enters the conversation. He tells James that he has it from his wife's own mouth that the whole story of marital infidelity was pure invention. And when James points out that Bill, after all, confirmed Stella's story, Harry launches into a savage attack on Bill:

> Bill's a slum boy, you see, he's got a slum sense of humour. That's why I never take him along with me to parties. Because he's got a slum mind.

James is ready to leave and to accept his wife's latest version of the story. But at that moment Bill offers to tell the truth:

> I never touched her . . . we sat . . . in the lounge, on a sofa . . . for two hours . . . talked . . . we talked about it . . . we didn't move from the lounge . . . never went to her room . . . just talked . . . about what we would do . . . if we did get to her room . . . two hours . . . we never touched . . . we just talked about it. . . .

James leaves. The last scene of the play is between him and Stella. He repeats Bill's latest story:

> He wasn't in your room. You just talked about it, in the lounge.
> (*Pause*)
> That's the truth, isn't it?
> (*Pause*)
> You just sat and talked about what you would do if you went to your room. That's what you did.
> (*Pause*)
> Didn't you?
> (*Pause*)
> That's the truth . . . isn't it?

(Stella looks at him, neither confirming nor denying. Her face is friendly, sympathetic.)

Any of the different versions of the incident around which *The Collection* revolves may be true – or none. The point is that we have an abundance of possible motivations for each possible version. For example: Bill is a homosexual, he is therefore unlikely to have raped Stella. Yet, from Harry's wild outburst about how he found Bill in the slums it is also possible to infer that Bill may have been made into a homosexual by an older man who offered him social advancement, a good job, life in a middle-class milieu, thus his homosexuality might have been imposed upon him, he might have adopted that way of life against his will or natural inclination. In that case a sudden heterosexual impulse would be understandable as a desperate attempt to escape from Harry's bondage. Or, indeed, not having the courage for a real assault on a lady, Bill might have confined his attempts to break away from the homosexual ménage to the world of fantasy, he might just have talked with a woman about the possibility of such an escapade, without ever thinking of actually indulging in it. Conversely: Stella is clearly a somewhat frustrated wife (perhaps because James is a latent homosexual – he certainly gives some indications in this direction), she may have invented her story to make James jealous and activate his interest in her; or, again, being sex-starved she may have provoked and seduced Bill. Moreover, each of the two chief 'culprits' has very good reasons why he should tell any particular version of the story at any particular moment. Bill, for example when first confronted by James, may well be *revenging* himself for the intrusion by increasing his suffering through tantalizing details; Stella would obviously deny the whole thing to Harry, a stranger whom she does not regard as qualified to partake of her family secrets. And even the final, most plausible version, which Bill tells James at the end, may be a subtle way of revenging himself on Harry, who has just castigated him in the most cruel manner about his slum origins. By saying that he talked with Stella about love-making, Bill is in fact telling Harry that he is dreaming of breaking away from him, of returning to a heterosexual life.

The two objects of jealousy in the play are matched against the two sufferers from jealousy: James is jealous of Bill, but Harry is not only jealous of Stella, he is also, and perhaps more so, jealous of the obvious love/hate relationship which seems to be developing between Bill and James. His outburst against Bill for example is clearly directed to James, whom he is warning of the ingratitude and baseness of mind of the slum urchin whom he has raised to his own level.

But *The Collection* is more than merely a highly ingenious construction, an equation with three or more unknowns which allows of a multitude of equally valid solutions. It also contains a social comment on the situation in those strata of English middle-class society (and they are, after all, by no means insignificant) where homosexual attitudes among the men play a decisive role in determining the social climate. This aspect of the play became much clearer on the stage than in the original television version. On television the scene shifted between Harry's and James's apartments, on the stage they remained juxtaposed all the time – with a narrow street set, containing the telephone kiosk in the centre. As a result, Stella remained in view during the scenes when the three men squabbled among themselves; she just sat on her sofa, playing with her kitten, terribly alone and neglected. And although Stella has a relatively brief part, measured by the lines she has to speak, she gradually emerged as the true tragic heroine of the piece: she may have been the original bone of contention between the men, yet she is soon lost from sight by them: their very involvement in fighting transforms their relationship into one of intimacy and strong personal concern with each other, a male world of rough and tumble from which the woman is forever excluded and condemned to sit at home, neglected, abandoned, playing with her kitten.

The Lover

Also originally a television play, *The Lover* was as successful when transferred to the stage as *The Collection*, with which it is frequently linked as a double bill.

The Lover develops the notion of the erotic wish-fulfilment fantasy – which may well have been the source of Stella's confession of adultery in *The Collection* – and shows its function in a *happy* marriage.

Richard and Sarah live in a detached house near Windsor; Richard is the typical commuter to the city who leaves his wife behind each morning and returns to her each evening.

But the very first line spoken in the play shatters the illusion of safe respectability; for as he prepares to leave in the morning, Richard, having kissed his wife on the cheek asks:

Is your lover coming today?

Equally casually Sarah confirms that, indeed, her lover will be coming around three o'clock. Richard leaves. We see him return in the evening. And again, quite casually, after having given an account of the traffic as he was driving home, he asks:

RICHARD: What about this afternoon? Pleasant afternoon?
SARAH: Oh yes. Quite marvellous.
RICHARD: Your lover came, did he?
SARAH: Mmnn. Oh yes.
RICHARD: Did you show him the hollyhocks?

Later, while the two are having an evening drink after supper, Richard questions Sarah about her feelings while she is with her lover and whether she ever thinks of *him* slaving away at his office. Sarah retorts that the picture of Richard in the office is not very convincing:

Because I knew you weren't there. I knew you were with your mistress.

Richard hotly denies this:

> But I haven't got a mistress. I'm very well acquainted with a
> whore, but I haven't got a mistress. There's a world of differ-
> ence. . . . [She] is a common or garden slut. Not worth talking
> about.

It seems as though Sarah has found Richard out. She didn't
expect him to admit the existence of that whore so readily.
Richard points to the importance of utter frankness in
marriage. Sarah wonders how he, who attaches so much
importance to wit and elegance in women, could be
interested in a whore. His answer is:

> Why? I wasn't looking for your double, was I? I wasn't looking
> for a woman I could respect, as you, whom I could admire and
> love, as I do you. Was I? All I wanted was . . . how shall I put it
> . . . someone who could express and engender lust with all lust's
> cunning. Nothing more.

The conversation returns to Sarah and her lover. What does
the lover think of her husband – Richard?

> He respects you.

Why does she like him so much?

> . . . His whole body emanates love.
> RICHARD: How nauseating.

We meet Richard and Sarah again next morning. Richard is
leaving. Again Richard asks whether her lover is coming.
Yes, he is. Richard promises he won't come home too early.
He'll go to the National Gallery to waste some time.

The same afternoon: Sarah has changed into a tight,
seductive dress. She lowers the blinds. The doorbell rings. It
is the milkman. Is he her lover? No. He is merely delivering
some cream. Again the doorbell rings. This time it is the

lover: Richard, dressed in 'a suède jacket, casual shirt with no tie and light slacks'. Sarah greets him:

Hullo, Max.

So it is the husband himself who returns in the guise of the lover. There now follows a sequence of erotic rituals: first Max/Richard is playing the part of a man who molests Sarah in the park; then Richard/Max becomes a kind gentleman who rescues her from the potential rapist and, when it starts to rain, offers to sit the rain out with her in the park-keeper's hut:

SARAH: Do you think we should? I mean, what about the park-keeper?
MAX: I am the park-keeper.

But soon it is Sarah who becomes aggressive, and Richard/Max who insists that he is married: he calls Sarah by a number of different names – Dolores, Mary. Eventually the two of them disappear under the table and the scene fades with Sarah's voice exclaiming Max's name.

When the light returns Sarah and her lover/husband are having tea. Max is in a thoughtful, post-coital mood. He has qualms about Sarah's husband, he cannot understand how he puts up with the situation. In fact, he has come to the conclusion that the affair must stop. Because of her husband, Sarah asks.

No, nothing to do with your husband. It's because of my wife. . . . I can't deceive her any longer.

Sarah cannot understand what has come over Max. But he goes on and on about his guilt feelings. Not only about his wife, but also about her children who will soon be out of boarding school. And anyway, Sarah is too bony for his taste. Sarah still thinks it is all a joke. But Max/Richard insists: It's no joke. He leaves.

As the clock chimes six, Richard returns home in his business clothes, complaining of the dreary conference that occupied his whole day. After a while he inquires about the lover's visit. Sarah is less than enthusiastic this time. She retaliates by asking about Richard's whore:

RICHARD: Splended
SARAH: Fatter or thinner?
RICHARD: I beg your pardon?
SARAH: Is she fatter or thinner?
RICHARD: She gets thinner every day.
SARAH: That must displease you.
RICHARD: Not at all. I'm fond of thin ladies.

Was the complaint about the boniness of the whore merely a joke? No. Richard returns to the subject. The arrangement with the lover, which seems to have been a feature of the whole ten years that their marriage has lasted, must stop. Sarah is stunned. Richard insists she should receive her lover where she wants, but not in his house. And what about his whore? She has been paid off. Why? Because she was too bony.

Then Richard takes the bongo drum, which has been a feature of the erotic ritual with the lover, from the cupboard. He asks what it is, and as he handles it he slips into the afternoon ritual of picking up a girl in the park. Sarah at first is horrified by this breach of the rules of the game, but gradually she also gets into her part. She starts to slip beneath the table. Remarking that it is a very late tea they are having, she suggests that she should change her clothes. The play closes with Richard agreeing:

Change your clothes. . . . You lovely whore.

Thus the fantasy world of their afternoons has irrupted into, perhaps permanently taken over, the 'respectable' portion of their day, of their lives. Or have they merely learned to treat their fantasies as fantasies and thus become able to switch them on and off at will, having converted a compulsion into a lighthearted game?

There is no indication in the text how we are able to take the final twist in the pattern. Again we have been confronted with the shifting nature of reality: is Sarah, deep down, a whore forced by society into a guise of respectability; is she a respectable woman seeking an occasional outlet for her desires in erotic fantasy? Is Richard unable to find sexual satisfaction with a respectable woman and mother, and therefore compelled to the fantasy that he is buying satisfaction from someone experienced in 'all lust's cunning'? Or is he really at heart a pimp whom society has forced into the mould of the bowler-hatted commuter?

The ambivalence of our social selves, the coexistence in all of us of the primeval, amoral, instinct-dominated sensual being on the one hand, and the tamed, regulated social conformist on the other, is one of the dominant themes of Pinter's writing: above all the oscillation of the image of woman between that of mother/madonna/housewife and that of the whore/maenad. We need only recall the respectable schoolteacher Virginia in the novel of *The Dwarfs* who turns almost overnight, and without any discernible motive, into a Soho call-girl; the whore in *A Night Out* who is revealed merely as another aspect of Albert Stokes's super-respectable mother; the dual image of woman in *The Birthday Party*, where the female principle is represented for Stanley by Meg and Lulu; Flora the middle-aged, middle-class matron in *A Slight Ache* who unexpectedly reveals herself as a sex-obsessed maenad thirsting after her husband's death; Stella in *The Collection* who, in reality or in fantasy, throws herself into the arms of a man she casually met in the lift in a hotel; and, of course, Ruth in *The Homecoming*.

The image itself – the female as mother and as whore, split asunder into two contrasting characters or coexisting in the same person – is, indeed, one of the basic archetypes of all literature. In *The Lover*, as in some of Pinter's other works, it is, however, most originally merged with another archetypal problem, the question of the dividing line between reality and dream. Max and his whore are dream images in the minds of Richard and Sarah, their ritual is a game played by Richard and Sarah. Are Richard and Sarah therefore their true selves, Max and his whore mere figments of their imagination? Or are not, rather, the respectable stereotypes, the clichés which they enact in their daily lives the figments, the masks, while the reckless lover and the promiscuous female represent their real selves, at a far deeper level of significance and reality? The conclusion of *The Lover* suggests that it is an integration, an interpenetration of the external mask and the subterranean instinct that a solution might emerge in the recognition that we must accept both our social self and our instinctive one, and by that acceptance learn to control them. Yet, here again, we might read the ending differently: that the luxuriant growth of erotic fantasy might take over altogether and destroy Richard's and Sarah's lives as respectable suburbanites altogether. Or, indeed, that the whole play does not represent reality, but a dream in the mind of one or the other of the two.

The Bacchae and Genet's *The Balcony* treat the same vast subject of the conflict between tamed, socialized and wild, instinct-dominated humanity on a vast and epic scale. *The Lover* deals with the same theme in miniature, with elegance and dry humour on the level of subtle and intimate comedy.

The Homecoming

Pinter's third full-length play, which was received with some bewilderment in London, became a sensational success in America and established him on Broadway.

The external action of *The Homecoming* is both simple and startling: Max, a retired butcher about seventy years old, shares his large old house somewhere in the industrial areas of North London with two of his three sons: Lenny and Joey. Joey the youngest is an amateur boxer who hopes to become a professional but in the meantime has a job with

125

a demolition firm. He is slow of speech and clumsy. Lenny, on the other hand, is sleek and intelligent and – at the start of the play – of uncertain occupation. Max's brother Sam, a hire-car driver, is the fourth inhabitant of Max's house.

Max talks a great deal about his boys' mother, his late wife Jessie, and of his life-long friend and companion MacGregor, also now dead. The sons, especially Lenny, treat their father extremely badly; the old man acts as housewife and cook and has to listen to a great deal of sarcasm about his cooking. He in turn is extremely rude to his brother, Sam, the hire-car driver. A great mystery seems to surround the personality of the now dead mother of the family, Jessie, and Sam somehow seems connected with this mystery. Apropos of nothing, for example, Sam feels compelled to assert certain facts about Jessie's past:

> I want to make something clear about Jessie, Max. I want to. I do. When I took her out in the cab, round the town, I was taking care of her, for you. I was looking after her for you, when you were busy, wasn't I? I was showing her the West End.

As to Max's great friend MacGregor – Sam has his own opinion too:

> Old Mac died a few years ago, didn't he? Isn't he dead?
> (*Pause*)
> He was a lousy stinking rotten loudmouth. A bastard uncouth sodding runt. Mind you, he was a good friend of yours.

Max's reaction to this outburst is equally brutal:

> Eh Sam. . . . Why do I keep you here? You're just an old grub. . . . As soon as you stop paying your way here, I mean when you're too old to pay your way, you know what I'm going to do? I'm going to give you the boot. . . . I mean, bring in the money and I'll put up with you. But when the firm gets rid of you – you can flake off.

When Sam draws Max's attention to the fact that the house is partly his as well, because it was their father's house, Max launches into reminiscences of his childhood:

> Our father? I remember him. . . . He used to come over to me and look down at me. My old man did. He'd bend right over me, then he'd pick me up. I was only that big. Then he'd dandle me. Give me the bottle. Wipe me clean. Give me a smile. Pat me on the bum. Pass me around, pass me from hand to hand. Toss me up in the air. Catch me coming down. I remember my father.

A few hours later. It is night. The inhabitants of the house have gone to bed. But two intruders stand on the threshold of the room: Teddy, Max's third and eldest son, and his wife Ruth. Teddy teaches philosophy at an American college. He and Ruth have been on a trip to Italy. On the way back they have decided to visit the house where Teddy was born and to introduce Ruth, whom he has not yet met, to Teddy's father, Max. Teddy still has a key to the front door, that is how he was able to get in without ringing the doorbell. Teddy does not want to wake anyone. He goes upstairs. His old room is still there. It is empty. There is some altercation between the couple. Teddy wants Ruth to come up to bed with him, she wants to stay up, perhaps go for a walk. Finally Teddy agrees. He goes upstairs. He gives Ruth the front door key and she goes out.

Lenny, wearing pyjamas, confronts Teddy. He could not sleep. The meeting of the two brothers after six years is very casual: Teddy merely says that he has come for a few days, he asks how his father is and where he could find sheets for his bed. Then he goes upstairs. Lenny too goes, the stage stays empty for a while, then Lenny returns, lights a cigarette and sits down. Ruth comes back. The meeting between Lenny and his sister-in-law – whose identity he does not yet know, her presence has not been mentioned in his conversation with Teddy – is also strangely casual. Only after polite nothings about the weather and whether he can offer her a drink have been exchanged does Lenny inquire who the mysterious woman who has just come into his house in the middle of the night might be:

> You must be connected with my brother in some way. The one who's been abroad.

When Ruth replies that she is his brother's wife, Lenny does not react at all. He merely asks her advice about his insomnia. And later in the conversation he makes it clear that he does not really believe, or has not really taken in the fact that Ruth is Teddy's wife.

> RUTH: We are on a visit to Europe.
> LENNY: What, both of you?
> RUTH: Yes.
> LENNY: What, you sort of live with him over there, do you?
> RUTH: We're married.

Again Lenny does not react to this remark. He merely recapitulates the previous information:

> On a visit to Europe, eh? Seen much of it?

And then almost immediately, after talking about Venice and his idea that, had he not been too young to serve in the war, he might have gone there during his war service, Lenny asks:

> . . . Do you mind if I hold your hand?
> RUTH: Why?
> LENNY: Just a touch.

And when Ruth asks again why he wants to hold her hand, Lenny tries to explain his request by telling her a long lurid story about a lady who was making certain propositions to him, whom he could have killed, but merely beat up brutally when he encountered her in a lonely spot by the docks. And that simply because she was 'diseased'.

> RUTH: How did you know she was diseased?
> LENNY: How did I know?
>   (*Pause*)
>   I decided she was.
>   (*Silence*)

The absence of a reaction from Ruth to this extraordinary long narrative of violence which, though it is never clearly stated, implies Lenny's connections with a world of prostitutes and gangsters, deepens the atmosphere of mystery.

Lenny changes the subject and inquires about his brother. A mention of Teddy's intelligence and sensitivity prompts Lenny to explain his own brand of sensitivity. He describes how, last Christmas, he decided to do some snow-clearing for the Borough Council, not because he wanted the money but because he liked the work in the early morning in the newly fallen snow. During a tea break he was, he reports, approached by an old lady who asked him to help her move a heavy iron mangle which had been left in the wrong room when it was delivered. He had consented to help, but when he found that the mangle was very heavy, and the old lady herself showed no sign of giving a hand with the job, he got extremely angry:

> So after a few minutes I said to her, now look here, why don't you stuff this iron mangle up your arse? Anyway, I said, they're out of date, you want to get a spin drier. I had a good mind to give her a workover there and then, but as I was feeling jubilant with the snow-clearing I just gave her a short-arm jab to the belly and jumped on a bus outside.

Both of Lenny's long – and brilliantly phrased – narrations describe acts of brutality against women. He is showing off to Ruth and telling her something about himself. And as we – or, indeed, Ruth – cannot be sure whether these stories are true or merely invented on the spur of the moment, it is by no means clear what it is that Lenny wants to communicate.

However, Ruth has understood something. When Lenny suggests that he should relieve her, first of an ashtray by her side, then of the glass from which she is drinking, a battle of wills develops between them:

RUTH: I haven't quite finished.
LENNY: You've consumed quite enough, in my opinion.
RUTH: No, I haven't.
LENNY: Quite sufficient, in my opinion.
RUTH: Not in mine, Leonard.
Pause
LENNY: Don't call me that, please.
RUTH: Why not?
LENNY: That's the name my mother gave me.
Pause
Just give me the glass.
RUTH: No.
Pause
LENNY: I'll take it, then.
RUTH: If you take the glass . . . I'll take you.

Lenny is thrown by Ruth's aggressiveness: he retreats: he just wants the glass. She offers him a sip from the glass:

RUTH: Put your head back and open your mouth.
LENNY: Take that glass away from me.
RUTH: Lie on the floor. Go on. I'll pour it down your throat.
LENNY: What are you doing, making me some kind of proposal?

Ruth has won the contest of wills. She laughs, drains the glass and merely says:

Oh, I was thirsty.

130

Then she goes upstairs. Lenny angrily shouts after her, asking whether she has been making him some sort of proposal.

The noise has woken Max. He comes down scolding and nagging Lenny and asking what is going on. Lenny does not – mysteriously enough – disclose the presence either of his brother or his wife and maintains that he, Lenny, had been sleepwalking. Finally he turns on his father – half in irony, half in deadly earnest – by putting a question to him:

> It's a question I've been meaning to ask you for some time. That night . . . you know . . . the night you got me . . . that night with Mum, what was it like?

He enlarges on the question, describes how this torments lots of people of his age. Max is speechless with rage. All he can say is:

> You'll drown in your own blood.

Max spits at him and goes back upstairs.

The next morning. Max and Joey are discussing what they will be doing during the day (evidently a Saturday at the end of August, as it's the first day of the football season). Max resents Sam's presence in the kitchen, where he would like to have breakfast, but cannot stand seeing Sam doing the washing up there. When Sam appears the endless bickering between the two brothers continues. Max complains about Sam's lack of virility which led to their father having to take MacGregor into the shop.

Teddy and Ruth come downstairs. Max is upset that he has not been told of his son's arrival. When he notices Ruth he gets very angry:

> Who asked you to bring tarts in here?

He does not want to hear Teddy's explanation that Ruth is his wife:

131

I've never had a whore under this roof before. Ever since your mother died. My word of honour. . . . Take that disease away from me. Get her away from me.

Again overhearing Teddy's insistence that Ruth is his wife, Max orders Joey to chuck them out. When Joey apologizes to Teddy that Max is an old man, Max hits him viciously; he himself is about to collapse from the exertion, but when Sam tries to come to his aid, Max hits him over the head with his stick. With Joey and Max on the floor and Sam holding his head, Lenny, who has appeared on the scene, and Teddy face each other in silence. Joey is at Ruth's feet, she looks down at him.

When they are back on their feet, Max's mood is changed. He asks Ruth is she is a mother, and when she answers that she has three children, he is pacified. He even offers Teddy a nice cuddle. And when Teddy consents to a cuddle and kiss he exclaims in triumph:

He still loves his father!

So ends Act One. Act Two opens the same afternoon. The whole family have had a lunch prepared by Max, who is flattered by Ruth's approval of his cooking. Max reminisces about Jessie, his late wife, who taught his boys every single bit of the moral code they live by, his generosity towards her, his exertions in building up his business, and inevitably also the exploits of the late MacGregor. But almost in the same breath he calls Jessie a 'slutbitch'. Teddy tells about his life on the college campus and about his and Ruth's three boys:

MAX: All boys? Isn't that funny, eh? You've got three, I've got three.

But the mood of genial goodwill begins to change. Lenny starts to needle Teddy about his philosophy. He wants Teddy to comment on the nature of reality: What is a table,

132

philosophically speaking, he asks. Teddy refuses to be drawn. But Ruth suddenly intervenes:

> Look at me. I . . . move my leg. That's all it is. But I wear . . . underwear . . . which moves with me . . . it . . . captures your attention. Perhaps you misinterpret. The action is simple. It's a leg . . . moving. My lips move. Why don't you restrict . . . your observation to that?

The association of ideas in Ruth's mind seems to be: if a table, philosophically speaking, is more than just a table, if there is another plane of reality behind its appearance, this to her is analogous to the contrast between the outward appearance of a woman, and what is beneath that appearance: the underwear, the flesh, the sex.

Teddy has got up; he is clearly alarmed. Ruth is in a mood to make revelations about her real background, her real feelings:

> I was born quite near here.
> *Pause*
> Then . . . six years ago, I went to America.
> *Pause*
> It's all rock. And sand. It stretches . . . so far . . . everywhere you look. And there's lots of insects there.
> *Pause*
> And there's lots of insects there.

The family are embarrassed. Sam has already left to go to work. Now Max, Joey and Lenny also leave. Teddy and Ruth remain behind alone. Teddy suggests that they should leave and go back to America immediately. But Ruth does not seem enthusiastic, although she neither accepts nor rejects the suggestion. Teddy goes upstairs to pack.

Lenny returns. He talks with Ruth about the weather, about clothes. Ruth asks whether he likes her shoes, and when he says he does, complains that they are unobtainable in America. She confesses that before she married Teddy and went to America, she was a model. Not for demonstrat-

133

ing clothes or hats, but 'for the body'. She describes a place in the country where she and other girls had been photographed in the nude by a lake.

Teddy comes downstairs with his and Ruth's luggage. He asks her to go. But Lenny suggests a dance, just one, before she leaves. He puts a record on the radiogram: they dance; he kisses her.

At this point Max and Joey return from the gym where Joey has been training. When Joey sees what is going on he exclaims:

> Christ, she's wide open.
> *Pause*
> She's a tart.

And now the youngest of the sons takes Ruth from Lenny's arms, sits on the sofa with her, and embraces and kisses her. Max, who was so shocked about Ruth when he first met her, is completely casual about her behaviour. He assures Teddy that he need not have been ashamed when he married Ruth (he went away to America without even informing his father that he had met and married her) and praises her beauty and quality. All this while Joey and Ruth have rolled off the sofa on to the floor. Lenny touches her with his foot to make her get up. She asks for something to eat and for a drink. She has become demanding and bossy. And now she begins to needle Teddy about his philosophy:

> Have your family read your critical works?

Teddy fights back with a defensive outburst against his family:

> You wouldn't understand my works. You wouldn't have the faintest idea of what they were about. . . . It's nothing to do with the question of intelligence. It's a way of being able to look at the world. It's a question of how far you can operate on things and not in things. . . . You're just objects. You just . . . move

about. I can observe it. I can see what you do. It's the same as I do. But you're lost in it.

The lights fade. When they come up again, it is evening. Sam and Teddy are alone in the room. Sam tells Teddy that he always liked him best among the three boys.

When Lenny appears the conflict between him and Teddy comes into the open in a quarrel about a cheese roll which Lenny made for himself, put into a drawer so that he could eat it when he got back, but which has been now been eaten by Teddy. Not just thoughtlessly, but intentionally. In a long speech Lenny scolds Teddy for having grown sulky in the States. Teddy hardly reacts.

Now Joey comes down from upstairs where he has clearly been spending the afternoon with Ruth. Lenny asks, coolly and clinically, how he got on with her. When Joey informs him that he didn't get all the way, Lenny is indignant. He reproaches Teddy with her being a tease. Teddy, quite unmoved and casual, merely comments:

Perhaps he hasn't got the right touch.

Lenny retorts with a long account of an exploit of Joey's and his, during which they drove two men away from their girl friends and raped them on a bombsite near Wormwood Scrubs. When Max and Sam come in, they are also informed that Ruth is a tease. Max is equally upset:

My Joey? She did that to my boy?

He asks Teddy if she treats him the same way. Again Teddy, quite detached, merely replies: 'No.'

And now, out of the blue, Max suggests that Ruth should stay in the house. Teddy, quite casually, doubts whether they should ask her to stay:

. . . She's not well, and we've got to get home to the children.

135

But Max insists. How could they bear the additional cost? Perhaps by each of them contributing a little from their wages. Lenny has a better idea: she could work for a living, as a prostitute. It now turns out that Lenny, in fact, is a professional pimp who runs a string of women in Soho. She could work part-time there, not more than four hours a night. Lenny even asks Teddy to recommend her to American professors planning to come to Europe. They could give her a nice professional name, print discreet cards with her name and address. Teddy does not object or protest. He merely says:

> She'd get old . . . very quickly.

But this objection is dismissed by Max: there is the health service, after all!

Ruth comes down. And now it is her husband, Teddy, who puts the proposition to her:

> Ruth . . . the family have invited you to stay, for a little while longer. As a . . . as a kind of guest. If you like the idea I don't mind. We can manage very easily at home . . . until you come back.

And when Ruth seems pleased with the idea, it is again Teddy who draws her attention to the fact that she will have to 'pull her weight. . . . Financially'. When Lenny mentions the flat in which she would have to spend a certain number of hours every night, Ruth, who instantly seizes the meaning of the suggestion, drives a hard bargain: she wants at least three rooms and a bathroom, a personal maid, and is not prepared to pay back the original outlay on clothes and furnishings.

> You would have to regard your original outlay simply as a capital investment.

Lenny, driven into a corner, agrees to all these conditions. Ruth wants it all drawn up as a legal contract.

136

At this moment Sam, who has been following the scene with growing consternation, comes forward and bursts out:

MacGregor had Jessie in the back of my cab as I drove them along.

He collapses. At first they think he is dead, but he is still breathing. They leave him lying there, while Ruth calmly concludes the bargain and Teddy merely regrets Sam's inability to drive him to London Airport. Max gives him elaborate instructions how to go by underground or taxi. He gives Teddy a photograph of himself, to show to his grandsons. Lenny and Joey also take their casual leave from Teddy. Ruth calls him, as he leaves, by a name she has not used before in the play: 'Eddie'. Will she change her mind? Come with him? Teddy turns. There is a pause. Ruth merely says:

Don't become a stranger.

Teddy goes, Ruth sits, relaxed, in her chair. Sam lies, motionless on the floor. Joey goes up to Ruth's chair; he kneels by it. She touches his head; he puts his head in her lap. Max goes to and fro, very agitated:

I am too old, I suppose. She thinks I'm an old man.
Pause
I'm not such an old man.

Ruth remains impassive. Lenny stands watching the scene. Max becomes more and more pleading, more and more insistent. He begins to stammer. He falls to his knees and crawls up to Ruth, pleading all the way that he is not an old man and begging for a kiss. But Ruth remains impassive, stroking Joey's head, while Lenny stands by watching. The curtain falls.

The Homecoming shocks it audiences not only by the casual and matter-of-fact way in which sex and prostitution are discussed in it, but also, and even more, by the apparently inexplicable motivations of its main characters: why should a woman, the mother of three children and the wife of an American college professor, calmly accept an offer to have herself set up as a prostitute, how could a husband not only consent to such an arrangement but actually put the proposition to his wife? Is the author merely out to shock for the sake of shock? Is the whole story not totally incredible? Alternatively, those who admired the play's obvious theatrical effectiveness, with its sudden surprises and unexpected turns, defended it as being a cluster of symbolic images and poetic metaphors which should therefore not be subjected to excessive scrutiny on counts of verisimilitude and realistic credibility.

It is my conviction that *The Homecoming*, while being a poetic image of a basic human situation, can also stand up to the most meticulous examination as a piece of realistic theatre, and that, indeed, its achievement is the perfect fusion of extreme realism with the quality of an archetypal dream image of wish fulfilment.

Let us first examine the validity of the play as a realistic and perfectly explicable series of events as they could, in fact, happen to a family living in the circumstances outlined and clearly indicated by the author. The sequence of events portrayed in *The Homecoming* is inexplicable only in terms of a convention of drama in which the past history of the characters and their motivations must be clearly outlined in the exposition. As Pinter regards this convention not only as contrary to strict realism (people don't explain each others' past lives and motivations, which are already well known to them) but also somewhat presumptuous (as it postulates an omniscient author), he does not supply a neatly worked out set of backgrounds and motivations; yet all the information is given in the most natural manner in the course of the play.

For example: there can be little doubt that Max was a butcher by trade, or that his friend MacGregor also started out as a butcher in the shop of Max's father. But that does not mean that Max and MacGregor could not also, and in addition, have been engaged in less savoury occupations, that in fact they might have been members of the London half-world of pimps and gangsters. In the very first scene, Max reminisces about MacGregor and himself:

> Huhh! We were two of the worst hated men in the West End of London. I tell you, I still got the scars. We'd walk into a place, the whole room'd stand up, they'd make way to let us pass. You never heard such silence.

At that point in the play the audience will tend to take this as empty boasting from an old man, but in the light of subsequent events it may well seem to contain at least part of the truth. And what would have been more natural than that Lenny should have followed a family tradition by taking up the profession of a Soho pimp? His story about the beating up of a diseased prostitute establishes his profession fairly early in the play. Moreover, in this story there is a hint that chauffeurs, like Sam, are an integral part of an organization like Lenny's:

> Don't worry about the chauffeur. The chauffeur would never have spoken. He was an old friend of the family.

Hence it becomes likely that Sam, who now works for a respectable hire-car firm, might, in his youth, have been a driver for prostitutes run by Max and MacGregor. His insistence to Max that he was always looking after Max's wife, Jessie, when driving her about the West End, may well indicate that indeed Jessie herself might have been one of the prostitutes involved. And this in turn would explain Lenny's bitter outburst when he asks his father about the circumstances of his conception. It would also explain Max's ambivalence about the mother of his children, whom he praises to the sky at one point and then calls a slutbitch. Even Max's statement that Jessie taught the boys all the morality they know would then become ironically double-edged: certainly Lenny and Joey have the morality of pimps and rapists which they may well have been taught by a prostitute. Even Max's indignant outburst when he first meets Ruth and immediately assumes that she is a tart has a double meaning:

I've never had a whore under this roof before. *Ever since your mother died.* My word of honour. [My italics.]

Which might well mean that Teddy's mother *had* been a whore.

In a family which had been living from prostitution for decades, Max's and Lenny's final proposition to Ruth would therefore be the most natural thing in the world. No wonder that it is made quite casually, and received quite casually also by Teddy, the son who became an intellectual and ran away from home precisely because he did not like the family's way of life, but nevertheless is wholly conversant with it.

So much for the husband's complacency. But what of the wife's equally casual acceptance of the offer? It is made quite clear by Ruth that when Teddy met and married her she was a nude photographic model – and this is widely known as a euphemism for a prostitute. The country house she so lovingly recalls as the scene for her nude posing by the lake and where there were drinks and a cold buffet sounds like the scene of orgies rather than a place for photography. If Ruth therefore had been a prostitute or near-prostitute when she first met Teddy (and she protests when Max praises her charm: 'I was . . . different . . . when I met Teddy . . . first') and if both Lenny on first meeting her – he does not pay any attention to her assertion that she is married to Teddy – and Max immediately recognize her as a tart, then surely it is quite possible that she does not like the life of a college professor's wife – she describes America as an arid desert infested by insects, an unmistakable image of her boredom in uncongenial surroundings – and that, indeed, her marriage to Teddy is on the point of breakdown. This would be a very believable motivation for the sudden and unannounced trip to Venice: just the kind of last minute attempt at a second honeymoon to save the marriage one would expect. The likelihood is that this trip did not produce the desired result. Ruth's refusal to go up to the bedroom with Teddy on her first arrival in the house could be seen in the light of her reluctance to be exposed to what might have become a tedious or unsatisfactory sexual relationship. No doubt in the narrow world of a university campus somewhere in Texas Teddy's marital crisis might have given rise to embarrassing gossip, perhaps there might even have been rumours about Ruth's previous life. What would therefore be more natural than that Teddy, having come to the conclusion that his marriage has broken down and that Ruth cannot be turned into a respectable college professor's lady, should regard the prospect of her not returning home with him with a certain amount of equanimity, even relief? Hence his eagerness to reassure Ruth that he and the boys might well be able to manage without her.

So much then for the credibility of the events of *The Homecoming* on a realistic level: once we realize that the family depicted is one which has always been living on the fringes of the respectable, normal world, that Ruth, although a college professor's wife, might well also have been a prostitute in the past, the actions and reactions of all the characters fall into place.

But, as do most of Pinter's plays, *The Homecoming* also exists on another level: its real, its realistic, action is a metaphor of human desires and aspirations, a myth, a dream image, a projection of archetypal fears and wishes. Just as the events in the *Oedipus* of Sophocles, or in *King Lear*, are both valid on a level of real, particular human beings, but can also be seen as dreams, nightmares of guilt and human suffering, *The Homecoming* also transcends the realistic level to become just such an archetypal image. And indeed it deals with the themes both of *Oedipus* and *Lear*: the desolation of old age and the sons' desire for the sexual conquest of the mother.

That there is a very strong antagonism between the two

younger sons, who live with Max, and their father is made clear from the very start of the play. In the first few minutes Lenny abuses his father in the rudest possible language:

Why don't you shut up, you daft prat?

And when Joey demands his evening meal from his father, Max complains:

They walk in here every time of the day and night like bloody animals. *Go and find yourself a mother.* [My italics.]

The absence of a mother, and the personality of the dead mother, Jessie, pervades the play. Max's inadequacy – or supposed inadequacy – as a cook is the most telling symbol of this state of affairs. But it is also made clear that at least one of the two younger sons, Lenny, also sees the mother as a sexual object. When he interrogates his father about the moment of his own conception, the act of sexual intercourse that gave him life, he is above all thinking of his own mother in that erotic context. And his violent hatred of his father is clearly also motivated by the suffering it causes him to imagine his mother in his father's embrace – in other words in that particular scene Lenny is a Hamlet figure.

Lenny and Joey closely resemble those other brothers, Mick and Aston in *The Caretaker* (who are also engaged in a conflict with a father figure); like Mick and Aston, Lenny and Joey are complementary: Lenny slick and fast, Joey slow and strong, and they act as one: Lenny arouses Ruth and then hands her, without a murmur, to Joey. In fact, these two could be seen as different aspects of one personality: Lenny embodying the younger son's cunning and cleverness, Joey his strength and sexual potency. Similarly Max, the father, and Teddy, the elder brother could be seen as two aspects of the father figure: Max embodies the father's senility and ill temper, Teddy his superior wisdom (hence Lenny's needling of his philosophy). At the end of the play Max and Teddy have been defeated, Lenny and Joey are victorious. And what was the bone of contention between the two sides in the conflict? Ruth.

It is surely no coincidence that Ruth, Teddy's wife, like Jessie, Max's wife, has three sons. The point is specially underlined by Max. As the elder brother's – a father substitute's – wife, Ruth is a mother figure, she is a reincarnation of Jessie. Max's violent reaction on first meeting Ruth could then be seen as the outcome of his sudden confrontation with the image of his dead wife. ('I've never had a whore under this roof before. Ever since your mother died').

At the end of the play Ruth again rules the household. This is the 'homecoming' of the title. It is not Teddy who has come back home – after all he left after one day – but the mother who has returned.

The mother whom the son desires in his infancy at the moment of the first awakening of his sexuality, is not an old woman but a young one. It is *her* image which still dominates his dreams when he is grown up. Ruth, the mother of three boys whose ages must range from five to three, therefore represents the dreams of Lenny and Joey in that period of their lives. The final image of *The Homecoming* therefore is the culmination of their Oedipal dreams: their mother, young and beautiful, has become available to them as a sexual partner, as a 'whore', while the defeated father grovels on the floor pleading for some scraps of her sexual favours. This wish-fulfilment dream is the exact reversal of the real situation that faces a young son: the father in proud possession and the son rejected, oppressed, dominated.

From the sons' point of view therefore, *The Homecoming* is a dream image of the fulfilment of all Oedipal wishes, the sexual conquest of the mother, the utter humiliation of the father. From the father's point of view the play is the terrifying nightmare of the sons' revenge.

The very ease with which Ruth is persuaded to take up a life of prostitution and to become a readily available sexual partner for Joey and Lenny seems, if the play is seen as a dreamlike myth, the most natural thing of all; it is merely the characteristic way in which wishes miraculously come

143

true in dreams. Even the way in which Lenny encounters Ruth in the middle of the night when she has turned up from nowhere bears all the characteristic features of the manner in which dreams develop from a consciousness of lying in bed and imagining what one would most desire to happen. Lenny's two long stories which he tells Ruth at this first encounter and which deal with his brutal treatment of women fall into place as a child's attempts to convince himself that he is strong enough and big enough to impress and conquer a grown woman like his mother. Ruth however, in the episode with the glass of water, has no difficulty in asserting her immediate and effortless superiority.

Like Sarah in *The Lover*, like Sally in *Night School*, like Stella in *The Collection*, Ruth is both mother and whore. A whore is the most passive of women, the one who can be treated as a sexual object without any consideration of her own feelings or desires. The more helpless a male, the more he will tend to dream of women as obedient slaves – prostitutes. Hence the stern, unapproachable mother image must, in the sexual dreams of a child, tend to turn into the image of the whore. And that is why both Jessie and Ruth are both mother and whore.

If the view that *The Homecoming* is a wish-fulfilment dream seen, primarily, from the viewpoint of the young son is correct, then the character of Ruth *must* be a passive one: she is the object of male desires and, being an image in a dream, yields to these desires without putting up any resistance. Yet the play must also function on the realistic level; and here Pinter's success in making Ruth a credible character even when seen as a real person and not just the passive object of archetypal desires, is a virtuoso achievement.

For Ruth sees herself – has resigned herself to be seen – as a passive object of desire. That is the significance of her speech about herself as a moving object in response to the discussion about the real nature of a table. Having failed in her marriage, Ruth is in a state of existential despair, a deep accidie, which is both fully understandable and completely motivates her behaviour. She has tried to fight her own nature and she has been defeated by it. Now she yields to it, and surrenders beyond caring.

The character of Sam, on the other hand, embodies the family's self-awareness about the true nature of the mother, Jessie, and the man who was her pimp, MacGregor – who indeed, on a deeper level, merely represents Max's own activity as an underworld character – Max, in fact, when he was like Lenny. Thus Sam is the family's conscience, its super-ego; hence it is only natural that he collapses at the moment when the situation about which he has felt ashamed and guilty all his life is restored.

The subject matter of *The Homecoming* appears in various guises in a number of Pinter's previous plays. In *The Birthday Party* a son-figure is brutally torn from a near-incestuous relationship with a loving mother-figure – and the chief agent of this traumatic experience, Goldberg, has much in common with the father-figure of Max. In *The Caretaker* two sons expel a father-figure (and again the old tramp Davies has much in common with Max's garrulousness and irascibility, while Mick and Aston are very close to Lenny and Joey). In *Night School* a son (Walter) is fighting with a father-figure (Solto) for the possession of a girl who is half schoolteacher (mother) and half night club hostess (whore). In *The Lover* the hero dreams of his wife (who is a mother) as a whore. But it is in *The Homecoming* that the Oedipal theme emerges most fully and most explicitly. It is as though it had gradually risen to the surface as Pinter gained the self-confidence and formal skill which enabled him to meet it head-on rather than merely obliquely.

The universality of the archetypal situation dealt with in *The Homecoming* on the other hand, and its immense relevance, however deep down in their subconscious, to theatre audiences everywhere, seems to me also to provide the explanation for the powerful impact of the play in spite of an initial reaction of incomprehension and puzzlement over its apparent surface 'implausibility'. However much audiences may reject the play on the rational level, they ultimately respond in the depth of their subconscious. Hence the abundance of discussion and probing about *The Homecoming*.

Tea Party

Based on a short story which Pinter himself recorded for the BBC Third Programme in April 1964 (it was broadcast on 29th April 1964) and which appeared in the January 1965 number of *Playboy*, the television play *Tea Party* was commissioned by the European Broadcasting Union as part of a project of simultaneous, or nearly simultaneous, transmissions of television plays by major European dramatists throughout the European television networks. Pinter's contribution was preceded by plays specially written for this 'largest theatre in the world' by Terence Rattigan, and Fritz Hochwälder; and followed by one from François Billetdoux.

Tea Party deals with the downfall of an industrial tycoon, Robert Disson, who from modest beginnings has risen to the position of one of the most successful manufacturers of sanitary installations in Britain. This allows Pinter to start the play with a tracking shot of an elegant office suite lined with showcases displaying a selection of wash basins, lavatory bowls and bidets. Disson's breakdown is the result of the tension between his desire for social status and respectability, represented by his second wife, Diana, a cool upperclass lady, and his sensuality which manifests itself in his lusting after 'the swelling body' – as it is repeatedly referred to in the story – of his secretary, Wendy. In other words: Disson's conflict is that of Richard in *The Lover*, except that in this case the chaste upper-class lady and the whore are different people rather than just one woman playing both parts.

The play opens with Disson's first interview with Wendy and his taking her on, on the eve of his marriage to Diana. So he acquires the pure wife and the sexual object – the secretary – at the same moment. Diana's brother, Willy, who is out of a job (it seems this upper-class family is very much in need of marrying into money) is asked, at the wedding reception, to deliver not only the eulogy of the bride, his sister, but also, owing to the unforeseen absence of Disson's best friend, the eulogy of the bridegroom which, as Willy does not know much good to say about his new brother-in-law, turns into a second eulogy on the bride. Thus starts Disson's feeling of embarrassment and inferiority towards his new wife's family. The fact that Disson's two teenage sons, twins, from his first marriage are going to a public school and are therefore also growing into his social superiors aggravates his loss of self-confidence. Wendy, the lusty, willing, social inferior becomes a kind of haven of rest and reassurance for Disson. When Diana, bored with being at home by herself, asks to be given a job in the family firm and becomes her brother's private secretary in the adjoining office, Disson's guilt and embarrassment grow. He suspects Wendy of flirting with his brother-in-law. When Wendy is called in to Willy's office, Disson tries to watch through the keyhole what they might be up to. In the story the scene is described as follows (Disson is the 'I' in the story):

With my eye at the keyhole I hear goosing, the squeak of them. The slit is black, only the sliding gussle on my drum, the hiss and flap of their bliss. The room sits on my head, my skull creased on the brass and loathsome handle I dare not twist, for fear of seeing black screech and scrape of my secretary writhing golden and blind in my partner's paunch and jungle.

In the play we see the door suddenly open: a pair of woman's legs stand by Disson's squatting body. He looks up. It is Diana, Disson's wife, who has been in the room with Wendy and Willy.

Disson's discomfiture manifests itself – as Rose's in *The Room*, as Edwards' in *A Slight Ache* – through a failure of his vision: he sees double or blurred images, and suffers from fits of temporary blindness. His friend Disley, who is an eye specialist, can find nothing organically wrong. Yet, while playing table tennis or doing carpentry with his sons, Disson is repeatedly handicapped by his failing eyesight.

And even in the office Disson's eyes give trouble. On these occasions Wendy bandages them with her chiffon kerchief, giving Disson an opportunity to touch her as she ministers to him.

The catastrophe comes during a tea party at Disson's office on the first anniversary of his marriage to Diana – and his acquisition of Wendy as his secretary. Disson's old working-class parents have travelled down to London from the North, Disley, the ophthalmologist, and his wife are there, as are the twins, Willy, Diana and Wendy. Disson's eyes have again given trouble. Disley has bandaged them, just for half an hour, till the guests arrive.

The guests assemble. Disson listens to the clatter of tea cups, the snatches of party conversation. We see the scene now objectively, now as Disson imagines it, not being able to see what is going on. And these imaginings become wilder and wilder: finally he sees Willy making love to both Diana and Wendy, who are stretched out on Wendy's desk. Or as the story puts it:

Meanwhile my partner had the two women half stripped on a convenient rostrum. Whose body swelled most? I had forgotten. I picked up a ping pong ball. It was hard. I wondered how far he had stripped the women. The top halves or the bottom halves? Or perhaps he was now raising his spectacles to view my wife's swelling buttocks, the swelling breasts of my secretary. How could I verify this? By movement, by touch. But that was out of the question. And could such a sight possibly take place under the eyes of my own children? Would they continue to chat and chuckle, as they still did, with my physician? Hardly. However, it was good to have the bandage on straight and the knots tight.

So ends the story. In the play Disson's downfall is far more concrete. He 'Falls to the floor in his chair with a crack. His teacup drops and spills. The guests try to lift him from the chair, but they don't succeed. Disley cuts the bandage away.

Finally they raise the chair. Disson sits in it, motionless, with open eyes in a catatonic trance. Diana asks him whether he can hear or see her. She can elicit no answer. The last shot is of Disson's face in close-up, his eyes wide open'.

Tea Party is unusual in Pinter's *œuvre* in that the age-old English theme of the upstart who feels uneasy in his new upper-class surroundings comes so much to the fore. Yet it is characteristic of Pinter that even here the social theme coalesces with a sexual one. Disson does not only feel himself socially, but also sexually inadequate when he is with his wife; her social superiority deprives him of his manhood; for virility to him equals dominance; hence he feels more manly, more at home, with Wendy, his social inferior. And the breakdown comes when he suspects Wendy of having been taken up by his wife and brother-in-law. Indeed, his final collapse in the play is preceded by his overhearing a snatch of conversation between them:

WENDY: What, me? Come to Spain?
DIANA: Yes, why not? . . .
WILLY: Yes, of course you must come. Of course you must come.
WENDY: How wonderful.

Albert Stokes in *A Night Out* goes beserk when he discovers that the prostitute who has taken him home has the same social pretensions as his mother; Disson's collapse comes when he suspects that the vulgar and willing Wendy will rise to the social status of his upper-class wife and brother-in-law. While he sits with bandaged eyes at the tea party Disson can hear the vulgar working-class accents of his parents on one side, the polished public school talk of his sons on the other. It is the tension between these two worlds that reduces him to paralysis and blindness.

In some ways Disson's emergence from the squalor of his working-class youth into the antiseptic respectability of upper-class life (beautifully symbolized by the spotless water closets and bidets) parallels Len's loss of the warm squalor of his life with the dwarfs, Aston's loss of the wild exuberance of the period before he underwent electric shock treatment, Stanley's squalid existence in Meg's boarding house in *The Birthday Party*; and Stanley too is propelled into respectability – and speechlessness – by an assault on his eyesight: his glasses are broken, he is reduced to near-blindness. Blindness is the punishment which Oedipus inficted upon himself for having lusted after his mother. Is it Disson's punishment for having aspired to the bed of the chaste, madonna-like Diana?

Thus, although at first sight *Tea Party* looks like a far more conventional treatment of a more conventional subject matter, the staple of innumerable English plays, it does, in fact, combine many of the thematic strands of Pinter's more ambitious plays.

The Basement

The Basement was first broadcast on BBC Television in February 1967. Yet the script dates back to ca. 1963. It appears, under the title *The Compartment* in the manuscript for a composite film planned by Grove Press, the title page of which is inscribed 'PROJECT I, Three Original Motion Picture Scripts by Samuel Beckett, Eugene Ionesco, Harold Pinter'. Of the three projected films only one, Beckett's *Film*, was made in 1964 by Alan Schnieder, with Buster Keaton in the lead. The filming of Ionesco's *The Hard-Boiled Egg* and Pinter's *The Compartment* was postponed indefinitely. Yet the basic idea of the play (or film) goes back even further than that: the short story *The Examination*, first published in 1959 but certainly completed by January 1958 (see p. 50), deals with a conflict between two men, one of whom is called Kullus, at the end of which the narrator who had been the examiner has become the examinee while Kullus has taken over the narrator's room. Here the conflict is, at least on the surface, not concerned with a girl. But the prose-poem 'Kullus' (see p. 33) included in the collection of Pinter's early poetry published in 1968, not only introduces the girl but also contains much of the plot of *The Basement*, except that in the end it seems that the room belongs to the girl. 'Kullus' goes back to a period when Pinter was only nineteen, it represents preoccupations which are as basic to his thinking as the subject-matter of the novel of *The Dwarfs*.

The Basement shows a struggle for a room and a struggle for a girl. At the beginning we see Stott, a young man in a raincoat standing in the falling rain on a winter night outside a basement flat. Behind him, leaning against a wall, is a very young girl, Jane. Inside the large, comfortable basement room Law, another young man, is reading a Persian love manual with illustrations. Stott rings the bell and is received as an old and long-lost friend by Law, who invites him to stay the night. After he has dried himself, exchanged some reminiscences of their previous life together with his host and been offered a drink, Stott asks whether a friend of his, who is still waiting outside, can come in. Law readily agrees, Stott brings Jane in, they undress and immediately get into Law's bed. Law, deprived of his bed, sits by the fire and tries to read, while long sighs and gasps by Jane can be heard from the bed.

There follows a sequence of scenes in which Jane is shown exchanging confidences with Law about Stott, whom she does not appear to have known long, on a beach in summer (in the first sequence we were in winter), in a cave by the beach and in the room, when Jane, in bed with Stott, smiles at Law who is sleeping on the floor.

We are back in winter. Stott and Law talk about Jane who, Stott maintains, 'comes from a rather splendid family, actually.'

And now we are in summer again. On the beach: Jane caresses Law who is afraid they might be seen by Stott.

As Law and Jane return from the beach, their towels over their shoulders, they find the room completely transformed: it is now hyper-modern in a Scandinavian style.

Back in winter: but the room is still in its Scandinavian guise. Stott and Jane are in bed, Law is sitting in a chair. Stott demands some music to be played on the hi-fi.

The two men and the girl are drinking in a bar, one of the haunts of the two friends' youth.

In a field in winter Jane is ready to act as umpire in a race between Stott and Law. She gives the sign to start. Law runs, Stott remains standing still; Law turns to look back and stumbles.

A winter night in the room with its Scandinavian look. Stott asks for some music, opens the window and sees Law and Jane sitting outside in the moonlight, clenching their bodies with cold.

Walking in the backyard on a winter's day, Law suggests to Stott that the basement flat might be too small for three people; the town council and the Church might well object. Stott merely says: 'Not at all. Not at all'.

Summer again: the three at lunch. Jane in Stott's lap. Stott demands music. Law in looking for the Debussy record angrily flings all the other records at the wall. Jane breaks away from Stott and runs out.

But now it is winter again, and the room looks as at the beginning. Stott and Jane, naked, are climbing into bed. Law puts the record down, sits in his chair and pokes the dying fire.

And now it's the backyard again, in summer. Jane is sitting by the table, Stott comes out and tries to touch her breast, she moves away. Law calls from the open window: he has found the record.

In the cave by the beach Jane asks Law to ask Stott to go. It seems now as though Jane and Law had once lived together by themselves. Jane says:

We had such a lovely home. We had such a cosy home. It was so warm. Tell him to go. It's your place. Then we could be happy again. Like we used to. Like we used to. In our first blush of love.

Winter again. The backyard. Law whispers to Stott that Jane is betraying him:

. . . She has no loyalty. After all you've done for her. . . . She sullies this room. She dirties this room. All this beautiful furniture. This beautiful Scandinavian furniture. She dirties it. She sullies the room.

And now Stott lies in bed. Jane and Law discuss him as though he was about to die.

And then we see Law and Jane in a corner 'snuffling each other like animals'. Stott is standing by the window.

He closes the curtains. The room has again been completely transformed: it is now in the style of the Italian Renaissance with a marble-tiled floor, tapestries, a Florentine mirror, an Italian old master on the wall. Jane offers Stott fruit from a bowl, Law, in a corner, plays the flute. Stott suddenly tosses the bowl of fruit across the room; he picks up a tray containing large marbles. As he throws them across the room at Law, Law uses his flute as a cricket bat: a savage and dangerous game of cricket develops; Law counters one marble by hitting it into a fish tank, the tank breaks, the fish swim across the marble tiles. Jane applauds. But then one of the marbles hits Law on the forehead; he collapses.

And now the room has become completely bare: Law and Stott advance on each other holding broken milk bottles. As the horrible weapons smash together, we see a record turning, playing Debussy's 'Girl with the Flaxen Hair'.

Law and Jane are standing outside in the area in front of the basement flat, Law wearing Stott's raincoat.

Inside, Stott is sitting by the fire, reading. The doorbell rings, Stott goes to open and lets in Law, greeting him as a long-lost friend.

That this sequence of images does not tell a realistic story is only too clear: the sudden switches from summer to winter, the changes in the furniture of the room leave no doubt on that score. Thus *The Basement* must either be a kind of dream or daydream: the first image of Stott standing outside in the rain may be a wish in Law's mind to see his old friend again – the rest would then express his hopes and fears arising out of the associations which the thought of a sudden visit by Stott would conjure up in his mind: he envied his friend's superior intelligence, taste and sexual prowess; so the thought of Stott would conjure up the image of the girl he would bring along and fears of the humiliation he would have to suffer seeing Stott make love to the girl in his bed, but also hopes of seducing her away from him. Knowing Stott's artistic leanings and wealth, he might imagine Stott furnishing the room in various sumptuous ways; and the thought of stealing the girl away from him would inevitably lead to fears of his revenge – hence the more and more savage dreams about fights with Stott (which follow the dream about Stott's sudden dying, a wish to kill him, causing instant guilt feelings). And finally, having imagined himself ousted by Stott, he begins to dream how he would reconquer his room by the same means that Stott had used. In fact he yearns to be as tough and ruthless as Stott, who would bring a girl with him and oust the owner of a room. The enigmatic scene in which it seems that Jane had in fact once been living with Law also fits into this pattern of a daydream. Here too Law merely tries out what it would feel like to be in Stott's shoes.

Alternatively, one might regard *The Basement* as no more than a sequence of images on the theme of two men fighting for a girl and for a room, an abstract, non-narrative pattern of moods and pictures which are all variations on the theme and composed after the manner of a symphony in a series of movements in which the different strands are contrasted, juxtaposed, varied, fused and separated again.

Both interpretations may well be equally valid: the dream might have been the starting point, but the abstract, symphonic pattern of images the ultimate and artistically highly satisfying and sophisticated result.

Certainly the prose-poem 'Kullus' and the short story *The Examination* radiate a dream-like atmosphere. Like Stott in the play, Kullus, both in the poem and the story, is associated with windows, the opening and closing of curtains:

154

Kullus took a room. The window was closed if it was warm, and open if it was cold. The curtains were open if it was night, and closed if it was day. Why closed? Why open?
   – I have my night,
said Kullus.
   I have my day. (Kullus)

Kullus's predilection for windows was not assumed. At every interval, he retired to the window, and began from its vantage, as from a source. . . . Neither was Kullus's predilection for windows a deviation from former times. I had myself suffered under his preoccupation upon previous occasions, when the order of his room had been maintained by particular arrangement of window and curtain, according to day and night, and seldom to my taste or my comfort. (*The Examination*.)

The room again, both in the poem, the story and the play is symbolized by the fire in the grate. In the poem, when Kullus and the girl invade his room, the narrator, after they had climbed into his bed,

   . . . placed a coat over the lamp and watched the ceiling hustle to the floor. Then the room moved to the flame in the grate. I shifted my stool and sat by the flame in the grate.

At the end of the poem, when the room has become the girl's, we have, as in the play, returned to the initial situation:

   The ceiling hustled to the floor.
      – You have not shifted the coat from the lamp,
   I said.

Which implies that all that had happened in between might have been dreamt. In the play Law 'unbuttons his cardigan. He places it over the one lit lamp, so shading the light. He sits by the fire'. The imagery of the poem has not been changed.
   The dreamer sitting by the fire in the grate is thus strongly

155

present both in the poem and the play, and to a lesser extent in the story.

The Basement therefore contains much of the youthful daydreams and preoccupations which form the matrix for Pinter's later development. Indeed, Stott and Law or the narrator and Kullus have much in common with the two rivals for the favours of the schoolteacher/call-girl Virginia in the novel of *The Dwarfs*; the *motif* of the change of role from the dominant to the dominated recurs in *A Slight Ache* when Edward's place is taken by the formerly despised matchseller; the fight for the room which in Pinter's other plays so often has a rather abstract character is here still very clearly linked with the fight for the bed and the girl who will share it; only in *Night School* is this equally explicitly stated in Walter's fight to get his bed back by becoming the lover of the girl to whom his aunts have let his room.

It is also noteworthy how the more directly visual medium of television brings out the relationship between realism and the dream image in Pinter. In *Tea Party* Disson's erotic nightmares while he is blind are made visible, and they are seen to arise directly from the naturalistic situation which has been painstakingly established. In *The Basement* it might be argued that we are being given *only* the nightmarish vision, while the realistic basis – which may be no more than the shot of Law sitting by the fire, trying to read his book – has been whittled down to almost nothing.

Landscape

A short play, written for the stage, but withdrawn by Pinter when the Lord Chamberlain (in the last year of his tenure of the stage censor's power) insisted on the omission of a few strong words, *Landscape* received its first performance on radio (not subject to the stage censor's influence) in the spring of 1968. It reached the stage, in a double bill with its companion piece, *Silence*, in the summer of the following year.

In its style and approach *Landscape* constitutes a new departure for Pinter: there is nothing here of the 'comedy of menace'. The difficulty of communication is, as in so many of Pinter's other plays, one of the main themes of *Landscape* as well; but now this difficulty emerges not from dialogue between people who talk at length without getting through to each other, but from what in effect are two *monologues*, simultaneously delivered and intercut, but each conducted on a different level of expression.

The scene is the kitchen of a country house. By a long kitchen table sits Beth, a woman in her late forties, in an armchair. At the opposite corner of the long table sits Duff, a man in his early fifties. It is evening. A note by the author stresses the difference in levels of awareness and expression between the characters:

> Duff refers normally to Beth, but does not appear to hear her voice.
> Beth never looks at Duff, and does not appear to hear his voice.
> Both characters are relaxed, in no sense rigid.

It seems therefore that Duff, who 'refers normally to Beth', is talking to her, or at least trying to talk to her, although she does not react. Beth, on the other hand, who 'never looks at Duff' and is not heard by him, seems to be talking merely to herself; her monologue is merely the stream of her thoughts, an *internal monologue*.

Beth's thoughts, moreover, are entirely about the past, she never refers to the present, or her present condition, while Duff is mainly concerned with telling Beth what he has been doing in the last day or two, with only an occasional reference to events further back.

Beth is dreaming of a day on the beach with a man, 'my man', from whom she wanted a baby. This is the main image of her 'landscape': the wide deserted beach, with only a few people passing by, someone glimpsed in the distance, and Beth and her man, lying in the sand. Occasionally Beth's thoughts wander away from the beach to a scene where she arranged flowers and 'he' (the same man or another? probably the same one!)

> . . . followed me and watched, standing at a distance from me. When the arrangement was done I stayed still. I heard him moving. He didn't touch me. I listened. I looked at the flowers, blue and white, in the bowl.
> *Pause*
> Then he touched me.
> *Pause*
> He touched the back of my neck. His fingers, lightly, touching, lightly, touching, the back, of my neck . . .

Other scenes Beth recalls – all related to the central landscape of herself and her lover at the beach – concern their visit to a hotel bar after their stay at the beach, and what preceded it: Beth meeting her man, having caught a bus to the crossroads and being picked up by him in his car to drive to the sea. And how she had got up early that day to do her housework; and how she wore her blue dress on that beautiful autumn morning. Beth speaks about her skill in drawing and says that on that day at the beach she might have drawn a portrait of her man. The final image of the play is Beth's memory of that day on the beach:

> He lay above me and looked down at me. He supported my shoulder.
> *Pause*
> So tender his touch on my neck. So softly his kiss on my cheek.
> *Pause*
> My hand on his rib.
> *Pause*
> So sweetly the sand over me. Tiny the sand on my skin.
> *Pause*
> So silent the sky in my eyes. Gently the sound of the tide.
> *Pause*
> Oh my true love I said.

Beth thus does not even try to communicate. She has shut herself off from the present, the world that now surrounds her. Duff, on the other hand, *wants* to tell *her* what he has been doing, and also, clearly, wants to elicit an answer from her.

Do you rememeber the weather yesterday? That downfall?

He informs Beth that the dog has disappeared, that he sheltered under a tree in the rain, that he went to a pub and had a beer and got into an argument with another man who complained about the quality of the beer.

But Duff's conversation also gives a lot more detail about his and Beth's background and how they come to be sitting in that large kitchen on that evening. It emerges that he and Beth were taken on by the owner of that large country house as a team of domestic servants, housekeeper/cook and handyman/chauffeur. And that the owner of the house was called Mr Sykes. And that now they are living in Mr Sykes's house by themselves:

That's where we are lucky in my opinion. To live in Mr Sykes's house in peace, no one to bother us.

That they are not just keeping the house warm for Mr Sykes, but, in fact, seem to have become its owners, emerges from Duff's next sentence:

I've thought of inviting one or two people I know from the village in here for a bit of a drink once or twice but I decided against it. It's not necessary.

Duff dwells on the fact that Beth was 'a first-rate housekeeper. . . .'

He could rely on you. He did. He trusted you, to run his house, to keep the house up to the mark, no panic.

Was it because of Beth's skill and reliability as a housekeeper that the couple were left the house by Mr Sykes? He must have had a very compelling reason, for he was by no means all alone in the world:

> Mr Sykes gave a little dinner party that Friday. He complimented you on your cooking and the service.
> *Pause*
> Two women. That was all. Never seen them before. Probably his mother and sister.

Or did Mr Sykes have other reasons? Although Duff considers that he was 'a gloomy bugger' who led a 'lonely life' he was very attentive towards Beth:

> That nice blue dress he chose for you, for the house, that was very nice of him. Of course it was in his own interests for you to look good about the house, for guests.

Was this the blue dress that Beth wore that day when she went to the beach with her man? It seems so, she does not seem to have had another one:

> I wore my blue dress.

How have Beth and Duff come to their present condition of non-communication? Duff recalls what must have been the decisive, traumatic incident:

> You used to wear a chain round your waist. On the chain you carried your keys, your thimble, your notebook, your pencil, your scissors.
> *Pause*
> You stood in the hall and banged the gong.

This was after Mr Sykes had gone, had in all probability died.

> Standing in an empty hall banging a bloody gong. There's no one to listen. No one'll hear. There's not a soul in the house.

Except me. There's nothing for lunch. There's nothing cooked. No stew. No pie. No greens. No joint. Fuck all.

(The last phrase was the principal cause of the Lord Chamberlain's ban.) It was seeing Bess banging on the gong, as no doubt she had always done when Mr Sykes was there, that made Duff very wild. He tore down Beth's insignia of her office of housekeeper:

I took the chain off and the thimble, the keys, the scissors slid off it and clattered down. I booted the gong down the hall. . . . I thought you would come to me, I thought you would come into my arms and kiss me, even . . . offer yourself to me. I would have had you in front of the dog, like a man, in the hall, on the stone, banging the gong. . . .

Is this merely fantasy, or did Duff, after tearing off Beth's chain with her keys and sewing things, really try to rape her there and then?

I'll bang the gong on the floor, if the sound is too flat, lacks resonance, I'll hang it back on its hook, bang you against it swinging, gonging, waking the place up, calling them all for dinner, lunch is up, bring out the bacon, bang your lovely head, mind the dog doesn't swallow the thimble, slam –

These are Duff's last words in the play. From them the image is cross-cut to Beth's final fantasy of her man lying tenderly above her at the beach.

Thus the play's main image is one of contrast; the contrast between the tenderness and delicacy of the woman's memory of her past love, and the man's brutal coarseness, whether he is talking about the duckshit that lay on the paths after the rain, whether he uses the strongest of taboo words, or dreams of sex in terms of banging a gong, bringing home the bacon, and slamming, beating, bashing.

There is, as always in Pinter's *œuvre*, a delicately balanced ambiguity in *Landscape*. Who is the man whom Beth remembers so tenderly? Is it Duff, who clearly is her husband, or another man, perhaps Mr Sykes, her employer?

That there might have been a period when Duff himself was as tender as Beth is suggested in the text. The man who watched her so tenderly when she was arranging flowers had remarked, says Beth, on her gravity –

My gravity, he said. I was so grave, attending to the flowers.

While Duff remembers:

I was thinking . . . when you were young . . . you didn't laugh much. You were . . . grave.

So it might well have been Duff who watched her arrange the flowers and who spoke to her about her gravity. Duff recalls another episode which shows not only that he had a certain delicacy in former times but that there had been genuine love and understanding between them. He speaks of an occasion when he returned from a trip to the north with his employer:

I told you that I'd let you down. I'd been unfaithful to you.
Pause
You didn't cry. We had a few hours off. We walked up to the pond, with the dog. We stood under the trees for a bit. . . . When we got back into this room you put your hands on my face and you kissed me.

If Duff is the man whom Beth remembers so tenderly, the man who loyally confessed his transgression to her and begged forgiveness and was forgiven, then what we are seeing is the tragic operation of time, which turns men coarse and brutal by throwing them together with coarse drinking companions in pubs where they argue about the quality of the ale and boast about their expertise in the handling of beer (there is a long passage in Duff's text in which he parades his knowledge of the professional jargon of cellarmen), while the women retain the warmth and delicacy of feeling which blossomed in the beautiful erotic experiences of their youth.

But the man whom Beth remembers may well not be Duff, indeed there is much in the text to indicate the likelihood that it was Mr Sykes who was Beth's lover, Mr Sykes who gave her the blue dress, and took her to the beach and to tea at a hotel, and who, when he died, left her his large, empty house. In that case it may well be the grief at her lover's passing which has turned Beth into a silent recluse, in which case there is an irony in the fact that Duff, when he was unfaithful, confessed, but that the tender and delicate Beth calmly went on deceiving her husband. If it was Duff who took Beth to the beach, for example, why should she have secretly gone off by herself by bus to the crossroads, to be picked up by him in the car later? If Mr Sykes allowed Duff to use his car, they could have left together from the house; after all, they were man and wife. But if, Duff having been given some other job, Mr Sykes had been driving the car himself, then he could not have set off together with Beth, and the subterfuge would have been necessary. And in that case *Landscape* would present us with another variant of the eternal triangle: the coarse, bluff fellow Duff, who loves his wife deeply but in a rough and ready, earthy way; the gentleman lover with his gentle ways; and the woman, who having tasted the delicacy and gentleness of a social superior, rejects the coarse wooing of her proletarian spouse, and cuts herself off from him in grief and loathing.

But, of course, the point is that we shall never be quite certain what the truth might be: perhaps Beth merely imagines all that beautiful episode by the sea, perhaps she only dreamt of having such an outing with her employer, or, indeed, her hust..nd. Or perhaps she did experience that beautiful day, but with an entirely different man. The landscape of memory, the landscape of the soul, is dark, inaccessible and shrouded in the mists of eternal uncertainty.[1]

[1] In a letter to the director of the first German performance of *Landscape* (Hamburg, 10 January 1970) which – very much against Pinter's intention –

What is remarkable about *Landscape* as a virtuoso piece of writing is not only the subtle control of its rhythms, but also the immense feat of compression which Pinter has accomplished. Like Beckett's *Play* – with which *Landscape* and its companion piece *Silence* have many affinities – the matter of what might otherwise have occupied a three-act play or a full-length novel is here compressed into a bare half hour. The sparseness of the style, the extreme skill with which minute clues are subtly inverwoven, creates a picture of depth and density with a bare minimum of words. It is out of the silence and the pauses that the landscape of these three lives emerges – a landscape which opens out into a vast horizon.

Silence

Of all Pinter's writings *Silence* is the most lyrical, but also the most mysterious and difficult. Like *Landscape*, *Silence* consists of cross-cut monologues, except that here there are not two but three characters; and, occasionally, two of the characters are shown in dialogues which are flashbacks to the past. Also, whereas in *Landscape* the two characters, though never making contact with their minds, are physically together in the same room, a realistically conceived kitchen in a definite house, in *Silence* they are also – except in the flashback dialogues – physically separated. The stage direction is extremely laconic:

---

was published in the programme brochure of that performance, Pinter stated: '. . . that the man on the beach is Duff. I think there are elements of Mr Sykes in her memory of this Duff which she might be attributing to Duff, but the man remains Duff. I think that Duff detests and is jealous of Mr Sykes, although I do not believe that Mr Sykes and Beth were ever lovers.

I formed these conclusions after I had written the plays and after learning about them through rehearsals.'

164

Three areas.
A chair in each area.

So, in fact, the three characters seem to live apart, each in his own room.

These three characters are – according to the list provided by the author – Ellen, a girl in her twenties, Rumsey, a man of forty, and Bates, a man in his middle thirties.

It is clear that Ellen has, or has had, relations with both these men. The play opens with Rumsey talking about going for a walk in the country with his girl:

> I walk with my girl who wears a grey blouse when she walks and grey shoes and walks with me readily wearing her clothes considered for me. Her grey clothes.

Ellen's opening passage starts with the essential information that:

> There are two. One who is with me sometimes, and another. He listens to me. I tell him what I know – I lead him to a tree, clasp closely to him and whisper to him, wind going, dogs stop, and he hears me.
> But the other hears me.

The other, it appears, is Bates, the younger of the two men. He seems less tender, a rougher type than the lyrical Rumsey: for he describes how he took a girl (who is clearly Ellen, as later appears from an enactment of the scene in flashback) to the town, by bus, walked with her through the back streets and:

> Brought her into this place, my cousin runs it. Undressed her, placed my hand.

Both Rumsey and Bates are country men; but it seems that Rumsey is socially superior to Bates. He has his own house, where, as Ellen tells in her next passage, she visited him once, while Bates, who had to take her to a place – a pub, or hotel? – run by his cousin, seems to be a farm labourer without his own house.

As Ellen says – clearly referring to Rumsey:

> One time visited his house. He put a light on, it reflected the window, it reflected in the window.

Whereupon Rumsey, taking up his cue, describes what seems to be the same visit from his point of view, how she walked from the door to the window –

> . . . to confirm that the house which grew nearer is the same one she stands in, that the path and the bushes are the same, that the gate is the same.

Bates on the other hand recalls how he used to stand waiting for the girl in the open:

> How many times standing clenched in the pissing dark waiting?
> The mud, the cows, the river.
> You cross the field out of darkness. You arrive.

And Ellen sums up:

> There are two. I turn to them and speak. I look them in their eyes. I kiss them there and say, I look away to smile, and touch them as they turn.

There follows the stage direction: *Silence*. That this is not just the usual *pause* which punctuates Pinter's dialogue is clear from the fact that the stage direction 'Pause' also occurs in the text. Here the 'Silence' – which gives the play its title has a doubtlessly far greater significance. It marks the end of a chapter. But it also has a dramatic meaning of its own.

At the end of this first caesura of silence we are no longer in the situation where Ellen was in contact with the two men. Now Rumsey speaks of his being alone with his animals. He has, he says, lost nothing. He finds it pleasant to be alone. Bates on the other hand describes his anger and dismay at living next door to young people who make noisy music, and noisy love. These young people have called him granddad. And he sighs:

Were I young . . .

So the Bates who is now talking is no longer 'a man in his middle thirties' but an old man. So presumably is Rumsey in the preceding speech, and Ellen in the one which follows Bates' complaint about the noisy young neighbours: for she speaks of a drinking companion, an elderly woman who constantly asks her about her early life and sexual adventures. That she is no longer in her twenties becomes clear when she muses about her appearance:

But I'm still quite pretty really, quite nice eyes, nice skin.

At this point Bates moves to Ellen's area. They enact the scene he had described in the first section of the play leading up to his invitation that they should take a bus to town to a place which his cousin runs. But Ellen's response in this flashback scene is: No. Followed by another *Silence*. Did she eventually accept the invitation? Or had Bates merely been dreaming about what might have been when he spoke of the visit to the place run by his cousin where he undressed her?

After the second silence we hear only Rumsey and Bates. Rumsey talks about the heat, about a visit to his horse. Bates speaks of his imagined walks, his inability, in the real world, to get out of the walls. And he remembers a little girl:

I took it for walks. I held it by its hand. It looked up at me and said, I see something in a tree, a shape, a shadow. It is leaning down. It is looking at us.
Maybe it's a bird, I said, a big bird, resting. . . .

Where, in the time scale of the play, are we here, in this brief section comprising just one short speech by Rumsey, one by Bates, between two silences? As Rumsey is alone, as Bates is living in town, we must assume that we are again in a period when they are no longer with Ellen, when, though perhaps not yet very old, they are older than at the time when they were having their relationship with her. Who then might the little girl be whom Bates took for walks? It seems that this too might have been Ellen at an even earlier stage in their relationship. For in a subsequent section, in a flashback scene between Rumsey and Ellen in which they re-enact her visit to Rumsey's house, Rumsey asks her whether she can remember when she last visited his house. She says she can remember. And Rumsey adds:

> You were a little girl.

So we must assume that Ellen grew up with both Rumsey and Bates having known her almost all her life.

But before we come to the passage which takes us back to Ellen's visit to Rumsey, there is a brief section, between two silences, in which Ellen as well as Rumsey speak of what seems to be an ecstasy of lovemaking:

> ELLEN: When I run . . . when I run . . . when I run . . . over the grass . . .
> RUMSEY: She floats . . . under me. Floating . . . under me.
> ELLEN: I turn. I turn. I wheel. I glide. I wheel. In stunning light. The horizon moves from the sun. I am crushed by the light.
> *Silence*

Then we are back with Rumsey and Bates much later, lonely and old. Then Ellen moves to Rumsey's acting area and we are in the scene where she visits his house. She offers to cook for Rumsey, Rumsey offers to play music for her. They notice her reflection in the window – which was mentioned by Ellen in the first section. The reflection is due to the darkness outside:

ELLEN: It's very dark outside.
RUMSEY: It's high up.
ELLEN: Does it get darker the higher you get?
RUMSEY: No.
 Silence

And now we are back in the old age of the three characters. Ellen talks of the night around her:

Around me sits the night. Such a silence. I can hear myself. Cup my ear. My heart beats in my ear. Such a silence. Is it me? Am I silent or speaking? How can I know? Can I know such things? No-one has ever told me. I need to be told things. I seem to be old. Am I old now? No-one will tell me. I must find a person to tell me these things.

Bates speaks about his landlady asking him for a drink and inquisitive about his former life: has there been no pleasantness, no loveliness in it? Bates reacts:

I've had all that. I've got all that, I said.

Ellen remembers that visit to Rumsey's house: he sat her on his knee by the window and asked her if he could kiss first her right, then her left cheek.

I said yes. He did.
Silence

There follows an enigmatic passage: both Bates and Rumsey recall a similar incident with Ellen. Rumsey talks about something which Ellen said and he could not hear, Bates about something he said which Ellen could not hear. Bates briefly recalls – presumably while old – how happy horses are in the country. Then Ellen moves to Rumsey's acting area: Rumsey is telling her to find a young man for herself. She refuses because they are stupid and she hates them.

Again there is silence. We are back, very briefly, in Ellen's

169

and Bates's younger life. Bates talks about the shapes in the trees, which are just birds. Ellen speaks of her two friends:

> There are two. They halt to laugh and bellow in the yard. They dig and punch and cackle where they stand. They turn to move, look round at me to grin. I turn my eyes from one, and from the other to him.
> *Silence*

Briefly Bates is interpolated – old again: the young people next door are silent now:

> Sleep? Tender love? It's of no importance.
> *Silence*

Ellen – old – speaks of her life in town among people through whom she walks without noticing them. Her drinking companion has asked her for the hundredth time whether she had ever been married:

> This time I told her I had. Yes, I told her I had. Certainly. I can remember the wedding.

And now with ever more frequent intervals of silence the rest of the play is taken up by brief snatches from the speeches we have heard, cross-cut in an intricate pattern of memory which, as the snatches of speech become briefer, seems to run down, to ebb away until they merge into one long silence as the lights fade.

Even more than *Landscape*, *Silence* recalls Beckett's *Play*, where the device of repeated fragments of speech running down is used to suggest the way in which the last moments of awareness of a dying person might remain suspended in limbo for ever, echoing on and on through eternity, while gradually losing their intensity but unable ever to fade away completely. Are the cross-cut thoughts and memories in *Silence* also the dying thoughts of the three characters before they are engulfed in total silence, the silence of death? The possibility is by no means excluded. But the play might, on the other hand, also try to portray the way in which memory gradually fades in the process of living and ageing, the way in which the most intense emotions gradually flatten out and lose their impact and intensity. As we age our awareness of the past dims and runs down – and the rest is silence.

Be that as it may, *Silence* is an attempt to tell a story by a technique which breaks the chronological sequence more decisively than is usually done even in intricately woven patterns of flashback: the story is presented simultaneously from three different points of *view* and from two, perhaps three, different points in *time*: the time of the relationship itself, and one, or even two later periods. It is remarkable that with this highly intricate technique the story which emerges is in fact probably less ambiguous than that of many of Pinter's other, and less intricately patterned, plays; Ellen, it seems pretty clear, grew up in the country and two men who knew her as a little girl fell in love with her. Rumsey the older of the two men later broke with her and advised her to look for younger men. She may have gone away with Bates, but as she loved Rumsey more, their relationship broke up. So Rumsey lived on, fairly contented on his lonely farm, while Bates and Ellen stayed in town, unhappy, isolated and longing for the country. It is a simple tale, but out of it Pinter has made an intriguing attempt at a truly lyrical theatre of strong images and vividly recreated emotions, interwoven like the themes of a symphonic poem.

Old Times

Pinter's fourth full-length play which opened, under Peter Hall's direction, at the Aldwych on 1st June 1971 develops the style of reminiscence which distinguished *Landscape* and *Silence* from Pinter's earlier works; it nevertheless also marks a return to a more readily accessible, one might almost say commercially viable, idiom: if *Landscape* and *Silence* are purely lyrical and static, *Old Times* contains drama in

171

presenting a clash of personalities, a battle for the affections of a woman by her husband and best friend; and while this is a deadly serious affair the dialogue sparkles with amusing lines; moreover, although the mood of the play is one of recall of things past, one of Pinter's main earlier themes re-emerges: the theme of the intruder who disturbs the peace of a home and a safe relationship.

The husband, Deeley, and his wife, Kate, inhabit a converted farmhouse somewhere in England. It is autumn – September. When the curtain rises Deeley and Kate are talking about the forthcoming arrival of Kate's friend Anna whom she has not seen for twenty years. (All three characters are in their early forties.) Yet while Deeley and Kate discuss Anna's impending visit, she is already seen, albeit in dim light, standing at the window, looking out.

From the opening dialogue between the married couple we learn that Anna was Kate's best and only friend in the London of the fifties and that they shared a room, i.e. lived together. Kate also mentions that Anna was a thief – she occasionally borrowed pieces of underwear from Kate. Quite suddenly and without any prepartion in the dialogue Anna turns from the window and launches into a description of the young women's life in the London of the early fifties, when they worked as secretaries in offices and went to concerts and spent their lunch-hours eating sandwiches in Green Park.

Are we to assume that Anna's sudden participation in the dialogue merely represents a cinematic cut? Or that she was in fact present during the opening dialogue in which she was being discussed? Or does her sudden inclusion in the action indicate that the action itself proceeds with the jerkiness of a dream?

This action develops into a duel of wits between Deeley and Anna; each seems to be using his memories and reminiscences to put the other at a disadvantage: when Deeley recalls how he first met Kate in some small fleapit of a cinema during a performance of *Odd Man Out*, Anna soon afterwards describes a Sunday afternoon, when she and Kate went to the cinema and saw *Odd Man Out*. Which of the two versions of the story is true? They can hardly both be correct, as Deeley has stressed that he and Anna were the only spectators in the cinema when he met her there. And Anna explicitly states what is one of the main themes of the play:

> There are some things one remembers even though they may never have happened. There are things I remember which may never have happened but as I recall them so they take place.

And Anna goes on to recount a scene when coming home at night she found a man, crumpled in the armchair, crying, in her and Kate's room. She went to bed. The man stood over her, but she would have nothing to do with him. He left the flat. But later in the night, Anna says, she woke and saw him 'lying across her [Kate's] lap on her bed'. The next morning he had gone.

Throughout this dialogue Kate is present, but she neither confirms nor denies the stories told about her. She merely says: 'You talk of me as if I were dead.'

Deeley's antagonism against Anna erupts in an exchange in which he questions her about her present home in Taormina. He does not seem to believe the tale of a sumptuous villa with marble floors and an elegant rich husband. In his exasperation he presents himself as a globe-trotting film-maker (Deeley's profession is never stated, but we are led to assume that he has something to do with television). 'My name is Orson Welles' he exclaims, while insisting that he made a film in Sicily which he both wrote and directed:

> As a matter of fact I am at the top of my profession, as a matter of fact, and I have indeed been associated with substantial numbers of articulate and sensitive people, mainly prostitutes of all kinds.

The inference is clear: while trying to assert that he is an artist or intellectual, Deeley simultaneously expresses his contempt of the snobs who claim to be artists or intellectuals – like Anna.

In the embarrassed silence that follows Deeley's outburst the two women revert to a re-enactment of their life in the old times. Again it is left open whether they are playing a game of reminiscence or whether the action, dreamlike, has actually shifted to the past (as it does in *Silence*). Anna and Kate are discussing whether they should go out or stay in, and Anna gives a description of the sordid park they would find if they went out, with people lurking behind bushes – an image of sexual menace and disgust. They then run through a list of boyfriends they might invite. Kate says she'll think about whom to invite in her bath. The first act ends with her leaving to have her bath.

Act Two takes place in the bedroom. While Kate is having her bath Deeley tells Anna that he remembers having met her twenty years ago, at a pub called The Wayfarers. He recalls an incident when having bought her a drink he took her to a party and sat at her feet gazing up her skirt. Anna is certain that this incident could not possibly have involved her. The conversation shifts to Kate in her bath: should Deeley dry her? Or Anna? The erotic overtones of this passage are clear. When Kate returns it seems as though the two women would again revert to their game – or dream – of living twenty years back. Deeley tries to intervene to drag the conversation into the present, but without success. When he finally does draw Anna into a reply about her present impressions of England, she, in turn, launches into her side of the story about the party at which a man looked up her skirt. And it gradually turns out that, *if* Deeley's story was true (Anna might well simply have decided to play along with him, having failed to impress him with her previous assertion that it could not possibly be true), then Anna in fact must have been wearing Kate's underclothes, which she used to borrow (or steal, as Kate had it previously).

Deeley reacts violently against this, be it mere teasing on Anna's part or real baiting. Kate merely replies, in defence

174

of her friend: 'If you don't like it, go.' So the intruder *has* taken over. . . .

Once more Deeley returns to the story of having taken Anna to a party and having looked up her skirt; but now he phrases it in trendy 1970 language ('We had a scene together. She freaked out. She didn't have any bread, so I bought her a drink etc.'). At the end of that story the two women seem to have merged: 'She thought she was you [i.e. Kate], said little, so little. Maybe she was you. Maybe it was you, having coffee with me, saying little, so little.'

Kate's reply is to tell Deeley what Anna must have seen in him: 'She found your face very sensitive, vulnerable. . . . She wanted to comfort it, in the way only a woman can.' Now it is Deeley who throws doubt on whether the woman in question could have been Anna at all. And now it is Anna who is certain: 'Oh, it was my skirt. It was me. I remember your look . . . very well. I remember you well.'

At this point – when Anna admits the incident – Kate turns on her. 'But I remember you. I remember you dead.' She describes how once she had found Anna 'dead' in her bed, her face dirty. It is quite clear that this death of Anna's is merely a metaphor, for Kate also speaks of her waking up. So what she is describing is the moment when her love for Anna died. And Kate goes on to describe how, after Anna's body had gone, she had brought a man into the room, a man's body. And how once when the man – Deeley no doubt – thought that at last she would be 'sexually forthcoming' she took earth from the window-box and 'plastered his face with dirt'.

Anna walks towards the door, Deeley starts to sob. Anna switches off the light and lies down on her divan. Deeley stands up and stops between them; he goes towards the door; then turns, goes towards Kate's divan and lies across her lap. After a while he gets up, slumps in the armchair. The lights come up brightly on Deeley in his chair, Anna and Kate on the two divans.

In other words: the scene which Anna had described in

the first act is re-enacted by the characters at the end of the play.

As always in Pinter's plays the ambiguity of the action is the very essence of the impact of *Old Times*. On a realistic level *Old Times* is simply a sparring match between a husband and the wife's former girlfriend for her affections. Each of the two contestants uses memories and evocations of the past as weapons in this confrontation. In the end the two women occupy the marital beds, the husband sits in the armchair between them, symbolically dispossessed of marital rights: the 'odd man out'.

But on another level one might see the play also as a dream, a nightmare of Deeley's. (Deeley is the only character who is actively involved in the *whole* play, Anna being present but not inside the action at the beginning of Act One, and Kate being in her bath at the start of Act Two.) Is Deeley merely anticipating, in a dream, or in his worried waking imagination, what would happen if the long-lost girlfriend from the past suddenly re-emerged?

There is even a third possibility: perhaps Anna is *really* present at the start of Act One; in that case the whole action of the play might be a kind of game – on the line of the game playing in *The Lover* – which three people involved in a triangular relationship might be playing every evening. The more playful aspects of *Old Times*, the sequences in which Anna and Deeley recall the popular tunes of the early fifties, for example, or the evocations of life in postwar London, would fit such an interpretation. The real antagonisms between the husband and the wife's woman friend would then naturally emerge from the playfulness of the ritual game, as the inevitable jealousies in such a *marriage-à-trois*.

In fact, of course, as always with Pinter, the three levels of possible interpretation do not exclude each other; they must *co-exist* to create the atmosphere of poetic ambivalence on which the image of the play rests.

On whichever level, however, that image is of Kate, at the still centre of the conflict, an ideal of purity around which the other two revolve. Kate's bath and the way Deeley and

Anna discuss it stands at the very centre of the action. And Kate found Anna dead when she found her dirty – i.e. sexually polluted. She dirtied Deeley's face when he wanted her to be sexually compliant. Kate thus has the superiority of the frigid wife for whom sensuality has no meaning. If it was Deeley who sobbed that night in Kate's and Anna's room, he must have been crying from frustration about his impotence, or his inability to arouse Kate. Why did Anna die for Kate? Perhaps because her story of what happened in that night was false, perhaps because Deeley *did* turn to her and she did *not* repulse him. After all, in the end Anna claims that it *was* Deeley who looked up her skirt when she wore Kate's underclothes . . . In that case Kate married Deeley to punish him for having soiled her love for Anna.

That might be the core of the story, if the action were wholly realistic. If it is a nightmare of Deeley's it would stand for what he is most afraid of. And if it is a game, it is a re-enactment of what might, or might not, be the basis of the relationship, an ever-shifting relationship, between these two women and this man. But, of course, the three levels must mingle: the dream is fraught with reality; reality and the memories of which it is composed has a dreamlike quality; and games are dreams made up from fragments of reality.

Monologue

'Man alone in a chair. He refers to another chair, which is empty' – that is the only indication Pinter gives as to the environment in which his short play is set. To judge from the text the Man is in his middle age; in fact, he seems to have much in common with Deeley in *Old Times* in that he seems both trendy and boastful about it. Why is he addressing an empty chair? The person imagined to be sitting in that chair is a friend of his youth and his rival, some time in the past, for the affections of a black girl ('my darling black darling,' 'my ebony love'). That rival cut a more dashing

177

figure, he rode a motorbike; and he was more beautiful than the speaker, 'Much more *aquiline* . . . more *ethereal*, more thoughtful, *slyer*.' The two friends were great sportsmen, they played ping pong, fives, golf together as well as cricket (Pinter's longstanding favourite game). And, like the young intellectuals in Pinter's early novel, *The Dwarfs*, they were indefatigable talkers about literature. The absent rival introduced the Man to Webster and Tourneur, but was in turn introduced to 'Tristan Tzara, Breton, Giacometti, Louis-Ferdinand Céline and John Dos Passos.'

The two rivals and the black girl formed a trio. 'We all walked, arm in arm, through the long grass, over the bridge, sat outside the pub in the sun by the river, the pub was shut.' In concise, evocative cameos like this the atmosphere of a whole period of their lives is intensely brought to life: it is a situation reminiscent of the constellation of characters in *The Basement*. The question at issue is: did the rival love the girl's soul and the Man her body? 'But I'll tell you one thing you don't know. She loved my soul. It was my soul she loved.' Which may be the reason she finally decided to love the rival's body. For it is with him she seems to be living now. The Man recalls her words, overheard behind a partition: 'Touch my body, she said to you. You did. Of course you did. You'd be a bloody fool if you didn't.'

A scene of parting from the black girl on the platform at Paddington Station is vividly recalled. Was that the moment she left London to live with the rival in another part of the country? It seems, from the stress which the Man puts on his own trendiness and energy, that the rival has relapsed into bourgeois mediocrity. And yet the Man implies that the affair between the black girl and the rival came to nothing, in his line, 'You could have had two black kids.' Yet in the following lines, the last of the play, he again contradicts that assumption:

I'd have died for them.
(*Pause*)
I'd have been their uncle.

(*Pause*)
I am their uncle.
(*Pause*)
I'm your children's uncle.
(*Pause*)
I'll take them out, tell them jokes.
(*Pause*)
I love your children.

The Man, boastful and superior, as he presents himself throughout the brief monologue, sits before the empty chair seemingly because he longs for the company of his ebony love *and* the friend and companion of his youth, not to mention the children. The empty chair thus appears to be the symbol and evidence of that Man's loneliness, the barrenness of his success as an intellectual whose frantic activity merely covers that emptiness.

The television production of *Monologue* in which Henry Woolf (the inspirer of Pinter's first play, *The Room*) played the Man failed, I believe, to produce the impact the play should have, because in concentrating on the Man's face in close-up, the camera neglected the empty chair, in its own way the protagonist of the play. Only on the stage could that tension between the speaker and the emptiness he addresses become fully manifest.

No Man's Land

'Magnificent parts giving rise to unforgettable performances by two of the greatest actors of our time – but what is Pinter saying?' seemed to be the question most frequently asked by audiences at the London performances of Pinter's fifth full-length play in 1975. To have provided a vehicle for what were undoubtedly great acting performances by two outstanding actors would in itself be a magnificent achievement for any playwright. But *No Man's Land* also has a very powerful statement to make – and, as so often with Pinter, on more than one level.

179

No Man's Land is in two acts. It is set in a room in the comfortable North-West London home of Hirst, a successful writer in his sixties. On a summer night Hirst has invited another elderly man, Spooner, also in his sixties, to come in and have a drink. He has met Spooner on Hampstead Heath. Throughout the first scene Spooner, the outsider, is voluble and ingratiating. He is obviously down at heel, almost a tramp, yet he is boastful about his past and exceedingly inquisitive as to Hirst's circumstances. Hirst, obviously drunk and continuing to drink, is morose and monosyllabic. Spooner is aware that his host is less than friendly: 'I speak to you with this startling candour because you are clearly a reticent man, which appeals, and because you are a stranger to me. . . .' And later: 'You're a quiet one. It's a great relief. Can you imagine two of us gabbling away like me? It would be intolerable.'

Spooner, who claims to be a poet, makes great play with his inner strength which he says derives from his detachment from human emotion: 'My only security, you see, my true comfort and solace, rests in the confirmation that I elicit from people of all kinds a common and constant level of indifference. It assures me that I am as I think myself to be, that I am fixed, concrete. To show interest in me or, good gracious, anything tending towards a positive liking of me, would cause in me a condition of the acutest alarm.' And again: 'I have never been loved. From this I derive my strength. Have you? Been loved?' These disclaimers of a need to be loved may well be negative exhortations, pleas for human contact, implying that Spooner is making a virtue out of the necessity of his solitary and loveless condition. Yet he insists on the advantages of being without emotional attachment:

> SPOONER: . . . The point I'm trying to make, in case you've missed it, is that I am a free man.

To which Hirst replies:

> HIRST: It's a long time since we had a free man in this house.
> SPOONER: We?
> HIRST: I.
> SPOONER: Is there another?
> HIRST: Another what?
> SPOONER: People. Person.
> HIRST: What other?

This is the first hint that Hirst considers himself less than free, and that there are others in the house. Although Hirst avoids answering the question we are left with the suspicion, the fear, that there are others who may be the cause of his lack of freedom.

As Spooner boasts of having been a fatherly friend and guide to poets in some dim past, keeping open house for them in a country cottage where he lived in idyllic circumstances with a gracious wife, Hirst makes the first reference to his own past. He too, he mutters, gave tea to visitors on the lawn at *his* cottage.

> SPOONER: . . . You've revealed something. You've made an unequivocal reference to your past. Don't go back on it. We share something. A memory of the bucolic life. We're both English.
> *Pause*
> HIRST: In the village church, the beams are hung with garlands, in honour of young women of the parish, reputed to have died virgin.
> *Pause*
> However, the garlands are not bestowed on maidens only, but on all who die unmarried, wearing the white flower of a blameless life.

The country cottage with teas on the lawn is thus for both Spooner and Hirst an image of a lost bucolic past, an age of innocence, the locus of a true Englishness, now lost.

Yet when Spooner probes Hirst's admission that he was once married and asks him to describe his wife, Hirst merely answers: 'What wife?' Hirst becomes so angry at this

181

questioning that he throws his glass at Spooner. After which, obviously with an immense effort to emerge for a brief moment from his drunkenness, he confesses:

> HIRST: Tonight . . . my friend . . . you find me in the last lap of a race . . . I had long forgotten to run.
> *Pause*
> SPOONER: A metaphor. Things are looking up.

Having effected something like an entry into Hirst's inner world, Spooner openly and even blatantly offers himself as a friend. Hirst's reply contains the first reference to the play's title:

> HIRST: No.
> *Pause*
> No man's land . . . does not move . . . or change . . . or grow old . . . remains . . . forever . . . icy . . . silent.

Having spoken these words Hirst falls to the floor and finally crawls out of the room on all fours.

> SPOONER: I have known this before. The exit through the door, by way of belly and floor.

And now, as in so many of Pinter's earlier plays, we experience the terror aroused by the appearance of a new and mysterious character. The surprise at the appearance of this young, casually dressed man in his thirties – Foster – is increased by his lack of surprise at finding Spooner, a perfect stranger, drinking alone in the drawing room. Foster is soon joined by Briggs, equally casually dressed, but older and stocky. Briggs, coarser and more brutal than the effeminate Foster, recognises Spooner as the man who collects the beer-mugs from the tables in a pub at Chalk Farm, The Bull. Spooner protests that he does that lowly job merely because the landlord of the Bull is his friend. Having been exposed as little better than a tramp, Spooner retreats into the pose of the gracious Englishman, inviting the two rude characters who are harrassing him to visit his house in the country, where they would receive a warm welcome from his gracious wife and his two daughters. At which Foster retorts with a story about a tramp he met during his travels in the Far East to whom he threw a coin – a clear reference to Spooner's arrogant pose when shown up. Hirst reappears and drinks with the three others. He asks who Spooner might be, having forgotten that it was he who brought him into the house. He begins to reminisce about people he knew in the past and whose faces are preserved in a photograph album. Suddenly Hirst has become very talkative: he recalls his recent dream about a waterfall in which someone was drowning. Who was it? When Spooner suggests, 'It was I drowning in your dream,' Hirst falls to the floor. Briggs' and Foster's contemptuous reaction to Hirst's incapacity shows that they, servants though they may be in the house, are also his jailers. And when Spooner offers help, he is brutally rebuffed:

FOSTER: Listen my friend. This man in this chair, he's a creative man. He's an artist. We make life possible for him. We're in a position of trust. Don't try to drive a wedge into a happy household. You understand me? Don't try to make a nonsense out of family life.

Briggs and Foster thus regard themselves as parts of Hirst's family. And yet, when Hirst briefly regains consciousness and rudely orders Briggs to bring some sandwiches, Briggs obeys. Foster speaks of having to prepare breakfast for Hirst's financial adviser who is due to visit him the next morning. Briggs reappears without the sandwiches. There is no bread in the house; he blames Foster whom he apostrophises as the housekeeper, a 'neurotic poof' and 'unspeakable ponce.' Brutally he leads Hirst out of the room. Foster leaves, turning out the light, so that Spooner remains in total darkness.

Act Two opens on the following morning. Spooner is locked in the room. Briggs serves him a sumptuous champagne breakfast which had been prepared for the financial adviser who has failed to turn up. When asked by Spooner who the cook is in the house, Briggs confirms that he and Foster are the only servants: 'We share all burdens, Jack and myself.' He then tells a long story of how he met Foster when standing at a street corner and Foster, in a car, asked him the way to Bolsover Street, one of those in the West End of London that are part of a one-way system so complex that they cannot be entered at all, or, once entered, trap the victim forever.

When Spooner has had his breakfast, Hirst briskly enters the room. He now acts as though Spooner was one of his oldest friends:

> HIRST: Charles. How nice of you to drop in.
> *He shakes Spooner's hand.*
> Have they been looking after you all right? Denson, let's have some coffee.
> *Briggs leaves the room.*
> You are looking remarkably well. Haven't changed a bit. . . .

There follows a long passage of reminiscences about Hirst's and Spooner's time at Oxford and their amorous exploits before the war. Hirst, it appears, had a love affair with Spooner's wife, Emily. Spooner retorts by revealing a number of occasions on which he deceived Hirst. When Spooner also questions Hirst's literary abilities ('. . . terza rima, a form which, if you will forgive my saying so, you have never been able to master'), Hirst is outraged:

> HIRST: You are clearly a lout. The Charles Wetherby I knew was a gentleman. I see a figure reduced. I am sorry for you. Where is the moral ardour that sustained you once? Gone down the hatch.

And as he begins to pour whisky down his throat, Hirst begins again to reminisce about the faces in his photograph album. Briggs brutally interrupts Hirst's musings and it becomes increasingly clear that Hirst is a prisoner in his own house. Foster appears and orders Hirst to go on his morning walk. Hirst feebly refuses. Spooner sees an opening for himself here. He offers to help Hirst with his literary work: 'Let me live with you and be your secretary.' But Hirst does not want to hear him:

HIRST: Is there a big fly in here? I hear buzzing.

Spooner launches into a long and desperate plea, listing his qualifications as a companion and cook and tops this with the offer to arrange a poetry reading for Hirst at the Bull in Chalk Farm where he will be heard by a crowd of eager young poetry lovers.

When he has finished, Hirst merely says: 'Let us change the subject.' At this point Briggs and Foster finally impose their will on Hirst. In a strange poetic passage, with the lines about the subject having been changed for the last time, and that it is now winter and that this winter will last forever repeated in a kind of incantation, as in a religious ritual, Hirst is entombed in the no man's land between life and death. Once more Hirst recalls the dream about someone who has drowned: 'I say to myself, I saw a body drowning. But I am mistaken. There is nothing there.' And Spooner, who has been silent throughout the whole ritual passage, agrees:

SPOONER: No. You are in no man's land. Which never moves, which never changes, which never grows older, but which remains forever, icy and silent.
Silence
HIRST: I'll drink to that.
He drinks.

And the lights slowly fade.

So much for the skeleton of the play's action. Superficially it echoes some of Pinter's basic situations. Like Davies, at the end of *The Caretaker*, Spooner's hopes of gaining a foothold in a new home are defeated; as in *Old Times* a duel of wits is conducted in terms of one spurious reminiscence topping another; Briggs and Foster are a pair of brutal thugs in the line of Ben and Gus of *The Dumb Waiter*, Goldberg and McCann of *The Birthday Party*, or, indeed, Lenny and Joey in *The Homecoming*. But, if they are more closely examined, these constellations of plot and character are seen to be serving a wholly different purpose in *No Man's Land*.

Taken at the most basic – and realistic – level, *No Man's Land* deals with a social situation, that of a successful and rich aging literary figure who lives with his servants and, being dependent on them, gradually becomes their slave. Pinter's film script of Robin Maugham's novel *The Servant* dealt with a situation of this kind, although the rich man in that case was younger. Such a situation is aggravated if the 'master' is a homosexual dependent on his servants not only for domestic but also erotic ministrations. There are suggestions that Foster was procured for Hirst by Briggs. 'I was in Bali when they sent for me. I didn't want to leave, I didn't have to come here. . . . I was only a boy. But I was nondescript and anonymous. A famous writer wanted me. He wanted me to be his secretary, his chauffeur, his housekeeper, his amanuensis. How did he know of me?. . . .' To which Briggs adds: 'You came on my recommendation. I've always liked youth because you can use it. . . . I recommended you.' Briggs' long speech which describes how Foster asked him the way into the one-way system of Bolsover Street, from which, once you have entered it, there is no escape, has its bearing on this aspect of the plot. Hirst, Briggs and Foster have become, as they clearly state, *a family*; inside that family there may be tension, even hatred and brutality, but it is a family nevertheless. A family – or a team. The names of all four characters are, incidentally, those of famous international cricket players. Pinter himself has confirmed this fact. There is thus the tension of a cricket match in the play; and cricket is a game of subtle positioning and indirect approaches, and a sport depending on immense staying power and team spirit. Hirst, Foster and Briggs are stonewalling against a powerful and subtle attacker.

It has been suggested that some elements of the play's situation might have been derived from Pinter's work in adapting another book, L. P. Hartley's *The Go-Between*, for the screen. In that novel, the narrator, an old man who has never married, describes a summer he spent with the family of a rich schoolfriend in the country – a summer of teas on the lawn and games of tennis and cricket – and how his discovery of the friend's sister making love to a lower-class farmer led to the lovers' tragedy and the boy's lifelong aversion to sex. The *motif* of a past – probably spurious – of teas on the lawn, country houses, and virgin garlands in the village church, enshrined in Hirst's photograph album as a picture of pristine innocence, and yet utterly false, riddled with sexual perversion and mutual deceit, thus may well have been inspired by Pinter's work on *The Go-Between*.

The past of country houses, wives and daughters, and tea in the afternoon in *No Man's Land* is clearly an attempt by Hirst to construct an image of an alternative life-style (whether he ever enjoyed it in reality or not – and he probably did) and by Spooner to find a common ground with the man to whose friendship he aspires. It is when, in the duel of reminiscences, Spooner is carried away into asserting his superiority over Hirst, that Hirst realises that Spooner, if taken into the household, would be as domineering as Briggs and Foster; and that is why he rejects him.

Hirst, as he says in the first scene, is in the last lap of a race he had long forgotten to run. His impulse to ask Spooner to come to his house is a last attempt at breaking out from the domestic situation he and his servants have created. In that last race he loses. Henceforth he will, forever, be in no man's land, the frozen region between life and death.

And here, I feel, is the real subject of the play: it projects and explores fear of old age. Hirst's situation is that of an old successful writer whose marriage has failed, or who has never been married, and who is condemned to a lonely old age, the prisoner of his domestic servants, with drink his only solace. Spooner also has grown old, his marriage having failed, or never taken place, but he is unsuccessful and poor. He is a free man longing for the bondage of a home; Hirst is fettered to his domestic situation, trying to break out into freedom but unable to muster the courage to break his bonds.

Throughout a man's life there remains at least the possibility of choice while some of youth's flexibility is preserved. But there comes a point, the onset of old age, when that possibility reaches zero. Then life congeals into the immutable winter of the no man's land between life and death.

The last scene, on the mundane level of realism, establishes the fact that the servants are telling their master that they have now achieved dominance, that he will never be able to break out again; on the more remote level of a poetic image that scene is a ritual of Hirst's entombment. But when Spooner, finally, repeats the ritual formula, he acknowledges that for him, as well, the last chance has passed. If Hirst will henceforth be imprisoned inside his home, Spooner will forever be condemned to homelessness.

Hirst was dreaming about a drowned man whom perhaps he might have rescued. Spooner felt that he might have been that drowned man. But in the end he too acknowledges that there was no one there.

Betrayal

Betrayal, Pinter's seventh full-length play, which opened at the National Theatre on 15th November 1978, represents a major stylistic change, even something like a new beginning in Pinter's development as a playwright. Hardly anything of the characteristic *Pinteresque* dialogue is left in the nine sparse scenes that constitute the action. Nor, on the surface at least, is there anything left of the comedy of menace, the allegorical overtones, the gaps in the characters' previous backgrounds and areas of deliberately unexplained motivation, the twilight zones between realism and dream which still gave the particularly Pinteresque flavour even to later plays like *Landscape, Old Times* or *No Man's Land. Betrayal* is the very realistically told story of a fairly trivial case of adultery among the London literary establishment: Jerry, a literary agent, has had an affair with the wife of his best friend Robert, who is a publisher. The affair started in 1968 and ended in 1975. We know the characters' backgrounds: Jerry and Robert were both born in 1937; Jerry went to Cambridge, Robert to Oxford, but they met in the course of student activities connected with literature. And when Robert married Emma in 1962, Jerry, his closest friend, was the best man at the wedding. Jerry, in turn, is married to Judith, a doctor who works in a hospital. Each couple has two children.

However, this trivial tale of adultery receives its special Pinter touch by being told backwards. The nine scenes start at the point when Emma's marriage finally breaks up – in 1977, two years *after* the end of her affair with Jerry – and finish at the point in the winter of 1968 when the affair began. Thus, thematically, *Betrayal* continues and develops Pinter's preoccupation with the operation of memory: the way in which the passage of time changes our perception of what the past was like and what we were like – *who* we were – in that past.

The unrolling of the story in reverse chronological order establishes a very characteristic dialectic from scene to scene; the audience perceives past events as they appear at a given moment in what is, as we watch it, the present for the characters on stage, only to be jolted into realizing a little later, what *actually* took place when those events occurred. And what is more: we also watch the way in which, over a period of time, the perception of those very past events undergoes various transformations in the minds of the people who lived through them.

The affair between Emma and Jerry, for example, which we first encounter as the typical stale dead husk of a burnt-out relationship in the spring of 1977 turns into a torrid, consuming passion when observed in its heyday, six years earlier, in the summer of 1971; but, when we witness the actual beginning of its consummation we see it arising out of a momentary drunken exuberance on Jerry's part to which Emma reluctantly yields partly out of pique at seeing her husband's indifference to having accidentally discovered the couple kissing in a bedroom during a party:

EMMA: Your best friend is drunk.
JERRY: As you are my best and oldest friend and, in the present instance, my host, I decided to take this opportunity to tell your wife how beautiful she was.
ROBERT: Quite right.
JERRY: It is quite right, to . . . to face up to the facts . . . and to offer a token, without blush, a token of one's unalloyed appreciation, no holds barred.
ROBERT: Absolutely.
JERRY: And how wonderful for you that this is so, that this is the case, that her beauty is the case.
ROBERT: Quite right.

JERRY *moves to* ROBERT *and takes hold of his elbow.*

JERRY: I speak as your oldest friend. Your best man.
ROBERT: You are actually.

He clasps JERRY's *shoulder, briefly, turns, leaves the room.* EMMA *moves towards the door.* JERRY *grasps her arm. She stops still.*
They stand still, looking at each other.

This is the end of the play, and the beginning of the affair; and its implication is clear enough: Emma has yielded to Jerry because she resents Robert's physical intimacy with Jerry, because she is jealous of Jerry's relationship with her husband. She decides to betray Robert because she feels betrayed by him in his indifference to what he has seen taking place, his acceptance of Jerry's claim to intimacy with her as her husband's best friend. In the very last moments of the play we are shown that the complex web of betrayals that is its subject matter started with what, to Emma, must have appeared as her husband's betrayal of herself.

190

This is the subtle and brilliantly differentiated subject matter that underlies what on the surface seems a straightforward and conventional marital triangle play. Pinter presents us with a symphonic structure of variations on the theme of betrayal that, ultimately, becomes an inquiry into the inextricable web of lies that constitutes the social relationships of the members of that segment of society to which the characters of the play – and most of the audience, and Pinter himself – belong.

In the opening scene, in a pub in 1977, Emma has asked her ex-lover to come and talk to her. Her marriage is finished, after fifteen years:

> EMMA: You know what I found out . . . last night? He's betrayed me for years. He's had . . . other women for years.
> JERRY: No? Good Lord.
>
> *Pause*
>
> But we betrayed him for years.
> EMMA: And he betrayed me for years.

But what interests Jerry more than anything else at this moment is another aspect of betrayal. Has Emma, in the course of this final confrontation, betrayed him to Robert?

> JERRY: You told him everything?
> EMMA: I had to.
> JERRY: You told him everything . . . about us?
> EMMA: I had to.
>
> *Pause*
>
> JERRY: But he's my oldest friend . . .

In the second scene – we are still in 1977, a few hours later than in scene one – Jerry has phoned Robert and asked him, urgently, for an interview. Robert has come to Jerry's flat. Jerry is deeply upset. He cannot bear the thought that Robert now knows of his affair with Emma. But what Emma has just told Jerry was a lie.

ROBERT: . . . She didn't tell me about you and her last night. She told me about you and her four years ago.

Pause

So she didn't have to tell me again last night. Because I knew. And she knew I knew because she told me herself four years ago.

And now Jerry realizes that *Robert* has betrayed *him* by not letting him know that he has so long been aware of Jerry's relationship to Emma. This amounts to Robert *and* Emma jointly betraying Jerry by leaving him in a fool's paradise, thinking that he is betraying Robert and basking in the – as it now turns out – spurious feeling of superiority that comes from knowing something important that another person does not. What Pinter is drawing attention to is precisely this element in betrayal, adultery, that makes it so attractive: the feeling of power, of superiority, it gives to the one who knows what is happening over the victim who is totally oblivious of it. A complacent husband who allows his wife to continue an adulterous relationship *after* he has found out about it, and does not confront the other man, turns the tables on him.

It is in the light of this knowledge we have gained in scene two that the ironies of scene three unfold. We are in the flat in Kilburn where Jerry and Emma have been meeting for their love-trysts in the afternoons since the early days of their affair. It is now the winter of 1975. The affair is ending. Emma is running an art gallery; it seems it is becoming more and more difficult for the lovers to find afternoons on which they are both free. The flat is being given up. What Jerry does not realize, but what the audience now knows, of course, is: that it is Emma's awareness that her husband knows about the affair and about the flat which has spoiled the relationship for her.

In the following scene, more than a year earlier, autumn 1974, we are shown the ironies of the situation in Robert's and Emma's house. Jerry has come for a drink, there is a lot of small talk between him and Robert. After Robert accompanies Jerry to the door,

> ROBERT *returns. He kisses her. She responds. She breaks away, puts her head on his shoulder, cries quietly. He holds her.*

The centrepiece of the play's action, the hub around which it turns, is formed by the three scenes – five, six and seven, all set in 1973 – that deal with the discovery of Emma's adultery by Robert and its immediate aftermath.

While on holiday in Venice with Emma, Robert is handed a letter for Emma from Jerry at the American Express Office, which she had given as a convenient – and, she thought, secret – accommodation address. Confronted with the letter in their hotel room, she confesses. Robert's reaction to her betrayal shows that he feels rather more betrayed by Jerry, his best friend:

> ROBERT: I've always liked Jerry. To be honest, I've always liked him rather more than I've liked you. Maybe I should have had an affair with him myself.
>
> *Silence*

The second scene of this 1973 triptych relates Jerry's and Emma's first encounter in their Kilburn love-nest after her return from Venice, and shows how she betrays Jerry by not telling him what had happened there. On the other hand Jerry tells her of his panic when he remembered that he had left one of Emma's love letters from Venice in his clothes where his wife, Judith, might well have found it. But she hadn't found it. All that Emma can say to that is: 'God.' This is the moment when, logically, she should tell the parallel story about the letter that was discovered by *her* betrayed spouse. With the hindsight that we, the audience, now possess, we can recognize the decisive turning point in the story of which the two characters to whom it is happening have to remain totally unaware.

The third 1973 scene is set a few days later in an Italian

restaurant with a picture of Venice on the wall, where Robert and Jerry are having one of their business lunches. Robert's emotions and excitement emerge merely in his getting somewhat drunk. The conventional small talk over lunch is given its subtext by the audience's knowledge that Robert knows but gives no inkling of it. The scene ends with Jerry's enquiry:

JERRY: How's Emma?
ROBERT: Very well. You must come and have a drink sometime. She'd love to see you.

In ironic contrast scene eight – in the lovers' flat, summer 1971 – shows them at the height of their involvement and passionate attachment. And here hindsight makes us recognize another turning point. After having told Jerry that she saw his wife having lunch with a lady at Fortnum and Mason's and hearing from Jerry that Judith has an admirer, a fellow doctor who takes her for drinks, Emma asks:

EMMA: Tell me . . . have you ever thought . . . of changing your life?
JERRY: Changing?
EMMA: Mmnn.

Pause

JERRY: It's impossible.

Pause

Having thus established that Jerry has no intention of leaving his wife and children – although he assures her that he has never been unfaithful to her since their affair started – Emma has another piece of news for Jerry (which, in some ways, amounts to another kind of betrayal):

EMMA: Listen. There's something I have to tell you.
JERRY: What?

EMMA: I'm pregnant. It was when you were in America.

Pause

It wasn't anyone else. It was my husband.

Pause

JERRY: Yes. Yes, of course.

Pause

I'm very happy for you.

It is from this scene, which shows the passionate affair at its height – and the worm in the bud – that we are transported to 1968 and the casual opening of the matter.

Betrayal thus centres on the complex web of betrayals and lies in the relationship of three people who are passionately attached to each other. It is a theme that runs through Pinter's *œuvre* from its very beginning: it dominates the early novel *The Dwarfs* and the play derived from it, and becomes fully articulated in *Old Times*; the suspicions of a lesbian relationship between the two women in that play are here echoed in the strong overtones of a subconscious homosexual attachment between Robert and Jerry. It is significant that Jerry stopped playing squash with Robert when the affair with Emma had got under way. Robert repeatedly asks Jerry why he has not been available for a game. That squash has a sexual connotation for Robert and Jerry (as cricket had for Hirst and Spooner in *No Man's Land*) is made clear from one of the very few longer speeches in the play – when, in scene four, Emma inquires whether she could not come to one of the after-squash lunches that had been a ritual with the two men in the past:

ROBERT: Well, to be brutally honest, we wouldn't actually want a woman around, would we, Jerry? I mean a game of squash isn't simply a game of squash, it's rather more than that. You see, first there is the game. And then there's the shower. And then there's the pint. And then there's the lunch. After all, you've been at it. You've had your battle. What you

195

want is your pint and your lunch. You really don't want a woman buying you lunch. You really don't actually want a woman within a mile of the place, any of the places, really. You don't want her in the squash court, you don't want her in the shower, or the pub, or the restaurant . . .

Note the phrase that Robert uses for the powerful orgasmic activity of 'the battle': 'you've *been at it*', an idiom that as often as not means sexual intercourse. (When Lenny, in *The Homecoming*, asks his father what he felt at the moment when he, the son, was conceived, he uses this phrase about the children who 'ruminate . . . about the true facts of that particular night – the night they were made in the image of those two people *at it*'.) Jerry's betrayal of Robert thus manifests itself in his ceasing to play squash with him, Robert's longing for Jerry appears in his repeated requests for a resumption of their squash games.

Yet the three central characters whom we see on stage in the play are not the only betrayers, not the only victims of betrayal in the play: Casey, the writer whom Jerry has discovered and whom Robert is publishing so successfully hovers, unseen, in the background of the relationship between Emma and Jerry. There are suggestions that Emma may be having an affair with Casey even during the time when she is involved with Jerry. And when, in the first scene, after their own affair has been over for two years, Jerry asks Emma about Casey, she clearly indicates that he is more to her than a casual acquaintance:

JERRY: Does Casey know about this?
EMMA: I wish you wouldn't keep calling him Casey. His name is Roger.

And there is Jerry's wife, Judith, whom Jerry is betraying with Emma; whom Emma has been observing at Fortnum's with a mysterious lady about whom Jerry knew nothing (so there might be even a hint of a lesbian relationship) and who has been telling Jerry about that fellow-doctor who admires her and who takes her out for what she assures Jerry (but how convincingly?) are purely platonic drinks. And, of course, there are 'the women' with whom Robert has been betraying Emma 'for years'.

The whole society here depicted – literary and artistic London – is thus shown as an inextricable network of adulteries and betrayals. And what is more: these sexual adventures seem to constitute the main preoccupation – almost to the exclusion of any other – of the people who make up that supposedly intellectual world. Yet at the same time, these sexual relationships are shown, by Pinter, to be superficial in the extreme; far from being passionate involvements, elemental and irresistible, they seem casual and trivial, hardly more involving than the occasional drunken binge, a form of amusement that will pass the time and alleviate the boredom of an affluent and meaningless existence.

It is this aridity of the protagonists, their lack of intellectual interest or passion, their failure to talk about anything but trivial everyday topics that constitutes a powerful element of satire in the play. Although Pinter, as the author, merely presents a clinical picture of his characters, without any comment, explicit or implicit, what emerges is a sardonically bitter portrait of the world of literary commerce and of ladies managing art galleries: they have no deep commitment to what they are doing. As Robert confesses when slightly drunk in the Italian restaurant in scene seven:

> . . . I hate books. Or to be more precise, prose. Or to be even more precise, modern prose, I mean modern novels, first novels and second novels, all that promise and sensibility it falls upon me to judge, to put the firm's money on, and then to push for the third novel, see it done, see the dust jacket done, see the dinner for the national literary editors done, see the signing at Hatchards done, see the lucky author cook himself to death, all in the name of literature.

Jerry, as a literary agent, is even more openly merely a parasite on the novelists, like Casey or Spinks, whom he peddles to publishers. And Emma never makes any reference to the art she deals with in her gallery. Deeley, the television director in *Old Times*, Spooner, the vagabond would-be-poet in *No Man's Land*, are still seen as deeply involved with an activity that means life to them; but there is no such attachment to art, or even the exercise of a profession as a life-fulfilling activity in *Betrayal*. It is as though the atmosphere of lies and deceit that pervades these lives had eroded all deeper concerns.

Structually, *Betrayal* is an intricate pattern of flash-backs and scenes that move forward in time: 1977 – scenes 1 and 2; 1975 – scene 3; 1974 – scene 4; 1973 – scenes 5, 6 and 7; 1971 – scene 8; 1968 – scene 9. The forward-moving sequence of three scenes – 1973 – is thus structurally as well as thematically the centre of the action. As the movement of the play in time is essential to its functioning, and as there is no exposition in the dialogue to indicate the year in which each scene takes place, the information would have to be signalled to the audience in some way or other outside the confines of the scene itself: thus, Pinter is making use of what must be regarded as an essentially Brechtian device by having the year displayed above each scene's setting.

The language of *Betrayal* is sparse in the extreme. There is no rhetoric in it, none of the long speeches through which Pinter's characters in earlier plays expressed themselves obliquely, but with virtuoso eloquence. There are no arias here, no self-consciously poetic passages. All the more powerful become the few recurring linguistic *leitmotifs* that Pinter now uses with masterly economy. One of these, which seems to stand as a symbol or image of the relationship between Jerry and Emma is the memory of when Jerry caught hold of Emma's daughter Charlotte and 'threw' her up and caught her':

JERRY: She was very light.
EMMA: She remembers that, you know.
JERRY: Really.
EMMA: Mmnn. Being thrown up.

198

The phrase 'throwing up' has a deep ambiguity: for 'throwing up' can also mean 'vomiting' and thus has an implication of disgust. And when Jerry and Emma are having this exchange, in scene one, their affair is over, Jerry has 'thrown her over' – so there is this echo also in the phrase. And significantly, the memory of that happy moment is a fallible one:

> JERRY: When I threw her up. It was in your kitchen.
> EMMA: It was in your kitchen.

In scene six, the central scene of the central triptych of the play's structure, that same memory is evoked in a happier context – although it is in that very scene that Emma conceals from Jerry the fact that she has confessed to her husband.

> JERRY: She was so light. And there was your husband and my wife and all the kids, all standing and laughing in your kitchen. I can't get rid of it.
> EMMA: It was your kitchen, actually.
>
> *He takes her hand. They stand. They go to the bed and lie down.*
>
> Why shouldn't you throw her up?
>
> *She caresses him. They embrace.*

By putting the evocation of the 'throwing up' of Charlotte and the conflicting memory about whose kitchen it happened in at the end of that climactic scene, Pinter underlines the symbolic significance of the incident – and of the phrase that embodies its ambivalent emotional colour. At the same time the repeated indication of a conflict of memories stresses the link between this play and Pinter's earlier work. The essential Pinter is very much present in *Betrayal*, but it is an essence that has been pared down and refined, purged of all exuberance and redundancy: mature and distilled Pinter.

Family Voices

Family Voices, a radio play written in 1980 and first broadcast by BBC Radio 3 on 22nd January 1981, is quintessential Pinter. It contains echoes of his very first play *The Room* – the leading character lives away from his family and is torn by longings for them as well as being clearly fleeing from them, and one of the characters is actually called Riley; echoes also of *The Birthday Party* – the hero is a young man mothered by his landlady, with his family looking for him and being turned away at the door; echoes of *The Caretaker* in the form of a highly ambivalent father figure – 'On his deathbed your father cursed you. He cursed me [the mother] too, to tell the truth. He cursed everyone in sight'; echoes also of *The Homecoming* in a mother-figure seen split into an old woman (Mrs Withers) and a young attractive one (Lady Withers) and with a further incarnation as an aggressively sexual schoolgirl (Jane Withers).

There are three voices in the play: a young man (at one point the mother speaks about his not yet being twenty-one) who has left home somewhere at the seaside (his mother reminisces about walks on the cliffs) for the big city. At first the exchange between this young man and his mother (the second voice) takes the form of letters that are probably never written and only exist in the mind of the speakers and certainly never reach their destination. The third voice, which twice makes an appearance towards the end of the play, is that of the father who explicitly states that he is speaking from his grave. It can thus be safely assumed that the entire exchange between these three voices takes place in the mind of the principal character – the young man – who is imagining the letters he would want to write to his mother as well as the letters his mother would probably write to him, and the voice of his father – whom he presumes dead but who may well still be alive. As the play progresses the letter convention is gradually dropped as the two – non-communicating – voices of mother and son are more and more rapidly cross-cut.

The young man in whose mind the play takes place is very similar to Stanley in *The Birthday Party* also in that he is struggling to find himself as an integrated personality. In his very first 'letter' he confesses:

At the moment I am dead drunk.
I had five pints in The Fishmongers Arms tonight, followed by three double scotches, and literally rolled home.

Only to withdraw that confession a few sentences later:

When I said I was drunk I was of course making a joke.
I bet you laughed.
Mother?
Did you get the joke? You know I never touch alcohol.

Only, a few further sentences on, to proclaim:

I get on very well with my landlady, Mrs Withers. She tells me I am her solace. I have a drink with her at lunchtime and another one at teatime and then take her for a couple in the evening at The Fishmongers Arms.

The house in which the young man lives, like the one that Rose inhabits in *The Room*, seems mysteriously expandable. Apart from Mrs Withers, who is in her seventies and cuddles the hero and tells him, 'You are my little pet', and Lady Withers and the schoolgirl Jane, there is an old man in the house, called Benjamin Withers, who, while clearly mad, intimidates the hero with a cataract of language akin to that with which Mick in *The Caretaker* overwhelms Davies:

You know where you are? he said. You're in my room. It's not Euston station. Get me? It's a true oasis.
This is the only room in this house where you can pick up a caravenserai to all points West. Compris? Comprende? Get me?
Are you prepared to follow me down the mountain? Look at me. My name's Withers. I'm there or thereabouts. Follow?
Embargo on all duff terminology. With me? Embargo on all

things redundant. All areas in that connection verboten. You're in a diseaseridden land, boxer. Keep your weight on all the left feet you can lay your hands on. Keep dancing. The old foxtrot is the classical response but that's not the response I'm talking about. Nor am I talking of the other response. Up the slaves. Get me? This is a place of creatures, up and down stairs. Creatures of the rhythmic splits, the rhythmic sideswipes, the rums and roulettes, the macaroni tatters, the dumplings in jam mayonnaise, a catapulting ordure of gross and ramshackle shenanigans, open-ended paraphernalia. Follow me? . . .

The other male inhabitant of the house is Riley, who speaks of himself as a policeman and takes a homosexually-tinged interest in the young man's body when he intrudes on him as he is lying in his bath to tell him that he has just sent away the hero's mother and sister, who were inquiring about him:

> He denied knowledge of me. No he had not heard of me. No, there was no-one of that name resident . . . I suggest, he said, that you both go back to where you come from, and stop bothering innocent, hardworking people with your slanders and your libels . . . so piss off out of it before I call a copper.

The affinity of these two male characters (Withers and Riley) to Goldberg and McCann of *The Birthday Party* and their verbal terrorism is also very striking.

Lady Withers has asked the hero to tea in a luxurious sitting room, much larger than one would have expected in what, at first, seemed a small suburban house with just one bathroom for all its inhabitants. During tea the schoolgirl Jane sits with her feet in the hero's lap, with her toes moving almost hysterically, so that the bun he is eating 'turned to solid rock'. But when the hero offers to 'help Jane with her homework' he is turned down by Lady Withers.

Everybody in the house is related, not only all the people called Withers, but Riley as well. He too is a relation of a sort.

What relation?
Is Lady Withers Jane's mother or sister?

If either is the case why isn't Jane called Lady Jane Withers? Or perhaps she is. Or perhaps neither is the case? Or perhaps Mrs Withers is actually the Honourable Mrs Withers? But if that is the case what does that make Mr Withers? And which Withers is he anyway? I mean what relation is he to the rest of the Witherses? And Who is Riley?

This exile into a large family with an intricate web of aristocratic connections at times greatly pleases the hero:

Oh mother, I have found my home, my family. Little did I ever dream I could know such happiness.

But towards the end of the play when the, perhaps dead, father's voice has resounded through his mind, the young man is overcome by nostalgia for his lost family and home:

I'm coming back to you, mother, to hold you in my arms.
I am coming home.
I am coming also to clasp my father's shoulder. . . .
I am on my way back to you. I am about to make the journey back to you. What will you say to me?

Yet the play concludes with the father's voice saying:

I have so much to say to you. But I am quite dead. What I have to say to you will never be said.

If, in *The Homecoming*, the dead mother returned to the sons that had longed for her, in *Family Voices* the son's homecoming, it seems, will never take place.

A Kind of Alaska

The quintessentially 'Pinteresque' *Family Voices*, which offered so strong a contrast to the 'realism' of *Betrayal* (where a philosophical and metaphysical dimension, an exploration of the nature of reality, memory and time, is evoked merely by the chronological re-arrangement of perfectly realistic scenes), in turn stands in stark contrast to the total realism of *A Kind of Alaska* (1982), a one-act play in which, again, very profound insights on the nature of time and the self are conveyed without recourse to extravagant language or areas of uncertainty.

A note on the title page of *A Kind of Alaska* – 'this play was inspired by Oliver Sacks' book *Awakenings*' – acknowledges Pinter's debt to one of the most remarkable medical books of the nineteen-seventies. First published in 1974, *Awakenings*, dedicated to W. H. Auden, is by a physician who, while working at the Mount Carmel hospital in New York, witnessed the awakening from some forty years of catatonic lethargia of a large number of patients who had been victims of a mysterious epidemic of 'sleeping sickness' (Encephalitis lethargica) that had swept Europe and the United States in the nineteen-twenties. Patients afflicted by this type of the disease had been virtually cut off from the world of consciousness until the discovery of the 'wonder-drug' L-DOPA suddenly opened up a chance of a return to a fully conscious and active existence. Oliver Sacks' book contains twenty detailed case histories of such patients, some of whom succeeded in regaining their full consciousness, while others failed. The book opens up fascinating insights into the nature of human personality, disease and physical and mental health.

A Kind of Alaska is an imaginative recreation of such a case of awakening, wholly fictional and transferred from America to England, but based on a deeply understanding reading of Sacks' book. Deborah who fell into a catatonic state when she was sixteen years old is now in her mid-forties. She is waking up in what appears to be a room in a hospital. Hornby, a man in his sixties, the doctor who has been caring for her, sits by her.

The play describes Deborah's gradual and painful realization that she has lost almost thirty years of her life. At the beginning she has the reactions and personality of a teenage girl in the nineteen-thirties; when her sister Pauline enters the room she does not recognize her and takes her for some old aunt she never met. She learns that her mother is dead, her father blind and being cared for by the third, elder, sister Estelle, that Hornby, the doctor by her bedside, had married the younger sister, Pauline, but has devoted most of his attention to Deborah:

> Your sister Pauline was twelve when you were left for dead. When she was twenty we married. She is a widow. I have lived with you.

And gradually she begins to feel the weight of those twenty-nine lost years descending upon her. She begins to remember what she felt like in the years of catatonic lethargia:

> . . . It's a vast series of halls. With enormous interior windows masquerading as walls. The windows are mirrors, you see. And so glass reflects glass. For ever and ever.
>
> *Pause*
>
> You can't imagine how still it is. So silent I heard my eyes move.
>
> *Silence*
>
> I'm lying in bed. People bend over me, speak to me. I want to say hullo, to have a chat, to make some inquiries. But you can't do that if you're in a vast hall of glass with a tap dripping.

The play ends with Deborah finally accepting her new reality:

> I think I have the matter in proportion.
>
> *Pause*
>
> Thank you.

Here Pinter's choice of subject has enabled him to produce a play with powerful intimations of the themes that haunt him – time, the self, memory and the nature of reality – without having to resort even to the manipulation of chron-

205

ological sequence which enabled him in *Betrayal* to combine outward realism with philosophical depth. The language of *A Kind of Alaska* subtly captures the girlish tones of the teenager's frozen self and its gradual transition to a resigned maturity without any of the more extravagant linguistic devices of earlier Pinter or even *Family Voices*.

Victoria Station

This short play, first performed together with *A Kind of Alaska* and *Family Voices* in a triple bill at the Cottesloe Theatre in October 1982, consists of a dialogue between a controller of taxis, whose office lights up one side of the stage, with one of the drivers, number 274, who is seen in his car at the other side of the stage. But as the play is confined to an exchange of radio messages and has very little visual or physical action it would work just as well in radio. In many ways this short play is related to Pinter's earlier cabaret and revue sketches and to the surrealistic world of *The Hothouse*.

The controller wants driver 274 to go to Victoria Station to pick up a little man coming from Boulogne on the 10.22 train and to take him to Cuckfield. The little man's name is MacRooney, he has a limp and can be recognized by the feather in his hat and by the fishing tackle he carries. But the driver declines on the grounds that he does not know Victoria Station. When asked where he is now the driver reports that he is near a dark park (which later turns out to be near the Crystal Palace) and that he has a passenger in his car, who, it later transpires is a beautiful woman with whom the driver has fallen in love and whom he therefore never wants to leave again. The controller moves from moods of anger and frustration about his inability to induce the driver to go to Victoria Station to eventual envy of the driver's happy disregard for routine. He finally decides to come and join the driver and his love at the Crystal Palace:

. . . I'm going to pop down to see you, to shake you by the hand.
All right?
DRIVER: Fine. But what about this man coming off the train at
Victoria Station – the 10.22 from Boulogne?
CONTROLLER: He can go and fuck himself.

The play ends with the driver promising to wait for the
controller's arrival.

Victoria Station is vintage Pinter, reminiscent of *The
Dumb Waiter* and *The Hothouse*. It is as though Pinter, after
the stylistic departure of *Betrayal*, was experimenting with
two different styles and approaches, searching for a new
synthesis between the grotesquely surrealistic on the one
hand and a metaphysical realism on the other.

One For The Road

This short play which opened at the Studio of the Lyric
Theatre, Hammersmith in West London in the spring of
1984 was generally considered to mark a new departure in
Pinter's *œuvre* – an openly *political* play, almost a political
pamphlet. And yet, these four short scenes between an
interrogator and his victims are clearly a direct continuation
of Pinter's preoccupation with 'man manipulating man' that
extends from *The Room* and *The Dumb Waiter* via *The
Caretaker* and *The Homecoming* to the sinister pair of
servants in *No Man's Land*. The difference merely lies in the
fact that here we are clearly in a totalitarian country, ruled
by a ruthless dictator who is brutally suppressing all dissi-
dence among intellectuals. There were many such dictators
in the news in the mid nineteen-eighties, and many reports
of leading intellectuals being persecuted. Pinter and his wife
had organised a PEN protest event against the imprisonment
of writers in 1982.

The interrogator, Nicolas – played in the first performance, and the subsequent television broadcast, by Alan Bates
– is himself a kind of intellectual using refined language in

an ironic mode of self-deprecatory affection which, however, at times slips into scatological coarseness. He is shown confronting the imprisoned intellectual Victor – whose house has been ransacked, his books rifled, his carpets pissed on – and mercilessly baiting him with reference to the beauty of his wife who is upstairs and obviously exposed to being raped by the brutal secret policemen there, and to his seven-year-old son, who is also under arrest.

In the second scene this little boy is interrogated by Victor about his love for his parents, and his hostile behaviour towards the soldiers who arrested them. Next we see the confrontation between the interrogator, Nicolas, and Victor's wife Gila; she is, as Nicolas implies, the daughter of a highly revered national hero, and has been repeatedly raped. Again the spectre of the possible fate of the little boy is raised and the scene ends with the suggestion that 'she might entertain us all a little more before you go'. In the final scene Victor himself, now terribly bruised after torture, is told that he can leave. But when he asks about the fate of his son, the reply 'Oh, don't worry about him. He was a little prick' clearly indicates that the child has been killed. This succession of unrelieved horrors gives no indication as to the country that is meant to be depicted, and thus conforms to Pinter's habitual refusal to provide chapter and verse in an exposition. The interrogator constantly refers to God, which might suggest a non-Communist country; yet these mentions of the Almighty might also merely be ironical mockery.

The most puzzling aspect of the play, however, is the fact that the interrogator clearly is not trying to elicit either information or a confession from his victim. While he is tormenting Victor with hints about the fate of his wife and son, he is not even using such threats to blackmail him into any of the meaningful objectives such secret-police interrogations might pursue in a concrete and real case. What is shown is unrelieved sadism, mental and physical torture for their own sake and finally the murder of an innocent child. There is no hint at anything Victor is accused of having done, no attempt to establish any concrete 'guilt' on his part. He and his family are simply tortured for what they are – intellectuals, people who are suspected of not liking the great dictator.

In that respect, in spite of the more 'realistic' setting of a recognizable political situation, the play is as mysterious as Stanley's torture in *The Birthday Party*. Whether the reference is to Ceausescu, the persecutors of Vaclav Havel in Prague, or the Chilean dictator Pinochet remains uncertain. Pinter carefully avoids being specific. What the play expresses is horror at the existence of such persecutions of intellectuals in general, wherever it may occur. As such it is an overwhelmingly powerful statement.

Mountain Language

Like *One for the Road*, *Mountain Language*, which Pinter himself directed at the National Theatre in October 1988, is an openly political tract, an anguished outcry against dictatorship and torture in a totalitarian society. It thus provided further evidence that Pinter had developed into an overt political crusader and activist in his work for the theatre as well as in his public persona as a signatory of Charter 88 and campaigner for other liberal causes.

There are still some 'Pinteresque' elements in *Mountain Language* – the speech patterns, repetition and inverted repetition of simple sentences – but beyond that the element of indeterminacy between a multiplicity of levels of possible interpretation and ultimate meaning, even the mysterious vagueness of *One for the Road*, is gone. The meaning here is clear, unidimensional and never in the slightest doubt: torture is obscene, the domination of human beings by other human beings is obscene, cruelty is obscene.

This point is being made with the utmost economy of means, in a succession of four terse scenes:

We are in a country in which the ruling regime has banned the use of the language of a minority, living in the mountains.

In the first scene we meet a group of women waiting outside a prison, wanting to be admitted to see their husbands and sons. An old woman has been savagely bitten in her hand by a guard dog; a younger woman who is not of the mountain people and might be English or American, protests about this.

In the second scene the elderly woman confronts her son in a visitor's room; she cannot speak the language of the capital, and is forbidden to speak to her son in her own language. The son protests, the guard calls the brutal sergeant to punish the prisoner.

In scene three the younger woman is confronted with the beaten and bruised body of her husband.

In the fourth scene we are back with the old woman and her son, who has now been brutally tortured. The guard informs the old woman that the regulations have now been changed, she will be permitted to speak her own language. Yet she has been so shocked and frightened that she cannot utter a word.

A novel feature for Pinter is the introduction of voice-overs of the thoughts of characters who do not speak. This is reminiscent of Brecht's introduction of the unspoken thoughts of characters in *The Caucasian Chalk Circle* or in some of the later plays of Beckett.

In its political explicitness this new phase of Pinter's *œuvre* is, in fact, getting nearer to Brecht than to Beckett – the short scenes are reminiscent of Brecht's sketches in *Fear and Misery of the Third Reich*. With further short works in this vein (the sketches *Precisely* and *The New World Order* and the play *Party Time* and others perhaps yet to come) Pinter might well assemble a major sequence that might add up to a full-length work of that kind – a kaleidoscopic sequence of scenes about the horrors and dangers of life in totalitarian or ostensibly democratic, but deep down essentially authoritarian, countries.

That *Mountain Language*, though set in an unspecified country, does in fact refer to Turkey, where for a long period the Kurdish language was brutally suppressed, is fairly clear, in view of the episode in which Pinter and Arthur Miller, as PEN delegates, interviewed Turkish dissident writers who told them of being tortured, and Pinter confronted the US Ambassador with strong criticism that his country should remain allied to such a regime. There is a technical problem in the play, which even the most skilful production will have difficulty in solving: how can the two distinct languages be effectively contrasted when the convention is that both are reproduced in English? Even Pinter's suggestion – in a stage direction at the beginning of scene 2 – that the 'prisoner and the woman should speak in a strong rural accent' cannot quite solve this problem. Nor does the intentional lack of specificity about the languages involved help: instead of what might be Turkish and Kurdish we have the 'language of the capital' and 'the mountain language' which is clumsy and incorrect, as other places in the country beside the capital clearly also speak that language, on the one hand, and the 'mountain language' on the other.

What this highlights is an underlying difficulty in writing political drama that cannot quite call a spade a spade or document its argumentation by being totally concrete and specific. In fact, the play only makes sense if the audience is actually aware that there really are countries where the native language of minority groups has been so brutally suppressed. And such knowledge cannot too readily be assumed in Britain or the United States.

Party Time

Although clearly another in Pinter's series of politically committed, not to say propagandist, plays, *Party Time*, which had its first professional production directed by Harold Pinter, in a double bill with *Mountain Language* at the Almeida Theatre in London on 31st October 1991, is also more directly linked to his earlier 'Pinteresque' use of language.

The play is set in an elegant drawing room: a cocktail

party is in progress, there is much small talk of the most trivial kind, yet there are repeated indications that something sinister is going on outside – a round-up of political opponents of a brutal totalitarian regime. As the play develops into a series of episodes picked out from the general party chatter, a number of pairs of characters reveal themselves: Gavin White, an elegant upper-class man of middle age, is the host of the occasion. His close friend is an elderly lady, Dame Melissa. Terry is a vulgar individual of forty married to Dusty, a young woman whose brother, Jimmy, has gone missing; she is brutally told off by her husband. Fred and Douglas, middle-aged men, are obviously big-shots in the regime. Liz, Douglas's wife, tells another young woman, Charlotte, of her infatuation with an unnamed man, not her husband. And Charlotte reveals in a conversation with Fred, the powerful man who once helped her to get a start in life, that her husband has died 'a short and quick' death, adding later: 'by the way he wasn't ill.'

At the climax of the party the host, Gavin White, makes a speech in which he regrets that some guests had not been able to come because 'they encountered traffic problems on their way here' and, in a somewhat ambiguous phrase, expresses his hope that after the end of the round-up 'normal services will be resumed shortly. . . . That's all we ask, that the service this country provides will run on normal, secure and legitimate paths and that the ordinary citizen be allowed to pursue his labours and his leisure in peace.' The lights go down, a hitherto unused door opens wide and reveals a burningly glaring white light. A young man appears in what seems prison dress. He is Jimmy, Dusty's missing brother, obviously now in detention. The play closes with his brief monologue about the dehumanizing effects of his imprisonment.

This short play – it runs for approximately forty minutes – does show the surface of life going on normally in the upper reaches of a totalitarian society, while people are detained, tortured and killed. Is it a South American dictatorship? Turkey? One of the East European countries before the overthrow of their communist regimes? Or is it meant to be a picture of Britain, destined to sink to that level if tendencies which the opponents of 'Thatcherism' thought they had detected continue indefinitely; yet the typescript of the play is dated March 1991, i.e. already after the downfall of Margaret Thatcher. Or is the suggestion that such conditions would be inevitable if Charter 88's demand for a 'Bill of Rights' is not implemented? Certainly the names of the characters, Gavin White, for example, or even the title 'Dame', with which Melissa is introduced, point towards a British background. This is somewhat confusing, as is the use of turns of clichéd small-talk idioms and idiosyncratic Pinteresque language, than which hardly anything could be more English. If the play was meant to be set in an English or British, milieu, it would be politically unconvincing. No such round-ups, disappearances or tortures and quick deaths are likely in this milieu and to suggest anything like it would amount to a case of paranoia. Are the British conditions and linguistic quirks thus meant to suggest another country? In that case the location is left too vague, and the English idioms and party manners become very much out of place.

Party Time thus remains an unhappy hybrid. On the other hand, the repetitious nonsense of the party small-talk is as amusing as ever, vintage 'Pinteresque' dialogue.

Moonlight

When *Moonlight* had its world premiere at the Almeida Theatre in London on 7th September 1993 it marked Harold Pinter's return from ten years of explicitly politically committed drama – *One for the Road*, *Mountain Language*, *Party Time* and the sketches 'Precisely' and 'The New World Order' – to the subtextual mode of his earlier creative period.

Party Time had prepared the transition: the dialogue of the partygoers, in which the horrors of a terrorist totalitarian regime were more or less clearly hinted at behind conventional cocktail banter, seemed to be relying on a subtextual technique until the point when the lights changed and one of the victims of the terror delivered a short, moving but painfully descriptive soliloquy about the sufferings of the political prisoner we had met in *One for the Road*, *Mountain Language* and 'The New World Order'.

Yet *Moonlight* was more than a return to the basically super-realistic mode of plays like *The Caretaker*, *The Homecoming*, *Betrayal* or *A Kind of Alaska*. It uses the dream-element that had briefly appeared in Pinter's earlier work, most clearly in *Silence* and perhaps, but only as one possible interpretation among others, in *Old Times*: two of the simultaneously visible acting areas in *Moonlight* are realistic, the third, above and behind them, is a dream area where Bridget, the protagonist's dead daughter, haunts his dreams and appears in flashbacks to earlier times.

It is this nostalgic dream-element which marks *Moonlight* as a new phase in Pinter's oeuvre: dying and the loss of children are its principal themes. And while the dialogue returns to all the brilliant comic absurdities of Pinter's uncanny rhythmic poetry of everyday speech, it presents a deeply tragic view of the human condition. Not only is Andy, a civil servant in his fifties, bedridden and supposedly on his 'deathbed', his two sons, Jake, aged twenty-eight, and Fred, twenty-seven, have left and refuse to communicate with him and their mother, Andy's wife Bel; his daughter Bridget seems no longer to be alive. In the list of characters she appears as 'a girl of sixteen' and in one of the flashbacks is described as two years younger than Jake, and thus seems to have been dead for ten years.

Andy, the civil servant, is far from civil in his use of language in which he is raging against the dying of the light. The two sons in their shabby quarters where they seem to be living on the state's social subsidies, on the other hand, spend their time in fantasy word games about their hypothetical inheritance from their father. Jake is said to have written poetry from his earliest youth, Fred seems more of a man of action. They are visited by an old friend of the family, Maria, an ex-mistress of their father and lesbian lover of their mother, and later by Maria's husband Ralph, who used to referee amateur soccer matches.

In a central flashback the three teenage children appear arguing whether Jake will take the two younger ones to a party in Amersham (an archetypical London suburban location). The following dialogue between Andy and Bel suggests that Andy either does not know, or want to know, that Bridget is dead. He demands to see his grandchildren, and Bel's evasive answers obviously want to shield him from the truth. Bel talks movingly about the little children's knowledge of death:

> Oh, the really little ones I think know about something about death, they know more about death than we do. We've forgotten death, but they haven't forgotten it. They remember it. Because some of them, those who are really very young, remember the moment before life began – it's not such a long time ago for them, you see – and the moment before life began, they were of course dead.

In the third, dream and flashback, area, Andy appears, cursing and swigging a perhaps illicit drink – Bridget appears silently in the background. Bel enters and she and Andy face each other and then turn away. Bridget remains, still, in the background.

This moonlit image obviously is the emotional climax of the play, which immediately descends to a scene in which the two sons seem to pay mock homage to their dying father, and one in which Andy and Bel discuss her lesbian attachment to Maria, his having Maria as a mistress and her lovemaking to Ralph. After this, again in ironic contrast, Maria and Ralph appear as conventional visitors making a polite social call to their friends.

Bel seems to have got hold of the sons' phone number: when she rings we see them pretending that she has reached a Chinese laundry. Here the play comes to a climax of wildly funny tragic irony.

In his bedroom Andy is more and more urgently demanding

to see his three grandchildren he believes to be Bridget's young family.

Fred and Jake are discussing some mock fantasy figure's, d'Orangerie's, memorial service. The subtext here may well be that their own father is now dead. Fred ends the scene by saying – about that fantasy figure, d'Orangerie: 'I loved him like a father'.

In the dream area Bridget speaks about being invited to a party which would only begin when the moon had gone down. She got to the house: 'I stood there in the moonlight and waited for the moon to go down'.

With that the play ends. The party to which she had been invited never happened.

The foregoing blow-by-blow summary of this puzzling play shows, I believe, a formal pattern different from any of Pinter's previous work which in all its wide variety adhered to one governing principle: total objectivity. Events – whether strictly realistic or 'surrealistic', like in the early *The Room* and *The Dumb Waiter* – were shown as happening before the audience's eyes as objective fact. The author clearly denied any knowledge of how these facts, real or surreal, should be interpreted. There were no transitions from one plane of reality to another. In some of Pinter's later plays the audience was left to choose whether to regard the whole play as being on a level of reality or taking place within the imagination or fearful anticipation of one of the characters, notably in *Old Times* where the action could be seen either as showing a real contest between Deeley and Anna for Kate's affections, or simply Deeley's nightmare about Anna's impending visit. If most of the play was a dream, it was quite clear *whose* dream it was.

Not so in *Moonlight*: here the play is framed by Bridget's, the dead character's, monologues. In whose consciousness is this vision located? Andy would be the likeliest answer, but then, Andy, by all other indications in the text, is already dead when she appears in the final image. Nor is Andy's mind likely to be the locus for the seeming flashback to the argument between the three teenagers, at which he was not present. None of the other characters is shown as likely to be the locus of Bridget's moonlit appearances.

It seems to me that the play can only be seen as taking place in the consciousness of its author, that it is its own author's dream or nightmare, and thus by far Pinter's most subjective play – in fact a return to his roots as a poet whose works are patterns of subjective images. If this is the case, I think that the scene-by-scene analysis above shows its structure as a structure of extreme contrasts: savage grotesquerie set against nostalgic wistfulness, relentless irony against free-flowing emotion, as well as variations on the extreme parameters of the play's theme of Love – ideal and carnal; Loss of children – ironic and heartfelt; and Death – as an aspect of maudlin self-pity or genuine tragedy.

The prevailing mode throughout the whole text – whether couched in satirical or lyrical terms – is one of the most biting irony: Bridget's opening moonlit soliloquy, for instance, is at first glance straightforwardly emotional when she talks of her parents as seeing her as 'all that they have left in their life'. Yet the irony of that statement is immediately brought out in the following scene which shows Andy and Bel with totally different preoccupations.

This particular type of ironical discourse is called, in London's East End, 'taking the piss'. In that very scene, the second of the play, this kind of discourse, as though to signal the play's leitmotif from the very start, not only becomes a subject for discussion but is also clearly defined: '. . . . it means mockery! It means to mock! It means a mockery Mockery! Mockery!', screams Andy at Bel, accusing her of taking the piss out of him. The two apostate sons, in all their scenes, are constantly taking the piss in their persistently ironic fantasising about their own position and mocking the English business classes' small-talk by endless references to strings of acquaintances' names:

JAKE: . . . . you must know Manning by his other name.
FRED: What's that?
JAKE: Rawlings.

217

FRED: I know Rawlings.
JAKE: I had no right to call him Manning.
FRED: Not if he's the Rawlings I know.
[. . . .]
FRED: Well, this quite clearly brings us straight back to Kellaway.
What's Kellaway's other name?
JAKE: Saunders.
Pause

[And so on. . . .]

The redoubled irony, however, lies in the fact that all this taking the piss must be hiding a subtext of deep unhappiness: they are taking the piss out of each other, and of the world in general, to cover up the underlying despair of their position.

From Michael Billington's biography, we know that Pinter's relationship with his only child, Daniel (born 1958), has been difficult and has led to a long period of non-communication between them. It would be too facile to establish a direct link between this fact and one of the main concerns of *Moonlight*. Yet pain about the loss of a child or children clearly lies behind the wild outburst of anguish that the play represents. The idealised dream image of Bridget becomes, in this perspective, merely another aspect of the same complex of feelings as the piss-taking duo of sons. They embody the rage and fury about that loss, Bridget its sheer sadness and nostalgia.

Weariness with the endless permutations of sexual activity implicit in the criss-cross relationships between Bel, Andy, Maria and Ralph, and the ultimate futility of such permutations, directly points to the play's third main theme – the injustice and iniquity of Death.

Moonlight thus ultimately appears as a sardonic, anguished and intensely-felt imagistic poem about the approach of old age and dying.

Ashes to Ashes

If *Moonlight* is thus a subjective, lyrical expression of its

218

author's feelings, *Ashes to Ashes*, which opened at the Royal Court's Ambassadors Theatre in London on 12th September 1996, returns to earlier, if ambivalent, modes of Harold Pinter's work: the kind of action which, presented with total objectivity but without exposition or closure, leaves the decision as to what kind of event is being witnessed – reality, allegory, dream, nightmare – entirely to the spectator.

The action takes place in a ground floor room, with a garden outside, in a house in the country on an early evening in summer. A man, Devlin, is standing, holding a drink; a woman, Rebecca, is sitting in an armchair. The man is interrogating the woman about what a former lover did to her. In answer to his questions she describes how she asked him to put his hand round her throat, starting to throttle her until her body sank back and her legs were opening. This, quite obviously, is a description of sado-masochistic erotic foreplay.

And this opens the question – are we witnessing a real act of confession, has Devlin really not known these matters before, or are we merely witnessing a recurring erotic ritual, a repetition of a permanent game between two partners who need this kind of fantasy to get into the right mood for love-making? The two partners in Pinter's earlier, much more straightforward piece, *The Lover*, a respectable suburban couple, perform a similar role-play by pretending to be a whore and her client. In a far more sophisticated way Pinter presented his audience with the same kind of question in *Old Times* when it was left entirely open whether the play depicted the anticipatory anxiety of the man, Deeley, about a forthcoming visit of his wife's girlfriend of earlier days whom he suspected of being her lesbian lover, or whether it merely represents the habitual foreplay in a long-persisting bisexual *ménage-à-trois*, by no means unusual in certain bohemian circles in London.

If *Ashes to Ashes* were to depict a sado-masochistic ritual, the fact that the course of the man's questioning elicits from the woman a series of vivid images of mass cruelty reminiscent of the holocaust – mass slave labour in the German armaments industry in World War Two (books by and on Albert Speer were in the news around that period), or ethnic cleansing in the

Balkans, genocide in Rwanda mixed with references to her own comfortable life, visiting her sister and her children for tea – would certainly fit the bill.

But something seems to go wrong. When Devlin tries to get the game back on track with, 'Let's start again', a discussion develops about whether one can end again, and again. And again. The title of the play is explained when Rebecca begins to sing lines from a popular tune, 'Ashes to ashes', and Devlin continues 'Dust to dust'. Rebecca, 'If the women don't get you. . . .', Devlin, 'Liquor must'.

Rebecca tells a story about a baby a woman was holding in an icy landscape. Suddenly she speaks of the baby as her own and, as Devlin puts his hand against her throat, he asks her to repeat the gestures described at the beginning. She does not react but remains caught in the vision of being forced to abandon the baby that was wrapped in a bundle. The play ends on Rebecca denying she ever had that baby, while a mysterious echo reverberates on variants of the word 'baby'. If we have been witnessing a love-ritual it seems to have gone wrong . . . perhaps Rebecca has become aware of her childnessness. . . ?

But if the play does not represent such a game between two lovers, then, I think, it should be seen as simply a way of presenting a series of images of the cruelty of our times. Just as T.S. Eliot's *The Waste Land*, the imagistic poem par excellence, strings such images of the desolation of the world at the start of the twentieth century together, *Ashes to Ashes* unfolds the far more cruel pageant of tableaux in its second half. In that case the play must be seen as its author's deeply felt subjective vision. That the act of love – with the past lover as well as the present one – seems to have to be introduced by a gesture of cruelty then becomes merely one more in a chain of such images of destructiveness, as does the pain of having lost or perhaps never having had a baby.

Pinter himself, when asked about *Ashes to Ashes*, during an interview at the department of English and German of the University of Barcelona in December 1996, seemed to incline towards that interpretation: 'From my point of view the woman is simply haunted by the world she's been born into, by all the atrocities that have happened. In fact they seem to have become part of her own experience, although in my view she hasn't actually experienced them herself. That's the whole point of the play. I have myself been haunted by these images for many years, and I'm sure I'm not alone in that. . . .'[1]

Yet, as always, Pinter avoids taking a firm stand on the interpretation of one of his own works. And, indeed, if the play did show us an erotic ritual, that would not exclude the fact that Rebecca would draw on her memories of the atrocities of her lifetime as a powerful ingredient to a game of sado-masochistic fantasies.

Celebration

Celebration – aptly titled for a play that opened on 16th March 2000, the year in which Pinter was to celebrate his seventieth birthday – returns, at least at first glance, to the far more straightforward fun of a hilariously comic and deadly accurate exploration of the language of certain of the London East End's shady business milieux and *nouveau riche* gangsters.

Two tables in a posh London restaurant are alternately lit up. At table one a wedding anniversary is being celebrated. Lambert, a loud – and foul-mouthed – individual, is treating his wife Julie and his brother Matt, who in turn is married to Julie's sister Prue, to a sumptuous dinner. At table two a shady investment banker, Russell, is dining with his wife Suki to whom he has just confessed a fling with a secretary.

These conversations abound in exchanges of insults and piss-taking: Russell calls his wife a whore; Julie invites her husband to 'go and buy a new car and drive it into a brick wall'. The degree of these characters' sophistication is shown not only by their ignorance of what kind of dish *Osso Bucco* might be, but also by the level of their acquaintance with the works of Sigmund Freud:

[1] 'Writing, Politics and *Ashes to Ashes*' in Harold Pinter, *Various Voices: Prose, Poetry, Politics 1948–1998*, Faber & Faber, 1998, p.64.

LAMBERT: All mothers want to be fucked by their mothers.

MATT: Or by themselves.

PRUE: No, you've got it the wrong way round.

LAMBERT: How's that?

MATT: All mothers want to be fucked by their sons. . . . [etc, etc.]

The posh restaurant's gentlemanly *maître d'*, Richard, visits table one; his female counterpart and assistant, Sonia, table two, to inquire how the diners are enjoying themselves – a confrontation of the rich vulgar with the servile pseudo-gentlemanly/ladylike. After Sonia has left the pair at table two a waiter comes to fill their wine glasses. He asks: 'Do you mind if I interject?' Under the pretext – quite obviously without foundation – that he had overheard the pair talking about T.S. Eliot, he proceeds to deliver a long speech about his grandfather who not only knew that poet but also Ezra Pound, W.H. Auden, C. Day Lewis, Louis MacNeice, Stephen Spender and a long string of other English literary giants right back to 'Thomas Hardy in his dotage'. He then adds a similar list of American greats from Ernest Hemingway, William Faulkner and others to Carson McCullers. He ends up with claiming that his grandfather 'stood foursquare in the centre of the intellectual and literary life of the tens, twenties and thirties. He was James Joyce's godmother'. All the stunned investment banker can say to that is: '. . . . next time we're talking about T.S. Eliot I'll drop you a card'.

As the celebration nears its drunken climax at table one the intellectual young waiter appears, and asks if he may make an interjection, reminiscing about his grandfather's connections with the great names of the golden days of Hollywood. After which, Lambert recognises the woman at the next table, Suki: 'I know her. I fucked her when she was eighteen'. The pair at table two join table one. Lambert and Matt introduce themselves as 'consultants . . . strategy consultants' and thus reveal themselves as members of the class that seems so dominant in Britain today. Lambert adds that the term strategy consultant 'means we don't carry guns'. As the spirits rise ever higher the two *maîtres d'* join in the proceedings and are duly cuddled –

the young waiter interjecting with another long speech, this time about his grandfather who had connections with the Austro-Hungarian Empire and knew Churchill, Mussolini, and a string of big names from Yeats and Brecht to Don Bradman, Kafka, the Inkspots and the Three Stooges.

The party disperses after Lambert has generously tipped the staff and assumed responsibility for Russell's bill.

As the light slowly fades, the young waiter remains behind, facing the audience, and talks about his grandfather who took him to the edge of the sea to look out on it through a telescope. 'My grandfather introduced me to the mystery of life and I'm still in the middle of it. I can't find the door to get out. My grandfather got out of it. He left it behind him and he didn't look back. He got that absolutely right. And I'd like to make one further interjection'. With that the play ends.

Celebration is a veritable feast of characteristically Pinter-esque linguistic satire; but it clearly also presents a microcosm of post-Thatcherite Britain, a society dominated by greed and dumbed-down educational and intellectual standards. The question arises whether the intellectually snobbish young waiter who constantly interjects his nostalgic memories of his grandfather is meant to stand for those lost values or whether he is there to take the piss of those very would-be chattering classes. I feel inclined to think that the character embodies both these tendencies at the same time – he reminds us of the topics of conversation of a now almost dying stratum of society and at the same time covers them with gentle ridicule. In some ways Pinter, himself the grandson of an emigrant from the Austro-Hungarian Empire, may be laughing about himself as an admirer of all those great names like Yeats, Auden, Kafka or Joyce, as an ardent fan of the Hollywood movies of the thirties, forties and fifties. . . . The fact that it is this character who ends the play, in a wistful coda that remains suspended in mid-air as the light fades, seems to point in this direction.

It may also not be without significance that all three plays of the seventh decade of Pinter's life have this common feature:

223

that they end in a melancholy soliloquy – Bridget's speech about the party that never happened, Rebecca's plaint about the lost baby, and the young waiter's unfinished interjection.

Sketches

The short sketches which Pinter contributed to two revues in 1959, some of which were broadcast or performed subsequently, are little more than limbering up exercises to try out characteristic innovations in dialogue technique. But precisely for this reason, they contain a good deal which is of interest for a deeper understanding of Pinter's style.

Here is a brief survey of Pinter's output of revue sketches:

The Lyric Revue, *One to Another* which opened at the Lyric, Hammersmith on 15th July 1959 and transferred to the Apollo Theatre on 19th August 1959 contained two sketches by Pinter:

TROUBLE IN THE WORKS: In a factory. Mr Fibbs, the manager, interviews a personnel officer, Wills, about the unrest among the workers. The reason, so Mr Wills asserts, is that 'they seem to have taken a turn against some of the products'. To his horror Mr Fibbs learns that they no longer like the brass pet cock, the hemi-unibal spherical rod-end, that 'they have gone vicious about the high-speed taper-shank spiral flute reamers' and a number of other wildly named mechanical contraptions. This is clearly an exercise for the much subtler use of technical language in *The Caretaker* – Aston's relish of the names of various saws, Mick's delight in new material for furniture.

THE BLACK AND WHITE: Two old homeless women late at night in a milk bar which stays open till the early hours of the morning discuss late-night buses, the chances of being picked up by the police and the dangers of talking to strangers. A study in the pathos of meaningless conversation. For example: '[An all-night bus] don't look like an all-night bus in daylight, do it?'

The revue *Pieces of Eight* (which opened at the Apollo Theatre on 3rd September 1969) contained four sketches by Pinter:

GETTING ACQUAINTED (the manuscript of which now seems lost).

REQUEST STOP: A woman who has asked a little man in a bus queue how she could get a bus to Shepherds Bush, showers abuse on him because he allegedly made insinuations about her in his reaction to the question. When the bus comes she remains behind and accosts another man, asking him how to get to Marble Arch. Clearly she is merely seeking an outlet for her hatred of foreigners.

SPECIAL OFFER (reprinted in Arnold P. Hinchcliffe's monograph on Pinter in the Twayne's English Authors Series): A BBC secretary is outraged by what happened to her in the staid London store of Swan & Edgar's: in the rest room she was handed a card offering 'men for sale'.

LAST TO GO: At a coffee stall the barman and an old newspaper seller muse on what was the last evening paper to be sold: 'Yes, it was the *Evening News* was the last to go tonight.' 'Not always the last though, is it, though? 'No. Oh no. I mean sometimes it's the *News*. Other times it's one of the others. No way of telling beforehand.' This speculation is cross-cut with musings about a man called George, whom neither seems to know and whom neither has seen for a long time. A study in the futility of human conversation.

A group of nine revue sketches broadcast by the BBC Third Programme in 1964 contained some of the above-mentioned sketches together with some hitherto unperformed ones:

THAT'S YOUR TROUBLE: Two men in a park discuss whether the sandwich board they see around a sandwichman's neck will give him a headache or a back and leg ache. They cannot agree:

> B: You just don't know how to listen to what other people tell you, that's your trouble.
> A: I know what my trouble is.

225

B: You don't know what your trouble is, my friend. That's your
   trouble.

THAT'S ALL: Two old women laboriously discuss the reasons
why a friend who used to visit Mrs A for a cup of tea on
Wednesdays now comes sometimes on Thursdays.

She comes in. She doesn't come in so much, but she comes in.
Pause
MRS B: I thought she didn't come in.
Pause
MRS A: She comes in. (*Pause*) She doesn't come in so much.
   That's all.

APPLICANT: A very efficient lady subjects an applicant for a
job to various very rigorous tests. This is a fragment from the
play *The Hothouse*.
INTERVIEW: A pornographic bookseller, Mr Jakes, is subjected
to the usual pre-Christmas radio or television interview about
seasonal trade. He puts holly round the shop but it doesn't
seem to make much difference. Gradually Mr Jakes reveals
that he is dreaming of imprisoning all his customers, because
every single one of them is a Communist.
DIALOGUE FOR THREE (also published in the quarterly review
Stand): A dialogue between two men and a woman. The first
man tells wildly extravagant stories of exotic adventure to the
second man (who only gets in one line) while the woman
pesters him with questions whether he thinks her too feminine,
too masculine or not masculine enough and reminds him of
their first meeting. Some of the lines also come from *The
Hothouse*, notably the memorable statement: 'The snow has
turned to slush.'

For a programme of miniature plays about marriage, in which
his wife took part, *Mixed Doubles*, Pinter wrote the sketch
NIGHT (1969): A man and a woman remember their first
meeting years ago which led to their getting married and
founding a family. But *her* memories contradict his. Did they

meet at a party or on a bridge? Did he 'take her' on a rubbish dump or pressed against some railings? Perhaps he remembers an incident with another girl, she with another man. . . .

In a completely different category are the political sketches which emerged as Pinter's preoccupation with totalitarian oppression became apparent in the early eighties:

PRECISELY (1983): Two civil servants discuss the hecatombs of death that would follow a nuclear attack and arrogantly determine the exact numbers to be expected 'precisely'.

THE NEW WORLD ORDER (performed as a curtain-raiser to Ariel Dorfman's *Death and the Maiden* at the Royal Court Theatre, London, in the spring of 1991): Two torturers address a man who sits, blindfolded and speechless, on a chair confronting them. They discuss what they are going to do to him. 'We haven't finished with him. We haven't even begun. And we haven't finished with his wife either.' They assure each other that they feel 'pure' because they are 'keeping the world clean for democracy'.

Screenplays

Apart from faithful transpositions of his own plays for the cinema and television and the short screenplay *The Basement* for the Grove Press project of a three-part film by Beckett, Ionesco and Pinter (of which only Beckett's *Film* was made) and the screen adaptation of Simon Gray's play *Butley* (1973), Pinter's work as a screenwriter is confined to the adaptation of other writers' novels. These are:

THE SERVANT from the short novel by Robin Maugham – 1963
THE PUMPKIN EATER from the novel by Penelope Mortimer – 1963
THE QUILLER MEMORANDUM from the spy story *The Berlin Memorandum* by Adam Hall – 1966
ACCIDENT from the novel by Nicholas Mosley – 1966
THE GO-BETWEEN from the novel by L. P. Hartley – 1969

227

REMEMBRANCE OF THINGS PAST by Proust. Screenplay written in 1972

LANGRISHE, GO DOWN from the novel by Aidan Higgins. The screenplay dating from 1970 was never made as a feature film, but produced in 1978 as a BBC television film

THE LAST TYCOON based on an uncompleted novel by F. Scott Fitzgerald – 1976

THE FRENCH LIEUTENANT'S WOMAN from the novel by John Fowles – 1981

VICTORY from the novel by Joseph Conrad – 1982 (not made)

TURTLE DIARY from the novel by Russell Hoban – 1985

THE HANDMAID'S TALE from the novel by Margaret Atwood – 1987

THE HEAT OF THE DAY from the novel by Elizabeth Bowen – 1988

REUNION from the novel by Fred Uhlman – 1989

THE COMFORT OF STRANGERS from the novel by Ian McEwan – 1990

THE TRIAL from the novel by Franz Kafka – 1990.

Clearly the adaptation of other writers' work for the screen is an exercise of craftsmanship rather than the wholly creative process of shaping themes and images which have entirely sprung from the artist's own imagination. Yet it is probably no more than the conditions under which the film industry works and which do not favour the commissioning of entirely original work from dramatists which provides the reason why Pinter has not as yet produced a film wholly his own. That the cinema as a medium attracts him is shown by his skill in writing television plays and the success of his screen adaptations. After all, the cinema is perhaps even more effective in mirroring the impenetrably mysterious surface of events, the silences between the words, than the stage. As Pinter himself has said in connection with *Accident*:

> In this film everything happens, nothing is explained. It has been pared down and down, all unnecessary words and actions are eliminated. If it is interesting to see a man cross a room, then we

see him do it; if not, then we leave out the insignificant stages of the action.

I think you'll be surprised at the directness, the simplicity with which Losey is directing this film: no elaborations, no odd angles, no darting about. Just a level, intense look at people, at things. As though if you look at them hard enough they will give up their secrets. Not that they will, for however much you see and guess at there is always something more. . . .[1]

Hence all Pinter's screen adaptations not only contain passages of dialogue highly characteristic of Pinter but also mirror some of his basic preoccupations and imagery. *The Servant*, for example, the story of a rich young man who is gradually being reduced to complete dependence and servitude by his manservant, is closely akin to Pinter's theme of 'changing places', as in *A Slight Ache* and *The Basement*; a comparison between the novel and the screenplay shows how Pinter made that *motif* which undoubtedly is already present in the story considerably more explicit in the concrete imagery of the action. In the novel the story is told by a narrator who was a friend of the hero – Tony. Pinter's screenplay eliminates the subjective source of the narration as the cinema can show the objective surface of events. Tony's fiancée (Sally Grant in the novel, Susan Stewart in the film), who is the sinister manservant's chief antagonist, steps into the narrator's shoes in incidents in which he was involved in the novel. For example, Barrett the manservant has brought his girl, Vera, into the house as his niece in the novel, his sister in the film, in order to seduce Tony away from his fiancée and to get a hold over him. In the novel, the *narrator*, passing Tony's house while he is out of London, sees a light burning in Tony's room, goes up and finds the servant in bed with his alleged niece. He then tells Tony and Tony sacks his manservant. In the film Tony, who wants to resume his relationship with his fiancée, returns from a visit to the country with her and has asked her to spend the night with him for the first time; when they go to Tony's

[1] Pinter interviewed by John Russell Taylor in *Sight and Sound*, Autumn 1966.

bedroom they find the manservant in bed with the girl whom he has introduced as his sister. Pinter's version of the incident has clearly greatly sharpened the situation and focused what is a series of loosely related coincidences in the story into a highly compressed image.

In the novel the final image is of the narrator visiting Tony for the last time and finding him completely under Barrett's spell; as he leaves, a girl arrives who has obviously been procured by Barrett for Tony's and his own amusement. In the film it is Susan who is coming to the house to try and redeem Tony from final subjection: she finds an orgy involving several girls in progress and, as though to arouse Tony into realizing his position, kisses Barrett, thus emphasizing the very Pinteresque point that the servant and the master have changed places.

There are many highly characteristic touches in the dialogue involving Susan's aristocratic relatives and, above all, there is the scene in the French restaurant in Soho, where Susan makes an attempt to get Tony to rid himself of Barrett. To counterpoint the action Pinter introduces three other dining couples in the background: a Bishop (played by Patrick Magee) taking out a Curate (played by Alun Owen – there is a private joke here in introducing two of Pinter's colleagues from the Anew McMaster company); an older woman giving lunch to a younger one, with hints of a lesbian relationship; and a society man (played by Pinter himself) lunching a debutante. There are delicious touches of absurd-sounding snatches of dialogue between these three pairs which are intercut with the tense scene between the hero and his fiancée who is struggling to save him.

The Pumpkin Eater – the story of a woman who wants more and more children, and her husband who escapes from too much domesticity into relations with other women – is more remote from Pinter's own preoccupations. He has, however, brilliantly dramatized the climactic situations of the plot and occasionally introduced passages of dialogue which bear his unmistakable hallmark, notably in the scene when Jake, the heroine's faithless husband, meets the jealous husband of his latest conquest:

> JAKE: . . . How is your wife, by the way?
> CONWAY: Tip top. She's at a reception tonight for the Duchess of Dubrovnik.
> JAKE: I thought she *was* the Duchess of Dubrovnik.
> CONWAY: My wife? No, not at all. Not at all. Not at all.
> JAKE: Well, you're not the bloody Duke anyway.
> JAKE'S *glass slips from his hand, falls on* CONWAY'S *lap and then to the floor. Whisky stains* CONWAY'S *trousers.*
> CONWAY: You've made me wet.

There is more than a hint here of the confrontations between the jealous men in *The Collection* or *The Basement*.

In *The Quiller Memorandum* Pinter's touch gave the modish spy story about a Western agent who penetrates a Nazi underground organization a gloss of tautness, dryness and economy, particularly in the scenes between Quiller and the German girl, where we sense that he knows that she is not what she pretends to be, and that she knows that he knows, and that he knows that too, while yet carrying on as though neither of them suspected anything beneath the surface of what looks like an ordinary love affair. The dialogues between two high British civil servants back in Whitehall which counterpoint the melodramatic action in Berlin with cosy upper-class aloofness also – and more obviously – display Pinter's style: the style of his revue sketches.

Accident, the second film Pinter wrote for Joseph Losey, whose direction of *The Servant* had revealed his affinity with Pinter's approach, is on an entirely different and higher level than *The Quiller Memorandum*. Nicholas Mosley's novel, set among dons and students at Oxford, was faithfully adapted and yet wholly transformed by Pinter. The screenplay follows the novel closely, and yet, by transferring the story from the subjectivity of its telling by the hero, Stephen, to a squence of images which, though most of them are a flashback in Stephen's mind and seen from his point of view, become

231

objectified merely by being deprived of any trace of reflecting commentary and description of feelings, Pinter and Losey succeeded in turning it into a wholly original work of art. The script is laconic, enigmatic and provides a minimum of explanation – and yet the theme emerges strong and clear: the tension between the university teacher's responsibility towards his pupils and his desire for the girl student, the tension between his love for his wife and childen and the urge to indulge in a last adventure, the way in which the actions of the other people around Stephen mirror and act out all his desires (his friend and fellow don, Charley, seduces the beautiful student) and his final fall from grace when, after the girl student's fiancé has been killed in an accident outside Stephen's house, and he has her in his power because he could testify that he found her in the driver's seat, drunk and without a licence, he takes advantage of her helplessness and dependence. (This last, telling touch is Pinter's; there is no hint of this consummation of Stephen's desire in the book.) Among the many original uses of the medium in the screenplay is the fusion of silent images with dialogue, belonging to the same incident but not synchronous, in the episode when Stephen recalls a brief escapade with a former girl friend whom he looks up in London to escape his preoccupation with the beautiful aristocratic student. The wild game involving the beautiful girl's equally aristocratic fiancé – a version of the Eton Wall Game played in that particular family at social occasions – is reminiscent of the confrontations between rivals in *The Collection*, *The Basement* or *Tea Party*. Pinter himself appears briefly as a television producer in an episode when Stephen tries to become a television don like his more successful rival Charley.

The screenplay for *The Go-Between* (also written for Joseph Losey) tackles a minor classic and a masterpiece. The screenplay, even more laconic and elliptic than *Accident*, does it full justice. In the book, the narrator finds his old diary which contains the account of the climactic episode of his childhood; he then tells the story which it recalls: his stay with a rich schoolfriend in Norfolk in the summer of 1900, his carrying of messages between a couple of illicit lovers, and his final discovery of them while making love which leads to the suicide of the man; and finally, in the epilogue his visit, half a century later, to the place of these dramatic events and his meeting with the girl involved, now an old woman. Pinter has telescoped the action into that last visit and brilliantly parallels the narrator's arrival, inspection of the place as it now is and meeting with the old lady, with the flashbacks of the ancient events, so that the whole culminates in the complete fusion of past and present in the mind of the spectator who has been gradually drawn into a complex pattern of past and present images and relationships.

What is most surprising in Pinter's work as a screenwriter is that he, whose work for the theatre is so eminently verbal and so economical with scenery, here displays a brilliant visual imagination and is able to tell much of the story in visual terms.

His most outstanding achievement in this area is his adaptation of Proust's vast novel *A la recherche du temps perdu* into the timespan of a single – if long – feature film. Proust uses a large number of *leitmotifs* in his work which he elaborates in long passages of intricate prose. Pinter has succeeded in transmuting these into instantly visible recurring images that sustain the structure of the action as wholly adequate cinematic equivalents. It is most regrettable that this masterly screenplay was denied its ultimate completion in a finished film owing to the financial and cultural shortcomings of the film-industry.

Pinter performed a similar tour de force of adaptation in his work on John Fowles' novel *The French Lieutenant's Woman*. Here the problem was to find a cinematic equivalent to the story's post-modern device of keeping the twentieth-century narrator and his opinions in parallel with the typically Victorian story. Pinter found the brilliant solution to this problem by translating the Victorian story into a film being made by a twentieth-century team of 'cineastes' and running the love story of the Victorian hero and heroine parallel to an affair between the two leading actors in the film.

Pinter likes to appear himself in his adaptations in cameo roles, only occasionally taking more extensive parts.

Pinter's work as a screenwriter shows his immense professionalism and the perfection of his craftsmanship, as well as the breadth of his understanding of other writers' world views (often diametrically opposed to his own). In whatever type of literary work he tackles – from the pulp novel to the sublime masterpiece – he enters into the spirit and style of his material and transmutes it with outstanding intelligence and empathy. This ability, moreover, to keep himself profitably at work has relieved him from the necessity – which so often leads other writers to hack work – of having to produce new original works at regular intervals. He can thus indulge in the luxury of producing original, truly creative material – for the stage, radio or television – only when he really has something urgent and personal to say or to express.

4

Language and Silence

That Pinter has added a new band of colours to the spectrum of English stage dialogue is attested by the frequent use of terms like 'Pinteresque language' or 'Pinterese' in current dramatic criticism. Some of the more obvious features of his use of language, such as recurrent tautologies on the pattern 'He's old – Not young – No, I wouldn't call him young – Not youthful, certainly – Elderly, I'd say – I'd call him old' have been copied to the point of parody by a large number of aspiring authors. And the bad imitations have, inevitably, cast a shadow over the original user – and indeed, discoverer, of these linguistic absurdities which had hitherto largely escaped the attentive ears of playwrights. Yet these most easily recognizable features of Pinter's dialogue are, on the whole, the most superficial aspects of his artistry; moreover, even their function in the overall picture has been largely misunderstood, for while Pinter undoubtedly *has* an uncannily accurate ear for the linguistic solecisms of the English vernacular spoken by ordinary people, it is neither his special intention or foremost dramatic purpose merely to amuse his audience by confronting them with accurately observed examples of linguistic nonsense and thus giving them the pleasure of *recognizing* the linguistic mistakes of others and feeling superior to them. It may be true that a good deal of Pinter's initial success was, indeed, perhaps due to this kind of audience reaction, and he may even, occasionally, have succumbed to the temptation of exploiting it; yet, if his work is seen as a whole it will be recognized that he has also resisted this temptation – and with considerable success – not only by at first discarding plays like *The Hothouse* (which might have been regarded at the time as an overindulgence in Pinterese), but also by moving out of the sphere of low-life dialogue in the plays which followed the success of *The Caretaker* (*The Lover*, *The Collection*, and later *Tea Party* and *The Basement*); by avoiding the tricks of the more obvious Pinterese in a play which might well have given a great deal of opportunity for self-copying and self-parody – *The Homecoming*; and, finally, by abandoning naturalistic action and dialogue altogether in the next phase of his development – the highly compressed stage poetry of recollected experience in *Landscape*, *Silence*, *Old Times*, *Betrayal* and *A Kind of Alaska*.

A true understanding of Pinter's use of language must, I believe, be based on deeper, more fundamental considerations: it must start from an examination of the function of language in stage dialogue generally – and indeed from considerations of the use of language in ordinary human intercourse itself. For here – at least as far as the English language is concerned – Pinter has given us added insight into – has, in a certain measure even *discovered* – the fact that traditional stage dialogue has always greatly overestimated the degree of logic which governs the use of language, the amount of information which language is actually able to impart on the stage – as in life. People on the stage have, from Sophocles to Shakespeare to Rattigan, always spoken more clearly, more directly, more to the purpose than they would ever have done in real life. This is obvious enough in verse drama which had to obey not only the rules of prosody, but also those of the ancient art of rhetoric, which concerned itself with the ways in which speech could be made as clear, well proportioned and easily assimilated as possible. So strong was this tradition that it even persisted in naturalistic drama although it was sometimes superficially disguised: the finest speeches in Ibsen or Shaw are as brilliantly constructed as those of Cicero or Demosthenes. And even in the scenes of light conversation in the exposition of these plays the main emphasis lies on the elegance with which the essential *information* about the antecedents of the plot and the motivation of the characters is conveyed, broken up perhaps into seemingly casually arranged fragments, but nevertheless in a discursive, explicit style.

It was only gradually that a certain defectiveness of communication between characters – who talk past each other rather than to each other – was introduced by dramatists like Strindberg or Wedekind; and that 'oblique' dialogue in which the text hints at a hidden sub-text was brought in by Chekhov: as in the climactic scene of *The Cherry Orchard* discussed in an earlier chapter of this book, when the real action – Lopakhin's failure to declare himself to Varya – is taking place beneath a trivial exchange about a missing article of clothing. But this scene was elaborately *prepared* by Chekhov: he had taken care in the preceding scene to make it quite explicit to the audience that they were to expect Lopakhin's offer of marriage. Pinter's technique continues Chekhov's use of such 'oblique' dialogue, but carries it much further.

A comparison between two climactic closing scenes by the two playwrights might serve to illustrate this point:

In the closing scene of Chekhov's *Uncle Vanya* the chief characters have lost their hope of love and fulfilment. Vanya turns to Sonia and expresses his feelings in a highly explicit outburst:

> My child, there's such a weight on my heart! Oh, if only you knew how my heart aches.

And Sonia replies:

> Well, what can we do? We must go on living! (*A pause.*) We shall go on living, Uncle Vanya. We shall live through a long, long succession of days and tedious evenings. We shall patiently suffer the trials which Fate imposes on us; we shall work for others, now and in our old age, and we shall have no rest . . .

Having described the reality of their lives to come, Sonia turns to talk of the remaining great hope of eternal rest – in death:

We shall rest! We shall hear the angels, we shall see all the heavens covered with stars like diamonds, we shall see all earthly evil, all our sufferings swept away by the grace which will fill the whole world, and our life will become peaceful, gentle and sweet as a caress. I believe it, I believe it. . . . Poor, poor Uncle Vanya, you're crying. . . . You've had no joy in life, but wait, Uncle Vanya, wait . . . we shall rest . . . We shall rest. . . .we shall rest!

A magnificent piece of writing, but surely very far removed from the way in which a girl like Sonia would use language in a real situation of this kind. The rhetorical heritage is still very strong in Chekhov's style. There *is* an element of 'obliqueness' present even here, however: for while Sonia professes to *believe* in the joys of eternal bliss in heaven, we know that what she is saying is *not* what she really believes; she is using the picture of heavenly bliss as a last despairing attempt at bringing consolation to Uncle Vanya. It is in the contrast between what is being said and what lies behind it that the poignancy and also the innovatory modernity of Chekhov's approach to language in drama appears.

Pinter, in the final scene of *The Birthday Party*, which portrays a situation that is analogous to the close of *Uncle Vanya* – the loss of the hope of love suffered by Meg – goes infinitely further than Chekhov. Pinter's characters do not talk explicitly about the situation at all. Meg knows, deep down, that Stanley has gone, but she cannot and will not admit it to herself; and Petey is too inarticulate to offer a speech of consolation like Sonia's:

MEG: I was the belle of the ball.
PETEY: Were you?
MEG: Oh yes. They all said I was.
PETEY: I bet you were, too.
MEG: Oh, it's true. I was.
  Pause
  I know I was.

Four times Meg repeats that she was the belle of the ball – the disastrous party through which her substitute son was destroyed and taken away from her. It is quite clear that she does not in fact want to say anything about the impression she actually made at that party. She is, in fact, merely trying to hang on to the illusion that everything is still as it was, that the disastrous party was not a disaster but the success she had hoped for it. The fourfold *repetition* of the statement does not derive from any desire to say the same thing four times; it is no more than a sign of the desperateness of her attempt, her pitiful determination not to let the realization of the disaster dawn on her. Hence the repetition of the statement is more relevant than the statement and the explicit, 'discursive' content of the statement, itself. Similarly Petey's affirmation that the statement is true merely has the function of expressing his compassion, his despair and, above all, his inability to do anything towards making Meg acknowledge or realize the true position. Thus the dramatic effect of this brilliantly moving, brilliantly economical and concise passage of dialogue is entirely due to the complete contradiction between the words that are spoken and the emotional and psychological *action* which underlies them. Here the language has almost totally lost its rhetorical, its informative element and has fully merged into dramatic action.

It is true that in a passage of dialogue like this there is little verbal communication between the characters in that Meg does not inform Petey of any fact she wants him to know, nor he her. Yet to sum up this state of affairs by labelling such a passage a dialogue of non-communication completely misses the point of the matter. For Pinter is far from wanting to say that language is incapable of establishing true communication between human beings; he merely draws our attention to the fact that in life human beings rarely make use of language for that purpose, at least as far as spoken, as distinct from written, language is concerned. People interact not so much logically as emotionally through language; and the tone of voice, the emotional colour of the words is often far more significant than their exact meanings, by their dictionary definition; we all know that an outburst of name-calling by one person against another is basically an act of aggression, an assault by verbal blows in which the violence of the emotion behind the words is far more important than their content. Where animals use physical action and physical contact (such as sniffing each other, catching each others' fleas) human beings, through the power of speech, can substitute verbal contact and verbal action (small talk about the weather, exchange of information about one's minor ailments, abuse or words of endearment). What matters in most oral verbal contact therefore is more what people are *doing* to each other through it rather than the conceptual content of what they are saying.

Thus in drama dialogue is, ultimately, a form of *action*; it is the element of action, the inter-action between the characters, their reactions to each other, which constitute the truly *dramatic* elements in stage dialogue, its essential aspect in the context of drama, apart from and over and above all the other values embodied in the writing such as wit, lucidity, elegance of structure and logical development, depth of thought, persuasiveness, rhythm, imagery, mellifluousness and sheer beauty as poetry – all the rhetorical and literary qualities which could also be appreciated outside the context of drama.

But being essentially action, dramatic dialogue is not necessarily the dominant element in the playwright's armoury: it may be equally or even less important than the non-verbal actions of the characters and, indeed, their silences. Traditionally, however because of the origins of dramatic writing in the art of oratory, dialogue has been the dominant element in drama. Hence the tendency for drama to involve highly articulate characters, the only ones who would naturally interact in terms of brilliantly phrased speech; this showed itself in the need to *stylize* the verbal expression by the use of verse, which relieved the playwright of the need to imitate the real speech of characters who in reality would have been inarticulate, or at least far from possessing the powers of expression with which they seemed to be endowed on the stage; or, in later, naturalistic drama the tendency to place the action among people who would be highly articulate in real life: the elegant wits of Wilde, the eloquent intellectuals of Shaw. Only when it was recognized that the verbal element need not be the dominant aspect of drama, or at least that it was not the content of what was said that mattered most, but the action which it embodied, and that inarticulate, incoherent, tautological and nonsensical speech might be as dramatic as verbal brilliance when it could be treated simply as an element of action, only then did it become possible to place inarticulate characters in the centre of the play and to make their unspoken emotions transparent. Pinter is among the discoverers of this highly significant aspect of drama.

If we examine some of Pinter's favourite linguisitic and stylistic devices in the light of these considerations, we shall find that far from being mere verbal absurdities held up to ridicule, they do in fact illuminate the mental processes that lie behind the ill-chosen or nonsensical words; and that in each case superficially similar quirks of language may serve quite different dramatic functions.

Take the most obvious of these, the one most frequently attributed to Pinter as a mere mannerism: repetition. Each time Pinter's characters repeat themselves, or each others' phrases, the playwright employs the device of repetition to fulfil a definite function in the action; if, for example, at the beginning of *The Birthday Party* Meg, having served Petey his cornflakes, asks:

MEG: Are they nice?
PETEY: Very nice.
MEG: I thought they'd be nice.

The emptiness of the dialogue clearly indicates the emptiness of the characters' relationship with each other, the boredom of their lives and yet their determination to go on making friendly conversation. So this short dialogue of no more than

241

ten words, three of which are repetitions of 'nice', which, on the surface, conveys no worthwhile *conceptual* information whatever, does in fact compress a very considerable amount of *dramatic* information – this being the exposition of the play – and dramatic action, i.e. the vain attempt at conversation, the desire to be friendly – into an astonishingly brief space.

If, on the other hand, Davies in *The Caretaker*, talking about his ex-wife's slovenliness, mentions the saucepan in which he found some of her underclothing, repeats himself, saying:

The pan for vegetables, it was. The vegetable pan . . .

the repetition serves a completely different purpose: it shows us this inarticulate man's struggle to find the correct word, the *mot juste*. Traditional stage dialogue always tended to err on the side of assuming that people have the right expression always ready to suit the occasion. In Pinter's dialogue we can always watch the desperate struggles of his characters to find the correct expression; we are thus enabled to see them in the – very dramatic – act of struggling for communication, sometimes succeeding, often failing. And when they have got hold of a formulation, they hold on to it, savour it and repeat it to enjoy their achievement, like Gus in *The Dumb Waiter* when he recalls the time they killed a girl:

. . . It was a mess though, wasn't it? What a mess. Honest, I can't remember a mess like that one. They don't seem to hold together like men, women. A looser texture, like. Didn't she spread, eh? She didn't half spread. Kaw!

The pleasure with which Gus dwells on the words *mess* and *spread* is evident: not because he enjoyed killing the girl, quite the contrary; but because, being an inarticulate person who has trouble in finding the expressive phrase, he loves to play with and savour it once he has got hold of it and does not want to let it go. He is delighted to have found the expressive image of the girl's body dissolving like butter: 'she spread'. So, while on one level he is worried and unhappy about his job as a killer and deplores having had to liquidate that girl, on another he revels in the happy feeling of having expressed his thought well. Another example of how dialogue which is primitive and crude when judged by the standards of rhetoric, can be astonishingly subtle, ironical and psychologically penetrating if considered as an expression of character in action – drama.

As against the use of repetition to show a character's *enjoyment* at having found the *mot juste*, there is repetition as a form of hysterical irritation: so obsessed, for example, is McCann in *The Birthday Party* with the unpleasantness of what he and Goldberg will have to do to Stanley, that he breaks out:

> Let's finish and go. Let's get it over and go. Get the thing done. Let's finish the bloody thing. Let's get the thing done and go!

McCann's hysteria emerges not only from the frantic rhythm with which these sentences are phrased but also from the obsessive permutation of the same elements – 'finish', 'go', 'get done'.

Conversely, Pinter uses repetition to show how a character gradually learns to accept a fact which at first he had difficulty in taking in. Having been terrorized by Mick, Davies in *The Caretaker* asks Aston:

> DAVIES: Who was that feller?
> ASTON: He's my brother.
> DAVIES: Is he? He's a bit of a joker, en'he?
> ASTON: Uh.
> DAVIES: Yes . . . he's a real joker.
> ASTON: He's got a sense of humour.
> DAVIES: Yes, I noticed.
> *Pause*
> He's a real joker, that lad, you can see that.
> *Pause*

ASTON: Yes, he tends . . . he tends to see the funny side of things.
DAVIES: Well, he's got a sense of humour, en'he?
ASTON: Yes.
DAVIES: Yes, you could tell that.
Pause

Here the manner in which Davies takes up Aston's phrase about the 'sense of humour' and the way in which he punctuates his realization of Mick's character with 'I noticed', 'you can see that' and 'you could tell that' allows the audience to witness the slow sinking in of the facts, the gradual evaluation of the man he met, the eventual and increasingly bitter coming to terms with these facts in Davies's mind. Two repeated phrases are interlocked in this passage ('he's a joker/got a sense of humour' and 'I noticed/can see/could tell that') and again their various permutations in the mouth of first the one and then the other character give the dialogue a definite poetic shape, a musical form of theme and variations, of strophe and anti-strophe: psychological realism and a poet's control over the formal element in language are here fused in a way highly characteristic of Pinter.

For repetition, which, as Pinter has discovered, is an aspect of real speech that stage dialogue had neglected under the influence of the rhetorical tradition (which rejects recurrence of the same word as stylistically inelegant) is, of course, also one of the most important elements of poetry – particularly in the form of whole phrases which recur as refrains, for example in ballad metre. On the realistic level Pinter uses the refrain-like recurrence of whole sentences to show that people in real life do not deliver well thought-out set speeches but tend to mix various logical strands of thought which intermingle without any permanent connection: while the structure of rhetorical or written language tends to be logical, that of spoken language is associative. In the first act of *The Caretaker*, for example, Aston tells Davies that there is a family of Indians living in the house next door. Davies immediately reacts with:

DAVIES: Blacks?
ASTON: I don't see much of them.
DAVIES: Blacks, eh?

The conversation then turns to other matters and Davies embarks on his story about his Odyssey to the monastery at Luton where he had been told the monks handed out shoes to the poor. Having reached the climax of that story, he is about to introduce the punch-line:

. . . You know what that bastard monk said to me?
Pause
How many more Blacks you got around here then?
ASTON: What?
DAVIES: You got any more Blacks around here?

Without any *logical* motivation the question about the Blacks re-emerges to the surface a minute or more after it was first mooted. But the association is clear enough: the hatred and indignation Davies feels for the monk who treated him so badly has re-awakened the emotion of fear and hatred against that other arch-enemy of his – the coloured community.

Similarly, in Davies' long speech of hatred against Aston, when he believes that Mick will support him in giving him control of the house and he tries to assert his superiority over Aston, as a former inmate of a mental institution, we find several lines of thought mixed to give a refrain-like effect:

. . . I'm a sane man! So don't start mucking me about. I'll be all right as long as you keep your place. Just you keep your place, that's all. *Because I can tell you, your brother's got his eye on you.* He knows all about you. I got a friend there, don't you worry about that. I got a true pal there. Treating me like dirt! Why'd you invite me in here in the first place if you was going to treat me like this? You think you're better than me you got another think coming. I know enough. They had you inside one of them places before, they can have you inside again. *Your brother's got his eye on you!* They can put the pincers on your head again, man . . . [My italics.]

It is clear that this type of associative structure in which several basic thoughts (I am better than you because I am sane, you have been in a mental institution – your brother is my friend, he has his eye on you) intermingle in ever recurring variations belongs on the whole to characters of Davies's primitive mentality. But Pinter also uses it, in an appropriately modified form, in the mouth of one of his most sophisticated characters, Harry, the rich clothing manufacturer in *The Collection*:

Bill's a slum boy, you see, he's got a slum sense of humour. That's why I never take him along with me to parties. Because he's got a slum mind. I have nothing against slum minds *per se*, you understand, nothing at all. There's a certain kind of slum mind which is perfectly all right in a slum, but when this kind of slum minds gets out of the slum it sometimes persists, you see, it rots everything. That's what Bill is. There's something faintly putrid about him, don't you find? Like a slug. There's nothing wrong with slugs in their place, but he's a slum slug; there's nothing wrong with slum slugs in their place, but this one won't keep his place – he crawls all over the walls of nice houses, leaving slime, don't you, boy? He confirms stupid sordid little stories just to amuse himself, while everyone else has to run round in circles to get to the root of the matter and smooth the whole thing out. All he can do is sit and suck his bloody hand and decompose like the filthy putrid slum slug he is. . . .

Here the structure is apparently one of rigid logic, even of syllogism, but only apparently. For the real motivation for the erection of this structure of pseudo-logic is to give an opportunity to hammer away at the humiliating terms *slum* and *slug*; the repetition here indicates the degree of Harry's obsession with Bill and his hatred of him, but it is also deliberately used by him as a means of aggression, of mental torture and humiliation towards Bill. And again the refrain-like recurrence of the same type of phrase (I have nothing against, There is nothing wrong) gives this highly realistic and closely observed reproduction of genuine speech patterns a musical-poetic structure.

In Harry's diatribe the emotional charge of jealousy, hatred and contempt underlies the associative structure of his speech. In other instances it is, on the other hand, the absence of emotion, the determination to avoid saying what ought to be said, that leads to associative and equally repetitious sequences of words. When Davies, in *The Caretaker*, first encounters Mick, is frightened by him and asks who he is, Mick, who wants to torment him by keeping him on tenterhooks, embarks on a long diatribe which is quite obviously intended to convey no information whatever:

> You know, believe it or not, you've got a funny kind of resemblance to a bloke I once knew in Shoreditch. Actually he lived in Aldgate. I was staying with a cousin in Camden Town. This chap, he used to have a pitch in Finsbury Park, just by the bus depot. When I got to know him I found out he was brought up in Putney. That didn't make any difference to me. I know quite a few people who were born in Putney. Even if they weren't born in Putney, they were born in Fulham. The only trouble was, he wasn't born in Putney, he was only brought up in Putney. It turned out he was born in the Caledonian Road, just before you get to the Nag's Head . . .

Not only is this passage, in its total nonsensicality, highly comic, not only does it prolong Davies's and the audience's suspence, it also shows the thought process which prompts Mick: one London place name simply leads him on to the next, we can clearly follow his method in making up a long and meaningless speech which ironically apes the exchanges of reminiscences between new acquaintances who want to break the ice between themselves by recalling mutual friends with a maximum of circumstantial detail. So transparent is the associative mechanism here that we are also fully aware that Mick is malevolently enjoying himself at Davies's expense.

It is by an analogous use of associative linguistic structure that Pinter indicates that a character is lying: here too the story is being made up as it goes along, and often merely from the *sound* of the words; as in Solto's reply to the question of how he got to Australia in *Night School*:

> By sea. How do you think? I worked my passage. And what a trip. I was only a pubescent. I killed a man with my own hands, a six-foot-ten Lascar from Madagascar.
> ANNIE: From Madagascar?
> SOLTO: Sure. A Lascar.
> MILLY: Alaska?
> SOLTO: Madagascar.
> *Pause*
> WALTER: It's all happened before.
> SOLTO: And it'll happen again.

It is quite clear that Solto thought of Madagascar only because the term Lascar suggested it. Walter's interjection, that it happened before, indicates that he is fully aware of the spuriousness of the story and the intention behind it, namely, the braggart's desire to impress. Hence by his remark he shows himself unimpressed, while Solto, by insisting that it happened and will happen again, feebly insists on his veracity, but without carrying any conviction.

The braggart is a stock figure of comedy and has been from time immemorial; so, of course, have been the braggart's stories and lies. Here Pinter, therefore, moves along very traditional lines; where his special talent shines through, however, is in his ability to make the often very pathetic thought processes behind the tall stories utterly transparent to the audience: these liars are carried along, almost passively, by the limited range of their imagination, the paucity of possible associations which can lead them on from one word to the next. When Walter, again in *Night School*, brags to Sally about his success as a prison librarian, for example, he is, very much against his will and better judgement, driven into a mention of rare manuscripts:

> . . . Well, funny enough, I've had a good bit to do with rare manuscripts in my time. I used to know a bloke who ran a business digging them up. . . . Rare manuscripts. Out of tombs. I used to give him a helping hand when I was on the loose. Very well paid it was, too. You see, they were nearly always attached to a corpse, these manuscripts, you had to lift up the pelvis bone with a pair of tweezers. Big tweezers. Can't leave fingerprints on a corpse, you see. Canon law. . . .

(The germ of this speech is already contained in Pinter's early novel *The Dwarfs*, where Pete tries to impress a girl during a party. In the passage in *Night School*, however, the idea has been considerably, and brilliantly, developed and expanded.) It is only superficially that a speech like this one is funny. On a deeper level it reveals an underprivileged individual's desperate attempt to impress the girl, the mixture of ignorance and half-baked information with which his mind is stocked, the vagueness of his ideas. Rare manuscripts to him suggest archaeology – archaeology, tombs – and somehow he has to invent for himself a way in which these two vague ideas can be related: hence the suggestion that rare manuscripts are found in tombs. Hence the association with skeletons; hence, again, the urge to mention one of the few technical terms from anatomy he knows – 'pelvis' – which again leads to the association with the cliché of the soap opera involving an operation: it is here that tweezers are always mentioned. And this brings the ex-convict Walter back to his own sphere: to explain the tweezers he gets back to his own world, that of the petty thief who does not want to leave fingerprints. To retrieve this lapse he has to take avoidng action into Canon Law. . . . While it is unlikely that the audience will be wholly conscious of the exact way in which such a chain of associations is built up, they can certainly follow the main line of the underlying thought process and thus partake in the *action* which this speech portrays, Walter's desperate attempt on the one hand to establish his intellectual and social superiority and his equally desperate efforts, on the other, to extricate himself from the more and more difficult traps and pitfalls he creates for himself.

Always, in Pinter's world, personal inadequacy expresses itself in an inadequacy in coping with and using language. The inability to communicate, and to *communicate in the correct terms*, is felt by the characters as a mark of inferiority; that is why they tend to dwell upon and to stress the hard or unusual 'educated' words they know. Solto, in the rodomontade quoted above, casually introduces the unusual, and to him no doubt highly refined, term 'pubescent', Walter talks about 'Canon Law', 'pelvis', 'rare manuscripts'; Mick in *The Caretaker*, on his first confrontation with Davies, speaks of someone of whom the tramp reminds him, who had a *penchant* for nuts:

> Had a penchant for nuts. That's what it was. Nothing else but a penchant. Couldn't eat enough of them. Peanuts, walnuts, brazil nuts, monkey nuts, wouldn't touch a piece of fruit cake.

Note, again, the laying bare of the mechanism of the lie: the false circumstantial detail contained in the associative use of the names of different kinds of nuts. The introduction of the 'refined' term *penchant*, however, serves to emphasize Mick's claim to superior education, intelligence and *savoir-faire*. It is, thus, equivalent to an *act of aggression*. Again and again veritable duels of this type develop among Pinter's characters. The memorable dispute about whether one says 'light the kettle' or 'light the gas' in *The Dumb Waiter* belongs to this category. Words like 'penchant' and 'pubescent' are proofs of superior general education. The use of technical terms and professional jargon, on the other hand, establishes the speaker's superiority in his own chosen field and gives him the advantages of belonging to a freemasonry, an inner circle of people who are able to exclude intruders and interlopers. The use of technical jargon thus corresponds to the enclosed rooms and protected spaces which Pinter's characters tend to covet and to defend against outsiders. When Mick finally turns against Davies and initiates the move which will expel him from the home he has been seeking, he overwhelms him with a demonstration of his ignorance of the skills he alleges Davies claimed when applying for the post of a caretaker in his house:

> ... I only told you because I understood you were an experienced first-class professional interior and exterior decorator.
> DVAIES: Now look here –
> MICK: You mean you wouldn't know how to fit teal-blue, copper and parchment linoleum squares and have those colours re-echoed in the walls?
> DAVIES: Now, look here, where'd you get – ?
> MICK: You wouldn't be able to decorate out a table in afromosia teak veneer, an armchair in oatmeal tweed and a beech frame settee with a woven sea-grass seat?
> DAVIES: I never said that!
> MICK: Christ! I must have been under a false impression!
> DAVIES: I never said it!
> MICK: You're a bloody impostor, mate!

Davies's inability to comprehend the technical jargon of the interior decorator seals what, in effect, is his death sentence. In fact he had never directly claimed any such knowledge, but had merely tacitly nodded his approval when Mick, using the self-same terms, had tempted him with the job of caretaker while outlining his grandiose plans for converting the derelict dwelling into a 'penthouse'. Incomprehension and the inability to express himself is clearly stated to be the reason for his loss of favour with Mick:

> Honest. I can take nothing you say at face value. Every word you speak is open to any number of different interpretations. Most of what you say is lies. You're violent, you're erratic, you're just completely unpredictable. You're nothing else but a wild animal, when you come down to it. You're a barbarian. . . .

The ability to communicate is here equated with civilization, even the possession of a claim to being human. The loser in a contest about words and their meaning loses his claim to live. Power, the power over life or death, derives from the ability to make one's opponent accept the meaning of words chosen by the dominant partner. When Davies, earlier in *The Caretaker*, ventures to remark that Aston, Mick's brother, is 'a bit of a funny bloke', Mick stares at him in indignant amazement:

MICK: Funny? Why?
DAVIES: Well . . . he's funny . . .
MICK: What's funny about him?
   Pause
DAVIES: Not liking work.
MICK: What's funny about that?
DAVIES: Nothing.
   Pause
MICK: I don't call that funny.
DAVIES: Nor me.

His surrender is both abject and complete. A disagreement about the meaning of a term has become a fundamental, existential contest of wills. Words, thus, are of vital importance. And yet, it is not so much the words themselves as the existential situations they conceal and reveal. It is no coincidence that the climactic turning point of *The Homecoming* arises from a 'philosophical' discussion, Lenny's attempt to draw his brother Teddy into an argument about being and non-being, words and the realities behind them:

LENNY: Well, for instance, take a table. Philosophically speaking. What is it?
TEDDY: A table.
LENNY: You mean it's nothing else but a table. Well, some people would envy your certainty, wouldn't they, Joey? For instance, I've got a couple of friends of mine, we often sit round the Ritz Bar having a few liqueurs, and they are always saying things like that, you know, things like: Take a table,

take it. All right, I say, *take* it, *take* a table, but once you've
taken it, what you going to do with it? Once you've got hold
of it, where you going to take it?

MAX: You'd probably sell it.

LENNY: You wouldn't get much for it.

JOEY: Chop it up for firewood.

Lenny looks at him and laughs

RUTH: Don't be too sure though. You've forgotten something.
Look at me. I . . . move my leg. That's all it is. But I wear
. . . underwear . . . which moves with me . . . it . . . captures
your attention. Perhaps you misinterpret. The action is simple.
It's a leg . . . moving. My lips move. Why don't you restrict
. . . your observations to that? Perhaps the fact that they move
is more significant . . . than the words which come through
them. You must bear that . . . possibility . . . in mind.

Perhaps the fact that the lips move is more significant than
the words which come through them! This key sentence not
only touches the basis of Pinter's practice of the use of
dramatic dialogue, it also reveals his fundamental philosophical attitude: his search, through and in spite of, an obsessive
preoccupation with language, its nuances, its meaning, its
beauty, for the area of reality that lies *behind* the use of
language. It is not the word table that matters, but the way
you *take* the table, how you *act* on it and how it *acts* on you,
what it does to you. The lips that move are more significant,
ultimately, than the words that come through them, the leg
and the underwear which moves with it has more reality,
because it is an action which creates an immediate response,
than any of the polite words that a respectable professor's
wife like Ruth might utter. Or, to put it differently, it
matters little whether Mick's or Davies's interpretation of
the word 'funny' is the correct one, what is essential and
existentially important is that Mick makes Davies accept *his*
definition of the word's meaning.

Thus, again and again in Pinter's plays language becomes
the medium through which a contest of wills is fought out,
sometimes overtly as in the disputes about the correct
expression to be used or about the correct meaning of a

253

given word or phrase, sometimes beneath the surfce of the explicit subject matter of the dialogue. The brainwashing of Stanley by Goldberg and McCann in *The Birthday Party* shows the transition from the one mode to the other with particular clarity; it opens with specific questions referring to Stanley's real situation:

> Why do you behave so badly, Webber? Why do you force that old man out to play chess?

Yet gradually the questions become more and more fantastic, more and more abstract, until in the end we are, indeed, made aware that it is the lips that are moving, and the rage with which they move, that matters rather than the words they utter. Nevertheless the words are of the utmost importance; not through their surface meaning, but through the colour and texture of their sound *and* the *associations* of meaning. At first Goldberg and McCann bombard Stanley with questions about specific crimes, which, however, are so contradictory that it is clear that he could not really have committed all of them: at one point he is asked:

> Why did you kill your wife?

A few lines later his crime is:

> Why did you never get married?

As the cross-examination proceeds, it becomes ever more obvious that it is an expression of Stanley's *general* feelings of guilt, of his tormentors' general conviction that he deserves punishment; the long list of venial and mortal sins, major and minor transgressions, which is unleashed upon poor Stanley –

> You stuff yourself with dry toast.
> You contaminate womankind.
> Why don't you pay the rent?

Why do you pick your nose?
What about Ireland?

– covers the whole gamut of possible sources of guilt feelings: from embarrassment over social gaffes (picking one's nose), collective national guilt feelings about crimes committed by one's country (Ireland for the Englishman Stanley Webber), minor lapses (such as eating too much toast) to the major sins of lechery and even the worst of all, cheating at the national sport:

Who watered the wicket in Melbourne?[1]

until it culminates in the final, existential question of why the chicken crossed the road, and which came first, the chicken or the egg – in other words, why Stanley has the effrontery of existing, of being alive at all. The proliferation of images, grotesquely juxtaposed and subtly intensified, establishes this long scene as a kind of poem, a structure of images which constitutes a set of variations on a basic theme. The chief character of the play is thrown, as it were, into a whirlpool of language which batters him into insensitivity.

(Ten years after Pinter wrote *The Birthday Party*, Peter Handke, a young protagonist of the theatrical avant-garde in Germany, achieved considerable success with a new kind of dramatic spectacle which he called 'Sprechstücke' (word plays); these consist of long structures of pure language uttered by speakers who do not represent any specific characters, but which, by confronting the audience with permutations of words and associations on a given theme (the future; cries for help; insults; or, indeed, the sources of guilt feelings) set up linguistic fields of force from which each member of the audience must, willy-nilly, assemble his own personal experience of hopes, helplessness, rage or guilt. Pinter not only anticipated this 'new' experimental

[1] Which so baffled the first translator of the play into German that he rendered it by a sentence which, translated back, reads: 'Who urinated against the city gate of Melbourne?'

form, but also demonstrated how it could be integrated and made to work within a more traditional framework of drama.)

Brilliant as the brainwashing scene in *The Birthday Party* is, Pinter's use of language became far subtler in his later plays. When Lenny first meets Ruth in *The Homecoming* he tells her two long, and seemingly gratuitous, stories. As in *The Birthday Party*'s brainwashing scene, these are linguistic structures designed to evoke feelings of guilt and terror in the listener; but they are far more subtly orchestrated, far less obviously abstract *tours de force*. Having just met Ruth late at night and alone in his house, Lenny at first engages her in the usual small talk. Then suddenly out of a speech about her visit to Venice and his feeling that he might have seen Venice had he served in the last war, he confronts her with a clearly erotic proposition:

> . . . Do you mind if I hold your hand?
> RUTH: Why?
> LENNY: Just a touch.
> *He stands and goes to her.*
> Just a tickle.
> RUTH: Why?
> *He looks down at her*
> LENNY: I'll tell you why.
> *Slight pause*

Lenny then launches into his first long story, which seems totally unrelated to the question he promised to answer – namely, why he wants to touch Ruth. The story starts on a formal linguistic level, almost like the opening sentences of a novel –

> One night, not too long ago, one night down by the docks, I was standing alone under an arch, watching all the men jibbing the boom, out on the harbour, and playing about with the yardarm –

Note the use of technical terms of nautical language as an indication of expertise, of being an insider! Ruth and the audience will now expect to hear that Lenny (whose occupation is a mystery) might turn out to have something to do with the sea. But at this point the story – and the language – suddenly change gear –

> when a certain lady came up to me and made a certain proposal.

Now we are in the terminology of the British popular press when it deals, as politely and respectably as is possible under the circumstances, with sexual matters and above all sex crimes:

> This lady had been searchng for me for days. She'd lost track of my whereabouts. However, the fact was she eventually caught up with me, and when she caught up with me she made me this certain proposal. Well, this proposal wasn't entirely out of order and normally I would have subscribed to it. I mean I would have subscribed to it in the normal course of events. The only trouble was –

and here the language again enters, abruptly, another sphere altogether –

> – The only trouble was she was falling apart with the pox.

This is another field of technical jargon: the professional talk of pimps and prostitutes. Lenny has shown his hand: he has indicated that this is his world. What is more: he goes on to discuss, very dispassionately and coolly, his desire to kill the girl there and then –

> . . . and the fact is, that as killings go, it would have been a simple matter, nothing to it.

– and concludes the story with his decision, *not* to kill her –

257

But . . . in the end I thought . . . Aaah, why go to all the bother . . . you know, getting rid of the corpse and all that, getting yourself into a state of tension. So I just gave her another belt in the nose and a couple of turns of the boot and sort of left it at that.

Again it is the switching from the polite language of the newspaper crime report to the brutal vernacular of the criminal himself which makes the point. In answer to Ruth's question why he made her an erotic proposal, Lenny has told her that being engaged in the business of prostitution, and being in a position to reject such proposals from other girls, he feels himself entitled to make such claims, and that, indeed, such claims should be regarded as an honour by the women to whom they are addressed. Ruth's reaction shows that she has understood the import of the story only too well. Displaying no surprise whatever, she instinctively, or deliberately, falls into the same technical jargon:

RUTH: How did you know she was diseased?
LENNY: How did I know?
  Pause
  I decided she was.
  Silence.
  You and my brother are newly-weds, are you?

Having, by her lack of surprise and the technical language of her question, revealed that she comes from the same world, Ruth is, in Lenny's answer, sharply reminded by him that his power over his girls is absolute. If he decides that a girl is diseased, then she is diseased. The point is made. Lenny can change the subject and return to polite small talk. But it is merely a short break in the contest of wills. Again, to establish his determination to be brutal to women, be they helpless and old, Lenny tells his second long story about the lady who asked him to move her mangle, while he was employed to clear the snow in the streets on a winter morning, but failed to give him a helping hand with the heavy object:

So after a few minutes I said to her, now look here, why don't you stuff this iron mangle up your arse? Anyway, I said, they're out of date, you want to get a spin-drier. I had a good mind to give her a workover there and then, but as I was feeling jubilant with the snow-clearing I just gave her a short-arm jab to the belly and jumped on a bus outside. Excuse me, shall I take this ashtray out of your way?

The narration of a brutal assault on an old woman is directly linked to the seemingly trivial question about the ashtray. But in fact the ashtray and the glass which stands beside it become the focus for the first direct confrontation between Ruth and Lenny. She does not want to move the ashtray and she wants to keep the glass as she is still thirsty. And Ruth, having been told of Lenny's capacity for being brutal to women, and having taken it all in, openly challenges him:

If you take the glass . . . I'll take you.

And she goes over to the attack:

> *She picks up the glass and lifts it towards him.*
> RUTH: Have a sip. Go on. Have a sip from my glass.
> *He is still.*
> Sit on my lap. Take a long cool sip.
> *She pats her lap. Pause.*
> *She stands, moves to him with the glass.*
> Put your head back and open your mouth.
> LENNY: Take that glass away from me.
> RUTH: Lie on the floor. Go on. I'll pour it down your throat.
> LENNY: What are you doing, making me some kind of proposal?
> *She laughs shortly, drains the glass.*

Ruth has turned the tables completely. She has become the girl who makes a proposal to Lenny; but Lenny fails to do to her what he had boasted he had done to the girl who had made him that certain proposal.

The audience, witnessing the play for the first time will, of course, not be consciously aware of *all* the information which the playwright has, subtly, supplied in the shifts of linguistic levels, the echoing and re-echoing of key-words (e.g. 'proposal'); to them the strange night scene with its long and seemingly pointless narrative passages and the sudden contest of wills must seem 'enigmatic', provocatively suggestive but barely penetrable. Dramatically this is an advantage, because it generates one of the most important elements in all drama – suspense. Yet, as in the best detective fiction, the clues are all provided, and with scrupulous fairness: they are present in the language itself which lets us see through it into the depths of the unspoken thoughts and emotions of the two characters: Lenny propositions Ruth because he has sensed that she is like the girls with whom he deals in his profession. When she asks *why* he has propositioned her, he tells her, by gradually falling into the brutal trade language of the pimp, what he is and – by implication – what he thinks she may well be. And by her reaction – or rather the absence of a shocked reaction, the acceptance of a man who uses that kind of language as a matter of course – she clearly indicates that she does in fact belong to that same world. Hence Ruth's acceptance of the role of a prostitute when it is offered to her towards the end of the play, which tends to shock audiences so deeply, has already been anticipated in this scene of her first confrontation with Lenny. And so has the sovereign, disdainfully businesslike attitude with which she settles the terms of her new life by driving an exceedingly hard bargain: for in that first contest of wills she had shown herself fully Lenny's equal in ruthlessness.

In fact, if one analyses Pinter's work closely, one will find that behind the apparently random rendering of the colloquial vernacular, there lies a rigorous economy of means: each word is essential to the total structure and decisively contributes to the ultimate, overall effect aimed at. In this respect also Pinter's use of language is that of a poet; there are no redundant words in true poetry, no empty patches, no mere fill-ins. Pinter's dramatic writing has the density of texture of true poetry.

That is why – as in poetry the caesura, as in music the pause – silences play such a large and essential part in Pinter's dialogue. Pinter uses two different terms for the punctuation of his dialogue by passages without speech: 'Pause' and 'Silence'. In the above example, which has been analysed in some detail, when, at the end of Lenny's first narration, Ruth asks how he knew the girl in question was diseased (and thus reveals her lack of surprise and familiarity with the vocabulary) Lenny's reaction is:

How did I know?
Pause.
I decided she was.
Silence.
You and my brother are newly-weds, are you?

The repetition of the question, 'how did I know' shows Lenny's surprise at Ruth's reaction; he can hardly, as yet, believe that she would react in so matter-of-fact a way. The 'pause' bridges the time he needs to take in the whole import of that reaction and to think out his reply. The 'silence' after his reply and before he changes the subject indicates the much deeper caesura of the end of that section of the conversation. When Pinter asks for a *pause*, therefore, he indicates that intense thought processes are continuing, that unspoken tensions are mounting, whereas *silences* are notations for the end of a movement, the beginning of another, as between the movements of a symphony.

The pauses and silences in Pinter's plays are the answer to Len's question in the novel *The Dwarfs* when he was speaking about those poets who climb from word to word like stepping stones:

What do they do when they come to a line with no words in it at all?

For the answer to that question is that *drama* is a kind of poetry which *can* find room for the emotional charge of the unspoken line: what speaks on the stage is the situation itself, the characters who confront each other in silence, what has gone before and the expectation, the suspense as to what will happen next. Pinter's pauses and silences are thus often the climaxes of his plays, the still centres of the storm, the nuclei of tension around which the whole action is structured: there is the 'long silence' at the end of *The Caretaker* when Davies's pleading for permission to remain in Aston's room elicits no answer. This 'long silence' is the death of hope for the old man, Aston's refusal to forgive him, his expulsion from the warmth of a home – death. But, as the curtain falls before he is seen to leave, it may also be the long silence before that final word of forgiveness is pronounced: the 'line with no words in it' thus has all the ambiguity and complexity of true poetry and it is also a metaphor, an image of overwhelming power.

Likewise, at the close of *The Collection* after Bill's 'final' confession, his last version of the incident with James's wife, Stella, namely, that nothing happened between them at all, Pinter calls for a 'long silence', after which James leaves the house. And then the silence continues as Harry and Bill remain sitting, facing each other. That silence contains an image of the despair and horror of their mutual dependence, above all of Bill's final failure to free himself from Harry's domination. As the light fades on that image, James is seen returning to his own home and confronting his wife:

> JAMES: You didn't do anything, did you?
> *Pause*
> He wasn't in your room. You just talked about it, in the lounge.
> *Pause*
> That's the truth, isn't it?
> *Pause*
> You just sat and talked about what you would do if you went to your room. That's what you did.
> *Pause*
> Didn't you?
> *Pause*

That's the truth . . . isn't it?
Stella looks at him, neither confirming nor denying. Her face is friendly, sympathetic.

Stella's silence, her refusal to confirm or deny the story, is, in the true dramatic sense, an *action*, the pause which echoes each of James's questions *is a line of dialogue*, it is also a poetic image of one human being's mystery and impenetrability for another. This, it must again be stressed, has nothing to do with man's *inability* to communicate with his fellow man: what is being demonstrated is man's – or this woman's – *unwillingness* to communicate, and indeed, her partner's inability ever to be certain that, whether she speaks or remains silent, he can get hold of the real, the inner, personal, truth of the matter.

That silence which is a *refusal* to communicate is one of the dominant images of Pinter's plays: from Bert's non-responsiveness to Rose in his first play *The Room* to Beth's inability or unwillingness to hear, and to respond to, what Duff tells her in *Landscape*.

There is another speechlessness, however, in Pinter's work, the speechlessness of annihilation, of total collapse: we find it in Stanley's inarticulate 'uh-gughh' and 'caaahhh' at the end of *The Birthday Party*, in Edward's silent acceptance of the matchseller's tray in the closing moment of *A Slight Ache*, in Disson's catatonic collapse at the close of *Tea Party*. This, also, is the silence which gives its title to the play *Silence* – the silence of the gradual fading of memory, the gradual, inevitable dissolution of human personality itself.

To be filled, to be meaningful, Pinter's silences and pauses have to be meticulously *prepared*: only if the audience knows the possible alternative answers to a question can the absence of a reply acquire meaning and dramatic impact; only because we know what Disson might want to say – and indeed the way in which he is torn between the conflicting desires and fears he is unable to keep under control – are we moved by his inability to speak. Thus the effectiveness of the pauses and silences is, by Pinter's technique, the direct consequence of the density of texture of his writing: each syllable and each silence is part of an overall design, all portions of which are totally integrated; another way to put this would be to say that Pinter's writing is of the utmost economy, there are no redundant parts in it. It is the economy by which a door, a simple, ordinary door, can become a source of nameless fear and menace, merely because the character in the room has been shown to dread the intrusion of the outside world: the economy of means through which a character who has been kept silent through most of the play can cause an effect of overwhelming surprise by suddenly starting to speak; the economy of words which can invest the most threadbare cliché with hidden poetic meaning.

Teddy's departure in *The Homecoming* might be cited as a telling, final example of this supreme economy of Pinter's dramatic technique. Ruth, Teddy' wife, has consented to stay behind with the family and to become a prostitute. Teddy is returning to America alone. He has said good-bye to all the men in the room. He has not spoken to Ruth. He goes to the door. Then Ruth speaks: she calls him – 'Eddie'.

Throughout the play Ruth has never addressed Teddy by his name. Talking to the others she has referred to him, as they have, as Teddy. The fact that she now calls him by a different name, the name which no doubt was the one she used when they were alone, thus acquires a particular force.

Teddy turns.

Quite clearly he feels that the use of a name which Ruth regarded as a part of their intimacy in earlier times may yet indicate that she has changed her mind, that she may yet come with him. But having turned, and having waited, he is greeted with silence. Pinter indicates a *pause*. Then Ruth merely says: 'Don't become a stranger.'

'Don't become a stranger' is a cliché, an idiom without any emotional force. It is what one says to a casual acquaintance after the holiday is over, the cruise has come to an end; if one were to explain the phrase in a dictionary of idioms one would translate it with no more than: we might meet again: or: see you some time. This, clearly, is also how Teddy understands it. For he goes and shuts the front door. Pinter indicates a 'silence'. But in that silence, which concludes Teddy's visit, which sets a full stop to his appearance in the play and probably in the lives of the other characters, surely there will also echo something of the *literal* meaning of that phrase 'don't become a stranger', rather like a last desparing lament of a wife for the husband she has now lost, who has, in fact, at that very moment become a stranger to her.

Only five words, only eight syllables are actually spoken in that whole passage: 'Eddie – Don't become a stranger.' But through the surprise use of a name, through a pregnant pause, and an utterly final silence, and through the subtle ambiguity of a phrase which is both a weak cliché and yet carries a literal meaning of deep, tragic impact, Pinter has put a wealth of drama, psychological profundity, suspense, irony and pathos into those eight syllables.

Such economy and subtlety in the use of language, such density of subtext beneath the sparseness of the text itself, is surely the hallmark of a real master of the craft of dialogue.

5

Summing Up

Having passed beyond sixty, Pinter, who started his career under the misleading label of one of the 'angry young men' of British drama, has, undoubtedly become a major public figure, already something of a 'great old man' of the theatre of his time. The main body of his work seems to lie behind him; his sorties into committed theatrical pamphleteering constitute a new departure, which, however, cannot, as yet, be regarded as more than a minor addition to his *œuvre*.

His having been thrown into the same pot as the other dramatists of the new wave of British theatre that transformed it in the late nineteen-fifties and the sixties – Osborne, Wesker, Arden, Bond – has since become evident as a misunderstanding. It is true that he, like these writers, came out of the first generation of the beneficiaries of the post-war reform of the educational system which allowed young people of all social origins access to higher education (Pinter went to the Royal Academy of Dramatic Art with a grant from the London County Council). These were the playwrights who replaced the middle-class idiom which had dominated the British stage with a wide variety of regional and lower-class vernaculars, and thereby, initially, shocked many of the older critics and playgoers. Yet apart from this superficial family likeness each of the playwrights concerned pursued totally different objectives and embodied very different basic attitudes. For all his brilliant use of lower-class idiomatic English, for all his mastery in reproducing the quirks and cadences of real spoken English as against the conventional stage rhetoric, Pinter's objectives were still fundamentally those of a lyrical poet, rather than a social realist or champion of revolution. Beckett and Kafka were his lodestars.

That his attitude of complete devotion to the demands of his work as a poet has been consistently maintained since his very beginnings as a writer, is shown by a letter which Pinter wrote to a friend of his who had deplored the lack of a 'moral' (i.e. ideological) standpoint in his writing, as long ago as 1955, when he was twenty-four:

> If I write about a lamp, I apply myself to the demands of that lamp. If I write about a flower, I apply myself to the demands of that flower. In most cases, the flower has singular properties as opposed to the lamp. . . . Flower, lamp, tinopener, tree . . . tend to take alteration from a different climate and circumstance and I must necessarily attend to that singular change with the same devotion and allowance. I do not intend to impose or distort for the sake of an ostensible 'harmony' of approach.
>
> What you want from my writing is not self expression but self confession, and you're not going to get it. You want me to open wide my doors (possibly from a 'moral standpoint'). That is neither my inclination, nor, more important, my purpose.

Here are the sources of Pinter's accuracy as an observer, the ability to hear the real speech of real people and to note it down with the objectivity of a tape recorder: this objectivity is *self-expression* insofar as it proceeds from an urge to communicate his own personal mode of experiencing the world – his own existential emotion:

> . . . I am not trying to assert myself when I write, or rarely. (My subjects) present themselves to me in their separate guises. I sharpen my tools for them. I stand them in front of the window with the light behind them. I place them in a corner in the shadows. I am there, of course – I am writing the stuff. There are many corridors and many rooms, many climates, in my possession. I am not a fixed star. Of course I am there – everywhere – I crawl on all fours – I declare war – I abdicate – it is my world. But I do not sit in a cosy didactic corner in *one* room, speaking through a loudspeaker. My preoccupation is not a cosy corner. It is the house.

I am stuck neither to a style, in the limiting, self conscious sense, to a room, or to a prophecy. I am concerned with penetration to the root of the immediate matter, the matter in hand. My aim is stringency, shading, and accuracy. Where I indulge in word-warfare, it is no longer for high jinks, but simply where I feel it demanded. Of course I recognize forms and employ them, or rather, go to meet them – a continuous voyage, and my seed within them, they expand or snap. There is no such thing as a static mode of expression. There is no form which does not take alteration with one artist's approach.

Sometimes, in poems, I am only dimly conscious of the grounds of my activity, and the work proceeds to its own law and discipline, with me as go-between, as it were. But as you say, if not conscious, so much the better. . . .

Thus this very early – and remarkable – self-examination goes, with penetrating insight, to the very heart of Pinter's method and artistic personality: on the one hand the objective, meticulous recorder of the world around him; on the other the poet who knows that his work flows from deep subconscious sources, by its own law and discipline; he records the world as dispassionately as he can, but, of necessity, this is a world recorded by *him*, seen through *his* eyes, which notice and select each detail by the inner law of *his* personality: hence the world thus recorded is *his*, the poet's own, personal world: at one and the same time it bears the lineaments of real, external objects, real people whom he has encountered, and yet, because it has been observed by that particular personality obeying its own inner law and discipline it is also an image, a metaphor of his *inner* world. The external world, objectively and meticulously recorded, must, of necessity, be fragmentary, disconnected, unmotivated and without a clearly discernible structure: segments of reality are like that. But, because these fragments have been noted down by a highly individual personality whose very act of perception must be an expression of his individual mode of experiencing the world around him, simply because certain objets or images will touch him more than others, the disconnected ingredients will coalesce into an organic structure, expressing its own inner consistencies – obeying its own inner law as an individual's personal vision of his own personal world.

Hence the dual nature of Pinter's work, the simultaneous co-existence within it of the most extreme naturalism of surface description and of a dreamlike, poetic feeling, which, as indeed often happens in dreams, is by no means inconsistent with an uncanny clarity of outline. This explains also the duality of the impact which Pinter's plays tend to have on their audiences: the amusement about the accuracy of observation, combined at a deeper level with the unease, the mixture of horror and fascination, evoked by a subconscious response to implications which spring from the author's own subconscious. On the surface we may laugh about Davies's impotent antics and stupid lies, but deep down we sense that this laughter expresses some of the contempt – and the fear – which sons feel for their fathers. We may feel amused by the game husband and wife play with each other in *The Lover*, yet deep down we respond to the fact that husbands do indeed dream of their wives as prostitutes, wives of their husbands as suave lovers or brutal rapists.

If, as it is sometimes suggested, the ambiguity and uncertainty of Pinter's plays really was no more than the outcome of a deliberate manipulation of his audience by a clever craftsman of theatrical trickery, his use of repetition and absurdly inconsequential conversation no more than mechanical mannerisms, his work would be highly ephemeral and have no chance of making an impact on future generations of playgoers who would no longer be taken in or shocked by such superficially effective devices. If, on the other hand, as I believe it to be the case, the uncertainties, ambivalences and ambiguities of plot and language in these plays are the expression of a genuine perplexity about the nature of our experience of the world, the distillation of a deeply felt, painfully sifted and conscientiously recorded creative process, then they will surely endure as works not only of brilliant craftsmanship (which is already beyond doubt) but as considerable artistic achievements.

What speaks for the latter view is the undoubted evidence of a steady development in Pinter's style, his consistent refusal merely to reproduce the mannerisms and technical achievements of his early successes. *Landscape* and *Silence*, *Betrayal* and *A Kind of Alaska*, in particular, are so radically different from the formula of what is commonly regarded as Pinteresque, so uncompromisingly remote from cheap seeking after success, that the view of Pinter as a mere manipulator of mechanical formulae surely must break down. In these plays the *poet* following his own inner law and discipline is again to the fore. '. . . My last two plays,' said Pinter in an interview before the first night of *Landscape* and *Silence*, 'are really rather different. They had to be from my point of view: I felt that after *The Homecoming*, which was the last full-length play I wrote, I couldn't any longer stay in the room with this bunch of people who opened doors and came in and went out . . .'[1]

If Pinter felt like that, one is tempted to think, it must be due to the fact that the fears and subconscious anxieties which were connected with his obsession by these images of menace, have been overcome. *The Homecoming* finally brought the true nature of these anxieties to the surface by showing the connection between these fears and the duality of the female figure who oscillates between mother and harlot. These anxieties were the anxieties of an adolescent, a young man coming to terms with his own personality. In *Landscape*, *Silence*, *No Man's Land* and *Betrayal* we are in an entirely different sphere: the area of nostalgia for lost love and innocence, regret for past mistakes and meditation about the gradual obliteration of consciousness in silence, in oblivion and death. This is the world of a young man no longer, but one which lies beyond the water-shed '*nel mezzo del cammin di nostra vita*' of middle age. The curve of the playwright's development as a human being is thus being followed by his work; yet, because the world he reproduced

[1] Interview with Michael Dean, BBC TV, reprinted in *The Listener*, 6th March, 1969.

in his plays was a poetic evocation, in precise and realistic images, of his *inner* world, Pinter's plays are free from the concentration of autobiographical subject-matter which has become a problem for such contemporaries of his as Osborne and Wesker (by presenting them with the difficulties of having to mirror a more opulent, but less interesting external life). Pinter's ability to transcend the merely autobiographical subject-matter puts him, in my opinion, into a different class from most of the other, social-realist, playwrights of his generation in Britain. Moreover, and surprisingly, since so much of his effect in his own country derives from his witty use of local speech patterns, Pinter's plays have been as successful in Amercia and in Europe across the Channel as they were in England. In English-speaking countries Pinter's language retains much of its appeal through his evident skill in the handling of rhythm, pace and pause and the fascination of his vocabulary. In translations – some of which, like the first (since revised) German version, were full of inaccuracies and downright howlers – these purely linguistic features are bound to lose much of their impact, although some elements, like the use of repetition, can be preserved. Yet enough remains to hold an audience: the 'oblique' character of the dialogue, the poetic power of 'motiveless' action, the menace and suspense, the philosophical implications of the existential uncertainties which are being demonstrated – but, above all, the depth of insight into the subconscious mainsprings of human action, the archetypal imagery, expressed through *situations* rather than explicit statement or discursive argumentation, by which they are brought to life by Pinter on the stage.

The unquestionable impact of Pinter's work notwithstanding, however, it has been said that his work lacks the wide sweep, the variety of subject-matter and character, which mark a major playwright, a Brecht, Shaw, Ibsen, or Shakespeare; that Pinter is no more than a miniaturist, a minor master with a narrow range. Yet, surely, the importance of a writer lies in the *depth* of his insights rather than in the width of his subject-matter; those writers who are primarily interested in society, politics, history and the external world certainly need this kind of richness; yet others, whose main preoccupation is the inner life of man, his basic existential problems, which, of necessity are few, have undoubtedly been of comparable stature: Beckett, one of Pinter's avowed literary models, is a case in point. These are, in the main, lyricists rather than epic poets, absurdists rather than realists. The extreme accuracy of Pinter's images from reality (which correspond to the meticulous descriptive pedantry of Kafka, the earthy naturalism of Beckett's detail) must not blind us to the fact that essentially his is a *lyrical* vision which builds up a communication of an individual's otherwise inaccessible and inexpressible experience of living from a complex structure of verbal and situational imagery; the observation of surface detail is not an end in itself, but a means to an end, which is the elevation of a situation (a man afraid of the persecutors behind a closed door; an old man being expelled from his home; two people separated by the gulf which yawns between the different levels of emotion on which they live – in *Landscape*) into a poetic metaphor, an image within a pattern of images. The range of such a work may *appear* narrow, and as a mere representation of external reality it may seem extremely simple: yet if we examine its ability to express the inexpressible, to transcend the scope of language itself and to evoke a response at the deepest level of direct communication of emotion and experience, then such a work will have to be acknowledged as in fact going *further* in range than anything that can be accomplished on a merely discursive level, and as being also far more complex: for to achieve such a communication a multitude of elements operating on a multitude of different levels must be brought to bear at one and the same time: it is from the tensions between the laughter about the accurately observed verbal blunder and the pathos of the situation, between the poverty of vocabulary and the wealth of emotion it hides, between the triviality of the outside circumstances and their power as an archetype of existence, that these high-points of poetry in the theatre are sparked into being and fused into flashes of insight which are communication on a higher level than can be attained by any prose: these are the 'lines with no words' in them of which one of Pinter's early characters spoke.

Clearly not all of Pinter's work can aspire to be judged on this high level. Some of his early plays are trial runs, his revue sketches are no more than exercises in the technique of dialogue; some of the radio and television plays were tailored to the needs of the media and their mass audiences. *A Slight Ache*, *A Night Out* and *Night School* are highly efficient and amusing examples of professional craftsmanship; *Tea Party* was written for a specific project involving a vast international audience; yet other television plays, notably *The Collection*, *The Lover* and *Basement* do achieve at least some degree of that higher level of communication. His major claims must, however, rest on his best work for the stage: *The Dumb Waiter* among his first efforts; and his impressive list of full-length plays: *The Birthday Party*, *The Caretaker*, *The Homecoming*, *Old Times*, *No Man's Land*, *Betrayal*; and the short lyrical pieces, *Landscape*, *Silence* and *A Kind of Alaska*.

The late short plays against torture and totalitarian cruelty make use of the techniques developed in the main body of his work, but stand, at least as far as can at present be seen, somewhat outside his central, major achievement. Yet in their pre-occupation with the cruelty of man against man, their horror at torture and their compassion with helpless individuals they clearly continue Pinter's more purely 'existential' concerns in his earlier work as a playwright.

Harold Pinter's supreme craftsmanship, his originality in treating the language, the depth and emotional intensity of his poetic vision, his refusal to compromise his artistic standards and integrity, give him the stature and assured position of a modern 'classic'. The numerous revivals of his early plays, thirty years after they first achieved their shock effects, their emergence as works of lasting impact, revealing ever new aspects, confirm that assessment. Moreover, Pinter can now be seen as being both a daring innovator who has enlarged the scope of stage dialogue by opening up wholly new perspectives on how real people communicate and fail to communicate, and, at the same time, as a supreme craftsman of the traditional techniques of the English drawing-room play, high comedy (Noël Coward admired his timing, he has a high regard for Coward) and the suspense thriller. As such he takes his place in the mainstream of the great tradition of British and world drama.

Bibliography

A. Pinter's Writings

Plays

Since January 1990 the following editions have been published by Faber & Faber, with the exception of the student editions indicated, which are published by Methuen.

The Birthday Party, London: Encore Publishing Co., 1959.

The Birthday Party and other plays, London: Methuen, 1960. Also contains *The Room* and *The Dumb Waiter*.

The Birthday Party (student edition), London: Eyre Methuen, 1981.

The Caretaker, London: Methuen, 1960.

The Caretaker (student edition), London: Methuen, 1982.

A Slight Ache and other plays, London: Methuen, 1961. Also contains: *A Night Out*, *The Dwarfs* and five Revue Sketches ('Trouble in the Works', 'The Black and White', 'Request Stop', 'Last to Go', 'Applicant').

The Collection and the Lover, London: Methuen, 1963. Also contains the story 'The Examination'.

The Homecoming, London: Methuen, 1965.

Tea Party and other plays, London: Methuen, 1967. Also contains *The Basement* and *Night School*.

Landscape, London: Emanuel Wax for Pendragon Press, 1968, edition limited to 2,000 copies, numbered 1–1,000 for Great Britain, 1,001–2,000 for the United States.

The Homecoming, London: Karnac/Curwen, 1968, edition limited to 200 copies, with nine lithographs by Harold Cohen, each signed by the author and the artist.

Landscape and Silence, London: Methuen, 1969. Also contains *Night*.

Old Times, London: Methuen, 1971.

Monologue, London: Covent Garden Press, 1973, edition limited to 100 copies, signed by the author.

No Man's Land, London: Eyre Methuen, 1975.

Betrayal, London: Eyre Methuen, 1978; revised second edition, 1980.

The Hothouse, London: Eyre Methuen, 1980; revised second edition, 1982.

Family Voices, London: Next Editions in association with Faber & Faber, 1981.

Other Places, London: Methuen, 1982. Contains *A Kind of Alaska*; *Victoria Station*; *Family Voices*.

One for the Road, London: Methuen, 1984.

Precisely, in *Harper's*, May 1985.

One for the Road, with production photos by Yvan Kyncl and an interview with Nicholas Hern on the play and its politics. London: Methuen, 1985.

Mountain Language, London: Faber & Faber, 1988.

Party Time, London: Faber & Faber, 1991.

Moonlight, London: Faber & Faber, 1993.

Ashes to Ashes, London: Faber & Faber, 1996.

Celebration & The Room, London: Faber & Faber, 2000.

Collected Edition:

Plays One, London: Faber & Faber, 1991. Contains: *Introduction: Writing for the Theatre*; *The Birthday Party*; *The Room*; *The Dumb Waiter*; *A Slight Ache*; *The Hothouse*; *A Night Out*; *The Black and White*; *The Examination*.

Plays Two, London: Faber & Faber, 1991. Contains: *Introduction: Writing for Myself*; *The Caretaker*; *The Dwarfs*; *The Collection*; *The Lover*; *Night School*; *Revue Sketches*.

Plays Three, London: Faber & Faber, 1991. Contains: *Mac*; *The Homecoming*; *Tea Party*; *The Basement*; *Landscape*; *Silence*; *Revue Sketches*; *Short Story*; *Tea Party*; *Old Times*; *No Man's Land*.

Plays Four, London, Faber & Faber, 1998. Contains: *Introduction: Speech on Receiving David Cohen Prize, 1995*; *Betrayal*; *Monologue*; *Family Voices*; *A Kind of Alaska*; *Victoria Station*; *Precisely*; *One for the Road*; *Mountain Language*; *The New World Order*; *Party Time*; *Moonlight*; *Ashes to Ashes*.

Poems, selection by Alan Clodd, London: Enitharmon Press, 1968. This selection contains most of Pinter's poems which have appeared in periodicals; it omits: 'Rural Idyll' and 'European Revels' in *Poetry London*, No. 20, November 1950, and 'One A Story, Two A Death', *Poetry London*, No. 22, Summer 1951. In both these issues Pinter's name is spelled Harold Pinta.

Mac, London: Emanuel Wax for Pendragon Press, 1968; limited edition, as *Landscape* (see above). A brief autobiographical sketch, recalling Pinter's association with the Irish actor-manager Anew McMaster.

'Tea Party' (story) in *Playboy*, January 1965.

'Memories of Cricket' in the *Daily Telegraph Magazine*, 16th May 1969.

'Between the Lines', Speech at the Seventh National Students Drama Festival, Bristol, in *The Sunday Times* (London), 4th March 1962. Reprinted as 'Writing for the Theatre' in *Evergreen Review* No. 33, August–September 1964.

Manuscript notes and a page of the typescript of *The Homecoming* are reproduced in *London Magazine*, New Series No. 100, July–August 1969.

'Speech: Hamburg 1970' in *Theatre Quarterly,* vol. 1, No. 3, 1971.

Poems and Prose 1947–1977, London: Eyre Methuen, 1978.

'Letter to Peter Wood', *The Kenyon Review*, New Series, vol. 3, Summer 1981.

The Dwarfs: A Novel, London: Faber & Faber, 1990.

100 Poems by 100 Poets, edited by Harold Pinter, 'Anthony Astbury and Geoffrey Godbert', London: Faber & Faber, 1992.

99 Poems in Translation, edited by Harold Pinter, 'Anthony Astbury and Geoffrey Godbert', London: Faber & Faber, 1994.

Various Voices: Prose, Poetry, Politics 1948–1998, London: Faber & Faber, 1998.

Screenplays

Five Screenplays, London: Eyre Methuen, 1971. Contains: *The Servant*; *The Pumpkin Eater*; *The Quiller Memorandum*; *Accident*; *The Go-Between.*

The Proust Screenplay, London: Eyre Methuen, 1978.

The French Lieutenant's Woman. A Screenplay, London: Jonathan Cape in association with Eyre Methuen, 1981.

The French Lieutenant's Woman and other screenplays, London: Methuen, 1981. Also contains: *Langrishe Go Down; The Last Tycoon*.

The Heat of the Day, London: Faber & Faber, 1989.

The Comfort of Strangers and other screenplays, London: Faber & Faber, 1990. Also contains: *Reunion, Turtle Diary* and *Victory*.

Interviews with Harold Pinter

Interview with John Sherwood, BBC European Service, in the series 'The Rising Generation', dated 3rd March 1960 (duplicated ms).

Interview with Hallam Tennyson, BBC General Overseas Service, 7th August 1960 (duplicated ms).

Interview with Kenneth Tynan, BBC Home Service, recorded 19th August 1960, broadcast 28th October 1960 (duplicated ms).

'Writing for Myself', based on an interview with Richard Findlater, in *Twentieth Century*, February 1961.

Interview with Carl Wildman and Donald McWhinnie, BBC Network Three, in the series 'Talking of Theatre', 7th March 1961 (duplicated ms).

Interview with Laurence Kitchin and Paul Mayersberg, in the programme 'New Comment', BBC Third Programme, broadcast 19th October 1963.

Interview with Marshall Pugh, 'Trying to pin down Pinter', in the *Daily Mail* (London) 7th March 1964.

Interview with Lawrence M. Bensky in *The Paris Review*, No. 39 (1966). Reprinted in *Writers at Work, The Paris Review* Interviews, Third Series, New York: Viking Press, 1967; London: Secker & Warburg, 1968; also in *Theatre at Work*, Methuen, 1967.

Interview with John Russell Taylor, in *Sight and Sound*, Autumn 1966.

Interview in *The New Yorker* ('Talk of the Town'), 25th February 1967.

Interview with Kathleen Tynan, 'In Search of Harold Pinter', part

1 in *Evening Standard* (London) 25th April 1968, part 2 ditto, 26th April 1968.

Interview with Michael Dean, BBC Television, 'Late Night Line-Up', reprinted in *The Listener*, 6th March 1969.

Interview with Joan Bakewell, BBC-2 TV, 11th September 1969 (typed transcript).

Interview with Mel Gussow, *The New York Times*, 5th December 1972.

Interview with Miriam Gross, *The Observer*, 5th October 1980.

Interview with Anna Ford, *The Listener*, 27th October 1988.

Gussow, Mel, *Conversations with Pinter*, London: Nick Hern Books, 1994.

B. On Pinter

The Pinter Review

This publication dedicated to Pinter-scholarship has been published annually since 1987 (with the exception of double numbers for 1992–3 and 1997–98). Originally entitled *The Pinter Review*, it has appeared as *The Pinter Review: Annual Essays* since 1990. The editors are Francis Gillen and Steven H. Gale. It is published by the University of Tampa, Florida. It contains original contributions by Harold Pinter, such as first drafts, etc., scholarly articles, and publishes full bibliographies of theatre reviews, articles and other material related to Pinter.

Bibliographies

Gale, Stephen H., *Harold Pinter. An Annotated Bibliography*, Boston, Mass.: G. K. Hall & Co., 1978.

Gordon, Lois, G., 'Pigeonholing Pinter: A Bibliography' in *Theatre Documentation*, Fall 1968.

Imhof, Rüdiger, *Pinter. A Bibliography*, London: TQ Publications, 1975.

Merritt, Susan Hollis, 'Harold Pinter Bibliography, 1977–88' in *The Pinter Review* No. 2, 1988.

Carpenter, Charles A., *Modern Drama: Scholarship and Criticism 1966–1980. International Bibliography*, Toronto: University of Toronto Press, 1986.

Monographs

Allgeier, Dieter, *Die Dramen Harold Pinters. Eine Untersuchung von Form und Inhalt* (Dissertation), Frankfurt: 1976.

Baker, William and Tabachnick, Stephen E., *Harold Pinter* (in the series 'Writers and their Critics'), Edinburgh: Oliver & Boyd, 1975.

Billington, Michael, *The Life and Work of Harold Pinter*, London: Faber & Faber, 1996.

Bloom, Harold (ed.), *Harold Pinter*, New York: Chelsea House, 1987.

Diamond, Elin, *Pinter's Comic Play*, Lewisburg: Bucknell University Press, 1985.

Burkman, Katherine H., *The Dramatic World of Harold Pinter: Its Basis in Ritual*, Columbus, Ohio: Ohio State University Press, 1971.

Burkman, Katherine H. and John Kundert-Gibbs (eds.), *Pinter at Sixty: Drama and Performance Studies*, Bloomington and London: Indiana University Press, 1993.

Dukore, Bernard F., *Where Laughter Stops. Pinter's Tragicomedy*, Columbia, Missouri: University of Missouri Press, 1976.

Dukore, Bernard F., *Harold Pinter*, 2nd edn, London: Macmillan, 1988.

Gabbard, Lucina P., *The Dream Structure of Pinter's Plays: A Psychoanalytic Approach*, Rutherford, N.J.: Farleigh Dickinson University Press, 1977.

Gale, Stephen H., *Butter's Going Up: A Critical Analysis of Harold Pinter's Work*, Durham, N.C.: Duke University Press, 1977.

Gale, Stephen H. (ed.), *Harold Pinter: Critical Approaches*, Rutherford, N.J.: Farleigh Dickinson University Press, 1986.

Ganz, Arthur (ed.), *Pinter: A Collection of Critical Essays*, Englewood Cliffs, N.J.: Prentice Hall, 1972.

Gordon, Lois, *Stratagems to Uncover Nakedness: The Dramas of Harold Pinter*, Columbia, Miss.: University of Missouri Press, 1969.

Gordon, Lois (ed.), *Harold Pinter: A Casebook*, New York and London: Garland, 1990.

Hayman, Ronald, *Harold Pinter*, in the series 'Contemporary Playwrights', London: Heinemann Educational Books, 1968.

Hinchcliffe, Arnold P., *Harold Pinter* in 'Twayne's English Authors Series', New York: Twayne, 1967 (rev. edn 1981).

Hollis, James R., *Harold Pinter: The Poetics of Silence*, Carbondale, Ill.: Southern Illinois University Press, 1970.

Imhof, Rüdiger, *Harold Pinters Dramentechnik*, Bonn: Bouvier Verlag Herbert Grundmann, 1976.

Kerr, Walter, *Harold Pinter*, No. 27 in the series 'Columbia Essays on Modern Writers', New York and London: Columbia University Press, 1967.

Klein, Joanne, *Making Pictures: The Pinter Screenplays*, Columbus, Ohio: Ohio State University Press, 1985.

Lahr, John (ed.), *A Casebook on Harold Pinter's The Homecoming*, New York: Grove Press, 1971.

Mengel, Ewald, *Harold Pinters Dramen im Spiegel der soziologischen Rollentheorie*, Frankfurt: Lang, 1978.

Quigley, Austin E., *The Pinter Problem*, Princeton, N.J.: Princeton University Press, 1975.

Sakellaridou, Elizabeth, *Pinter's Female Portraits: A Study of Female Characters in the Plays of Harold Pinter*, London: Macmillan, 1966.

Salem, Daniel, *Harold Pinter, Dramaturge de l'ambiguité*, Paris: Denoël, 1968.

Scott, Michael (ed.), *Harold Pinter: The Birthday Party, The Caretaker, The Homecoming: A Casebook*, London: Macmillan, 1986.

Strunk, Volker, *Harold Pinter: Towards a Poetic of his Plays*, New York: Lang, 1989.

Sykes, Alrene, *Harold Pinter*, Santa Lucia: Queensland University Press, 1970.

Taylor, John Russell, *Harold Pinter*, London: Longmans, 1973.

Thompson, David T., *Pinter: The Player's Playwright*, New York: Schocken, 1985.

Trussler, Simon, *The Plays of Harold Pinter. An Assessment*, London: Gollancz, 1973.

C. Books on Which Pinter Based His Screenplays

Bowen, Elizabeth, *The Heat of the Day*, London: Jonathan Cape, 1949.

Conrad, Joseph, *Victory*, London: Collins.

Fowles, John, *The French Lieutenant's Woman*, London: Jonathan Cape, 1969.

281

Hall, Adam, *The Berlin Memorandum*, London: Collins, 1965.
Hartley, L. P., *The Go-Between*, London: Hamish Hamilton, 1953.
Higgins, Aidan, *Langrishe Go Down*, London: Calder, 1966.
Hoban, Russell, *Turtle Diary*, New York: Random house.
Ishiguro, Kazuo, *The Remains of the Day*, London: Faber & Faber, 1989.
Kafka, Franz, *The Trial*, London: Penguin Books, 1970.
McEwan, Ian, *The Comfort of Strangers*, London: Jonathan Cape.
Maugham, Robin, *The Servant*, London: Falcon Press, 1948; republished by Heinemann, 1964.
Mortimer, Penelope, *The Pumpkin Eater*, London: Hutchinson, 1962.
Mosley, Nicholas, *Accident*, London: Hodder & Stoughton, 1965.
Proust, Marcel, *A la recherche du temps perdu*, Paris: Gallimard.
Scott Fitzgerald, *The Last Tycoon*, New York: Scribners, 1941.
Uhlman, Fred, *Reunion*, London: Penguin Books.

Index

Bergman, Ingmar, 78

Berlin Memorandum, The (Hall), 227; *see also Quiller Memorandum, The*

Betrayal: London production, 21; film, 22; theme of, 188–99; language, 236; nostalgia in, 270; qualities, 273; related to *The Dwarfs*, 195; related to *The Homecoming*, 196; related to *A Kind of Alaska*, 206; related to *Moonlight*, 214; related to *No Man's Land*, 198; related to *Old Times*, 195, 198

Billetdoux, François, 146

Billington, Michael, 218

Birthday Party, The: submitted to Codron, 6; first production, 7–10; Tavistock Players production, 10, 11; first German production, 11; first TV production, 11; Actors' Workshop production, 13; Tynan on, 13; Aldwych Theatre production, 17; film, 19–20; Pinter's comments on, 28; Pinter replies to enquiry about, 29; theme of, 32, 66–77; dramatic tension in, 35; linguistic techniques in, 40–1, 48, 76–7, 238–9, 241–2, 243, 254–5, 256, 263; symbolism in, 70–7; early failure, 87; qualities, 273; related to *The Caretaker*, 94–6; related to *The Collection*, 124; related to *The Dumb Waiter*, 66; related to *The Dwarfs* (novel), 124; related to 'European Revels', 49; related to *Family Voices*, 200–2; related to *The Homecoming*, 124–5; related to *The Hothouse*, 85; related to *The Lover*, 124; related to *A Night Out*, 81; related to *Night School*, 102, 105; related to *No Man's Land*, 186; related to *One for the Road*, 209; related to *The Room*, 66, 72, 74, 75, 78; related to *Silence*, 263; related to *A Slight Ache*, 78, 80; related to *Tea Party*, 150; related to 'A View of the Party', 71–2

Black and White, The, 10, 16, 224

Blake, Leila, 15

Blakely, Colin, 20

Blin, Roger, 14

Blithe Spirit (Coward), 21

Bogarde, Dirk, 19

Bond, Edward, 266

Bond, Philip, 16

Bowen, Elizabeth, 23, 228

Brasseur, Pierre, 18

Bray, Barbara, 13

Brearley, Joseph, 2–3

Brecht, Bertolt, 40, 107, 210, 271

Briers, Richard, 14

Bryant, Michael, 17

Burton, Richard, 16

Butley (Gray), 227

first London stage
production, 15; Gate Theatre
production, 15; theme of,
81–4; realistic dialogue in,
83, 84; qualities, 273; related
to *The Birthday Party*, 81,
83; related to *The Caretaker*,
99; related to *The Collection*,
112, 124; related to *The
Dumb Waiter*, 105; related to
The Dwarfs (novel), 112,
124; related to *The
Homecoming*, 112, 124;
related to *The Hothouse*, 85;
related to *The Lover*, 112,
124; related to *Night School*,
104–5; related to *A Slight
Ache*, 81; related to *Tea
Party*, 149

Night School: first TV
production, 13, 102; radio
version, 102; theme of,
102–5; linguistic techniques
in, 248–9; qualities, 273;
related to *The Baseement*,
156; related to *The Birthday
Party*, 102, 105; related to
The Caretaker, 145; related
to *The Collection*, 105;
related to *The Dumb Waiter*,
105; related to *The Dwarfs*
(novel), 111; related to *The
Homecoming*, 105, 144–5;
related to *The Lover*, 105;
related to *A Night Out*,
104–5; related to *The Room*,
105

No Man's Land: first London
production, 21; themes of,
179–88, 189, 270; qualities,

273; related to *The Birthday
Party*, 186; related to *The
Caretaker*, 185; related to
The Dumb Waiter, 186;
related to *The Go–Between*,
187; related to *The
Homecoming*, 186; related to
Old Times, 186; related to
One for the Road, 207;
related to *The Servant*, 186
'Note on Shakespeare, A',
45–6

Observer, The (newspaper):
profile on Pinter (15
September 1963), 3n; on *The
Birthday Party*, 13; on *The
Caretaker*, 13
Oedipus (Sophocles), 45, 141
Old Times: first (Aldwych)
production, 20; first French
production, 20; first German
production, 20; first New
York production, 20; TV
production, 23; theme of,
171–7, 189; dream element
in, 214; language of, 236;
qualities, 273; related to
Ashes to Ashes, 219; related
to *Betrayal*, 196, 198; related
to *Landscape*, 171; related to
The Lover, 176; related to
Monologue, 177; related to
No Man's Land, 186; related
to *Silence*, 171, 174
'One a Story, Two a Death', 5,
48–9
One for the Road: London
production, 22; New York
production, 22; themes of,

to *The Birthday Party*, 150;
related to *The Collection*,
232; related to *The Lover*,
146; related to *A Night Out*,
149; related to *The Room*,
147; related to *Silence*, 263;
related to *A Slight Ache*, 147

Thatcher, Margaret, 213

That's All, 16, 226

That's Your Trouble, 225

themes and images: anti–war,
3–4, 26, 63, 227;
non–communication between
people, 12, 36–9, 104–5,
156–7, 160, 239, 250, 251–2,
261–3; political content,
24–7, 207–14, 226–7; racial
tension, 25, 27, 58–9, 88–9,
95, 245; sexual, 26, 59–60,
74–5, 79, 83, 112, 114–19,
120, 123–5, 137–8, 142–5,
149–50, 161–2, 196, 219,
256; existential nature of,
27–36, 41–3, 45–6, 59, 64,
76–7, 144, 252–3;
symbolism, 28, 29, 94, 97,
100–1, 215; problem of
human identity, 29–30,
108–10; struggle for
self–expression, 36–7, 63–5,
242–3, 250–2; use of
language, 36–41, 62–5, 70,
76, 80, 112–13, 235–65; use
of silence, 37–8, 101–2,
164–71, 261–2; use of
psychoanalytical approach,
44–6, 56–7, 74–6;
re–emergence of early
themes in later plays, 47–51;
struggle for territorial
possession, 50–1, 94, 99,
102–3, 104, 150–1, 154–5;
image of blindness, 54, 56,
57, 72, 78, 79, 80, 101,
147–9, 150, 156; alienation
of individual in industrial
society, 63–4; position of
artist in society, 73, 76, 96;
process of dying, 73–4, 76,
78, 79–80, 170, 263, 270;
transition from adolescence
to maturity, 74–5, 108;
desolation of old age, 98–9,
142–5; Oedipal, 98–9,
142–5, 150; conflict between
instinct and social
conditioning, 125, 146;
dream elements, 214; loss of
children, 214–15; surrealism,
216; irony, 217–18;
atrocities, 219, 221; social
class, 222; torture, 227;
totalitarian oppression, 227;
changing places, 229; use of
repetition, 241–7

Thomas, Dylan, 47

Three: inclusion of *A Slight
Ache* in, 14

Time (magazine): Pinter on *The
Room* in, 6n

Times, The: on *The Birthday
Party*, 8; compares Pinter to
Webern, 11; on *The
Caretaker*, 12; reports
Pinter's divorce, 21

Trial, The (Kafka), 23, 77, 228

Trouble in the Works, 10, 16,
224

Turn of the Screw, The (Henry
James), 9, 10

THE LEARNING CENTRE
HAMMERSMITH AND WEST
LONDON COLLEGE
GLIDDON ROAD
LONDON W14 9BL

Lightning Source UK Ltd.
Milton Keynes UK
10 April 2010

152588UK00007B/1/P

The three following stanzas are variations on the key words – house, night, leaf, bud, open, night and room: the house of bells, for example, becomes the house of night; the leaf, which obeyed the bud, now alarmed the bud, etc. Thus the poem anticipates the kaleidoscopic effect of the changes in the furniture and situation in the room which is the scene of *The Basement*. The character of Kullus makes a third appearance in the short story 'The Examination', first published in the review *Prospect* in the summer of 1959. Here the narrator is engaged in a contest of wills with Kullus which takes the form of some sort of examination. As one or the other of the contestants attains a position of dominance over the other, the room in which the contest takes place becomes his property.

There is nothing surprising in the re-emergence of early preoccupations and imagery in the mature work of a writer. Yet the presence of these basic motifs helps to show us some aspects of the genesis of the author's world and its particular, highly personal atmosphere after 'the dislocated word' had 'become articulate'.

The Room

Pinter's first play shows the emergence of a firm dramatic structure and well-observed characters from the world of lyrical dream images, which pervaded his early poetry, with particular force and clarity.

The basic situation, which was so frequently to recur, is that of a room, a room with a door; and outside the door a cold, hostile world. The room is warm and light. Outside it is winter, cold and dark. The second basic component of the play is equally characteristic of much of the later Pinter: a couple; the man, large, brutal, fifty years old; the woman, older than the man, almost sixty, motherly, sentimental. The woman is completely devoted, completely absorbed in looking after the man. The man just sits there, reads his paper, and allows himself to be fed and pampered. And he never utters a word. Rose, the woman, seems to be married to the man, Bert Hudd; but that is by no means certain; already Pinter manages to maintain an aura of ambiguity, uncertainty, around his characters. Rose certainly seems very anxious to please Bert, to make herself as useful and agreeable to him as possible. She forces her solicitude upon him. But he shows no reaction whatever.

A warm room surrounded by a cold and hostile world is, in Pinter's case, already in itself a very dangerous situation. Somebody will be pushed from the warmth of the room out into the cold. And likewise, a couple, man and woman, where the woman so obviously wants to give love and the man so obviously does not accept her gift, must be a dangerous, ominous constellation. The woman is fighting to maintain the relationship. The man remains cold. When will he abandon the woman?

From the very first moments of the play Pinter stresses Rose's fears by her constant insistence on the cosiness and warmth of the room, as against the dampness and obscurity of the basement flat which had at first been offered to them. Again and again she asks herself whether there are any tenants still living in that basement, and congratulates herself on living on the first floor. Bert, who drives a van, still has a delivery to make, he will have to go out into the cold of the winter evening. But even when Mr Kidd, an elderly man who is hard of hearing and whom Rose treats as the landlord, though he seems to be no more than the caretaker, enters the room, Bert Hudd remains completely silent, so that we ask ourselves whether he will ever speak, whether indeed he can speak at all.

Rose tries to interrogate Mr Kidd about the tenants down in the basement. But he does not hear her questions – because he is deaf, or perhaps for other, more sinister reasons? – and does not even seem to know how many floors there are in the house: 'Well, to tell you the truth, I don't count them now . . . Oh, I used to count them once. Never got tired of it, I used to keep a track on everything in this house. . . . That was when my sister was alive. But I lost track a bit, after she died.'

There is nothing intrinsically improbable or unreal in an old man who is so dotty that he talks nonsense. And, yet, very characteristically already, by an accumulation of such basically realistic detail, Pinter succeeds in building up an atmosphere of menace, of Kafka-esque uncertainty. The silent giant van-driver, the anxious woman clinging to the warmth of her room, and the room being situated in a house of uncertain size, so that it seems suspended between an unexplored basement and a top that loses itself in a dim, unending flight of stairs, each of these details may in itself be explained away – in accumulation they create tension and foreboding.

Mr Kidd leaves, and so, after a while, does Bert Hudd. Now Rose is alone. She is about to put the dustbin outside the door. When she opens the door, she is terrified: there are people standing outside – a young man and a girl. So subtly has Pinter created the atmosphere of menace that surrounds the room, of the hostility of the cold world outside, that the mere presence of people on the landing – an ordinary enough occurrence – strikes not only Rose but the public as well as a veritable shock; with such simple means has *a coup de théâtre* of great impact been produced.

At first it seems as though all this terror would turn out to have been a false alarm. The young couple are looking for a room, what could be more normal and reassuring; they were looking for the landlord to ask him whether there was one available in the house. But Mr Kidd, whom Rose regards as the landlord, but whose name is not recognized as the one they have been given as the owner's by the young couple, has just been saying that there were no rooms to be let in the house. And then – to heighten the menace again – Mrs Sands, the young woman, tells Rose how in their search for the landlord they had gone down to the basement:

. . . and we couldn't see where we were going, well, it seemed to me it got darker the more we went, the further we went in, I

53

thought we must have come to the wrong house. So I stopped. And Toddy stopped. And then this voice said, this voice came – it said – well, it gave me a bit of a fright, I don't know about Tod, but someone asked if he could do anything for us. So Tod said we were looking for the landlord and this man said the landlord would be upstairs. Then Tod asked was there a room vacant. And this man, this voice really, I think he was behind the partition, said yes there was a room vacant. . . .

Even the vagueness and uncertainty with which the story is told – in Pinter's masterly handling of the vernacular – the very woolliness of the syntax adds to the atmosphere of horror and fear which it must strike in Rose's mind – and the audience's, now totally identified with her. When Rose insists that Mr Kidd told her the house was full up, Mr Sands replies:

The man in the basement said there was one. One room. Number seven he said:
Pause
ROSE: That's this room.

Again, with the simplest of means, a real shock has been produced. To Rose the very idea that the room which she regards as hers should be talked about as being to let is tantamount to a death sentence.

Rose violently denies that her room is going to become vacant. The visitors leave. Now Mr Kidd returns, in a state of considerable excitement. He is so agitated that he does not even hear Rose's indignant questions of how people could get the idea that her room might be to let. For Mr Kidd discloses that for days now he has been plagued by an intruder, who does not give him a moment's peace, a man, who wants to talk to Rose, is constantly asking for her, is lying down there in the basement and refuses to budge. He wants to see Rose as soon as her husband is out of the room. For two days Mr Kidd has been waiting for that moment. That's why he had come earlier – to see if Bert had not gone yet. Rose refuses to receive the mysterious intruder. She